12

Public Archaeology in Annapolis

View up Pinkney Street to the Shiplap House site, 1986.

Public Archaeology in Annapolis:
A Critical Approach to History in Maryland's Ancient City

Parker B. Potter, Jr.

Smithsonian Institution Press

Washington and London

Edited by Vicky Macintyre.
Production editing by Rebecca Browning.
Designed by Alan Carter.

Library of Congress Cataloging-in-Publication Data

Potter, Parker B.
    Public archaeology in Annapolis : a critical approach to history
in Maryland's ancient city / Parker B. Potter, Jr.
        p. cm.
    Includes bibliographical references and index.
    ISBN 1-56098-318-3.—ISBN 1-56098-410-4 (ppb).
    1. Archaeology and history—Maryland—Annapolis.   2. Annapolis
(Md.)—Antiquities.   3. Annapolis (Md.)—History. I. Title.
F189.A647P68   1994
975.2'56—dc20   93-20779

British Library Cataloguing-in-Publication Data is available.

Manufactured in the United States of America.

03   02   01   00   99   98   97   96   95   94

10   9   8   7   6   5   4   3   2   1

Contents

Acknowledgments

Many people have stood beside me to help me shepherd this text through its evolution from dissertation proposal to dissertation to this most recent incarnation.

I am grateful to my cohort of fellow graduate students in the Department of Anthropology at Brown University. The advice, support, and collegiality offered by Steve Mrozowski, Lee Kossin, Marsha King, Mary Moran, Jordy Kerber, Imogene Lim, Dick Waldbauer, Sue Reed, and Dennis Blanton set me up well for my journey south from Providence to Annapolis. Dick Gould and my dissertation committee—Pat Rubertone, George Hicks, and Peter Schmidt—all left their unique marks on me and my dissertation. Words alone cannot describe the contributions they have made. As if one department were not enough, Randy McGuire at the State University of New York at Binghamton (now Binghamton University) gave me a place to work in the fall of 1986 when I discovered that I could do almost anything I wanted to in Annapolis—except write. The hospitality of Randy and the denizens of DeForest House contributed enormously to my ability to produce the first draft of this book.

Even more important has been the assistance of dozens of people with whom I worked in Annapolis; without their help, there would have been nothing for me to send back to Providence. The staff and volunteers of Historic Annapolis offered me information and friendship in equal measure. St. Clair Wright, Pringle Symonds, Pat Kohlhepp, Judy Sweeney, Melissa Marsh, Jean Russo, Sandra Paskin, Caryl Cryer, Julie Fife, Jane Anderson, Carolyn Godesky, Shirley Brown, Susan Finley, Cackey Jansens, Eleanor Barr, and Naomi Kinnard were all, in their own ways, helpful to me and a pleasure to work with. I would like to give special thanks to Linnell Bowen, Madelon McDonald, and Dorothy Callahan, who showed me the Historic Annapolis interpretive program and invited me in. Only for them would I have spent an afternoon as a lipstick boy at the Macy's grand opening. As I have said before: Linnell, Madelon, and Dorothy and their fellow interpreters are among the most valuable assets of Historic Annapolis, and I admire their work greatly. On Maryland Avenue, Baldwin & Claude always provided a friendly front stoop and a unique perspective on local goings on, past and present. Wendy Dennis is a good friend who I could always count on for a break from whatever was going on.

In addition to the folks I had the good fortune to find in Annapolis upon my arrival, there are many members of Archaeology in Annapolis whose work has contributed directly to my research and to this book. On the archaeological side, I have benefited from working with Anne Yentsch, Joe Dent, Connie Crosby, Don Creveling, Jody Hopkins, and Dorothy Humpf. On the interpretive side, Pam Henderson, Stacia Gregory, Nancy Jo Chabot, Kris Stevens, Christine Hoepfner, Patty Secreto, and Elizabeth Kryder-Reid all served as public program crew chiefs for Archaeology in Public. Their work was excellent and vital. I would also like to thank everyone who served on the front lines as an archaeologist/guide during my tenure with Archaeology in Annapolis. This roster includes Samuel T. Brainerd, Nancy Jo Chabot, Vince Chick, Simon Coleman, Lynn Clark, Henry Cone, Mark Cramer, Rob Fernandez, Chelle Feutz, Stacia Gregory, Terri Harris, Bill Helton, Pam Henderson, Philip Hill, Heidi Hoffman, Nigel Holman, Elizabeth Hughes, Matthew Johnson, Lawrence Konefal, Elizabeth Kryder-Reid, Naomi Leach, Barbara Lichok, Barbara Little, Peter McGoon, Carey O'Reilly, Patricia Mitzel, Kris Stevens, Barbara Ray, Lisa Royse, David Sachs, Todd Sachs, Ellen Saintonge, Etta Saunders, Patty Secreto, Sam Shogren, Jim Sorenson, Charles Stearnes, Helen Sydavar, Anne A. Tschirgi, Raymond Tubby, Patsy Walker, Wendy Wolf, Danielle Wood, and Melissa Wood. Their work has contributed directly to the success of Archaeology in Public, and much of what I know about public interpretation, I owe to working with these people.

Turning from my time in Annapolis to the period after I left, I would like to thank George Logan for all his hard work in extending and improving upon the interpretive efforts begun while I was with the project. All of the interpreters listed in the previous paragraph are indebted, along with me, to Philip Arnoult, media consultant to Archaeology in Public, for teaching us things we did not know we did not know about talking with the public. The public interpretative programs described in this book have been funded by the National Endowment for the Humanities (grant GM-21645-83) and the Maryland Humanities Council (grants 546, 738-F, 780-G, 842-G, and 880-H). A final group of Archaeology in Annapolis colleagues who offered good advice and tremendous encouragement are my fellow students in the "Archaeology in Annapolis Graduate School": Paul Shackel, Barbara Little, Elizabeth Kryder-Reid, Julie Ernstein, Mark Warner, and Paul Mullins.

During the final stages of revising the manuscript of this book, I was aided considerably by the encouragement of Daniel Goodwin of the Smithsonian Institution Press and the good advice of an outside reviewer. Rebecca Browning and Vicky Macintyre have done their usual excellent editorial jobs. I am grateful to Marion Warren for permission to use many of his photographs in this book, and I would like to thank George Logan for his assistance in getting me prints from the Archaeology in Annapolis photo archives.

Finally, there are the "big three." Mark Leone invited me to join Archaeology in Annapolis, and for over a decade he has been a teacher, a colleague, and a friend. I owe him a great deal, and my ongoing scholarly partnership with Mark is far more important than any of the articles or other specific products that have resulted from our working together. Bob Sonderman, whom I met when we joined Archaeology in Annapolis at the same time, has been a housemate and a best man and remains today the second most important thing I ever found in Annapolis. The best thing I ever found in Annapolis is my wife, Nancy Jo Chabot, who has been an integral part of everything that has gone into this book and who has helped me with every stage of its development.

For support of all kinds throughout the writing and revision of this book, I am grateful to three families: my family of colleagues at the New Hampshire Division of Historical Resources, the family I married into, headed by Aleen and Herb Chabot, and the family I was born into, headed by my parents, Carol and Parker Potter.

Last, but certainly not least, I would like to dedicate this book to my father's mother, Mavis Benedict Potter. Mavis kindled my interest in antiques, took me to England for the first time, and in many other ways taught me to care about the past.

1

Introduction

Perhaps the best way to give a sense of what this book is about is to "unpack" the various elements in its title. Archaeology in Public is a program of archaeological interpretation started by Mark Leone in 1981, along with its parent program, Archaeology in Annapolis. *The Ancient City* is the main title of Elihu Riley's benchmark history of Annapolis, written in 1887 and still consulted regularly, more than a century later. Riley's book is both a nineteenth-century commentary on things already ancient in 1887 *and* a historic artifact in its own right (copies in good condition fetch nearly $100 in antique shops). The doubly historical quality of Riley's book provides an excellent introduction to the content of *this* book because an important part of my work here is to examine three related phenomena: contemporary versions of Annapolis history, historical versions of Annapolis history, and the history *itself*, to the extent that the past can be known by historians and archaeologists. Finally, the phrase "critical approach" refers to critical theory, which is the tool I use to link all these views of Annapolis to the city's contemporary needs and interests by means of a program of archaeological interpretation.

Stated another way, this book is a study of the creation and use of history in Annapolis, Maryland, undertaken as a part of Archaeology in Annapolis, a citywide research project sponsored jointly by the University of Maryland, College Park, and Historic Annapolis Foundation, a private, nonprofit, preservation organization, known until 1990 as Historic Annapolis, Inc. (For the sake of simplicity, I will refer to the organization simply as Historic Annapolis.) This book is concerned with two main topics: (1) the use of contemporary social context in the formulation of research questions for Archaeology in Annapolis and (2) the creation of a public interpretive program, Archaeology in Public, intended to make the products of Archaeology in Annapolis available to people in contemporary Annapolis.

The fact that I focus on Annapolis does not mean that I think every archaeological project should attempt to become another Archaeology in Annapolis. Archaeological interpretation requires a variety of resources and may be impossible or unadvisable to undertake in some instances. Furthermore, I recognize that the goals (and resources) of most archaeological projects fall somewhere between those of Archaeology in Annapolis—which was designed from the outset as a laboratory for archaeological education—and those of the handful of projects that must be conducted out of the public eye for a variety of legitimate reasons. Recognizing this range of archaeological circumstances, I have written this work for a wide audience of archaeologists—including those working outside of academic settings—in order to offer a sustained example of how to think about the context in which archaeology takes place and how to put archaeological work to use in such a context.

The historical, ethnohistorical, and ethnographic data collected and analyzed here have been used by Archaeology in Annapolis in its role as one of the first full-scale, long-term experiments in applying critical theory to American historical archaeology. The result is a critical archaeology, an instance of historical archaeology informed by a political philosophy based on the following two principles. First, the circumstances under which knowledge is produced exert an influence on the shape and the substance of the knowledge created. Second, there is no neutral or value-free knowledge; intentionally or not, all knowledge serves—or can serve—certain particular interests at the expense of other particular or general interests. These two principles are summed up by the statement that "knowledge is historically rooted and interest bound" (Held 1980: 253). Furthermore, this is the case for both the histories I have studied *and* the historical interpretations I have helped create while working for Archaeology in Annapolis.

The particular critical archaeology developed in Annapolis consists of a three-part program. The first part employs *ethnography* to determine how a community uses its past. The second part employs *archaeology* to illu-

The Main Street archaeological site, decorated to attract visitors.

minate what is hidden or mystified by the community's manipulation of the past. The third part employs *archaeological practice*, which in this case means presenting the techniques, methods, and findings of ethnographically informed archaeological research to the local community. At the very least, this kind of archaeological interpretation is intended to explain the techniques and methods of archaeology. In the ideal case, it strives to provide people with enlightenment. Within critical theory, the term "enlightenment" is used to denote information about and ways to question aspects of modern life that people are not normally encouraged to consider (Leone, Potter, and Shackel 1987). Knowledge derived by using critical theory helps people better understand their interests and overcome domination. This book is the result of research connected with the first step of the program outlined above and also of my effort with Leone to implement the third step, Archaeology in Public, a program of interpretation for the public inspired by critical theory.

Situation

Another feature of critical theory is that it demands self-reflection of those who use it. If the circumstances surrounding the collection of data influence the data collected, then the particular situation of any researcher must be considered a part of those circumstances. Thus, at the beginning of this book (but in the main text, rather than in a preface or a foreword) I present a brief autobiography to indicate the context of my research. This strategy was suggested to me by Alison Wylie (personal communication) and was also employed by Martin Jay in the introduction to *Marxism and Totality* (Jay 1984: 18–20).

My interest in the social context of archaeology began in the late 1970s when I worked in Rockbridge County, Virginia, doing historical archaeology as a student of John McDaniel at Washington and Lee University. In particular, I was concerned about the social structure of the project I was working on. I was one of many students who had come from outside Rockbridge County to excavate sites associated with local history and to earn wages, academic credit, and professional recognition in the process. By the time I left Rockbridge County, I had begun to see my work there as an example of the appropriation of local history by outsiders. This is, of course, an increasingly important issue throughout historical archaeology, perhaps most visible in the area of plantation archaeology, but worth considering *any time* that archaeology is used by one identifiable group of people to study the ancestors of another group. In Rockbridge it became important to me to learn whether local residents stood to benefit from archaeological uses of their history. If they could benefit, I wanted to understand how. And if they did not benefit, I wanted to do something about it. The conclusion I reached was that scholarly interest in the history of Rockbridge County—and the archaeological products of that interest— had the potential to enable residents of Rockbridge County to compete with places like Colonial Williamsburg in attracting historically minded tourists. This was my first serious consideration of the social context of archaeology.

I maintained this interest during my three years as a graduate student at Brown University. There I was influenced by Peter Schmidt's work with African iron technology (Schmidt 1977, 1981, 1983), Pat Rubertone's work at RI 1000 (Robinson, Kelly, and Rubertone 1985), and Richard Gould's modern material culture studies (Gould 1984; Gould and Schiffer 1981). Exposure to these various projects led me to further develop my own interest in the contemporary social context of archaeology.

Given my background and interests, I considered myself fortunate to have the chance to join Archaeology in Annapolis in 1982, at the invitation of Mark Leone. I was, at that point, already familiar with Leone's work, and I decided to go to Annapolis so I could work with him directly while at the same time conducting dissertation research on the social context of an ongoing archaeological project. I worked for Archaeology in Annapolis for three weeks during the late summer of 1982 and joined the project full-time in June, 1983. I stayed with Archaeology in Annapolis until September 1987, when I became a historical archaeologist and preservation planner for the New Hampshire Division of Historical Resources. The period from June 1983 through September 1987 constitutes the ethnographic present that I describe and analyze here.

From the beginning, my principal job with Archaeology in Annapolis was to manage the day-to-day operations of Archaeology in Public. My salary was paid occasionally by the University of Maryland, but usually by Historic Annapolis with funds raised by Leone from a number of sources, including the National Endowment for the Humanities, the Maryland Humanities Council, the Maryland Heritage Committee, and the city of Annapolis. Leone, as a codirector of Archaeology in Annapolis (with Anne Yentsch and Richard Dent) and a consultant to Historic Annapolis, was always my direct supervisor, although in specific circumstances I answered to various members of the Historic Annapolis professional staff. I had office space in two Historic Annapolis museum facilities, occasional access to Historic Annapolis clerical services, and day-to-day contact with the organization's staff members and volunteers during my stay in the city.

My relationship with Leone and my relationship with Historic Annapolis are two important elements of the environment in which this book was researched. Regarding the former, the only relevant factor is that Leone's invitation to me to join Archaeology in Annapolis was contingent upon my agreement to write a Ph.D. dissertation using Annapolis materials. Regarding the latter, the situation is slightly more problematic. Before I joined Archaeology in Annapolis, Leone negotiated with Historic Annapolis to establish academic freedom for the project's scholarly products. That academic freedom covers this book; no part of it has been previewed by anyone associated with Historic Annapolis. Many of the arguments I make here have been tried out on various staff members and volunteers, but as informants, not as censors.

While Historic Annapolis has played no role in the writing of the dissertation on which this book is based, my association with the organization contributed to a variety of minor constraints on my research activities. These constraints were both external and self-imposed, and the implied purposes of these tacit agreements were to avoid agitating Historic Annapolis and to avoid jeopardizing its position in the local power structure. These partly unconscious attempts to avoid rocking the boat are certainly represented in this book, most visibly in my limited treatment of power relations in the city. The point is that I have been free to write what I want to write, but that freedom has been tempered by certain limitations on access to the contemporary political scene. Although these limitations clearly diminish the depth of my analysis, I am confident that I would not have had any greater freedom on any other similar archaeological project.

The academic freedom negotiated by Leone for scholarly works does not cover the interpretive materials produced by Archaeology in Public for use in Annapolis. Historic Annapolis has interests clearly defined by its primary objective, the preservation of historic buildings. What Historic Annapolis wants from Archaeology in Annapolis above all else is specific archaeological information that it can add to its preservation data bank and use to aid its preservation efforts. Says Ramirez (1975:326), "The leader of Historic Annapolis . . . believed that research would protect the buildings by the sheer weight of the documentation." Given this orientation, the organization does not give a top priority to archaeological or historical interpretation, at least not in and of themselves. But Historic Annapolis supports Archaeology in Public because doing so provides good public relations. In light of Historic Annapolis's complex position in the community and its long-standing history as a political entity, Historic Annapolis asks to preview and edit interpretive materials intended for local use when those materials list Historic Annapolis as a sponsor, and Leone agrees. Historic Annapolis has usually limited its editorial input to correcting factual errors and softening language, although on one occasion, and under strong pressure from the organization, Leone (and I) eliminated a discussion of gentrification from a guidebook produced by Archaeology in Annapolis. To the extent that this book reports on Archaeology in Public, the editorial constraints placed on the interpretive program are reflected here.

Further constraints shaping this book are a set of assumptions about how the world works and a set of data collection decisions based on those assumptions. My first assumption is that there is deeply rooted, institutionalized social inequality in contemporary America. My second assumption is that history is one of the things that some individuals, groups, and institutions use, in some circumstances, to legitimize relations of inequality. My third assumption is that all versions of the past, accurate or inaccurate, serve some contemporary interest or another, whether or not they were constructed explicitly to do so. On the basis of these three assumptions, I have, in the analyses that follow, adopted certain observational strategies, certain ways of looking. These ways of looking will be important to bear in mind when reading the descriptive passages in the earlier chapters; these chapters contain description but also a point of view.

Following my assumption of social inequality, I have chosen to pay attention to social conflict in Annapolis and to the issues around which such conflicts take place. In the presentation of these conflicts, impartiality is impossible. My point of view is probably best characterized as the liberal academic version of advocate anthropology, a defense of the relatively powerless against powerful interests. This point of view is informed by critiques of anthropology and archaeology as tools of colonialism (D. Miller 1980). Following my assumption that history always serves contemporary interests, I have searched for themes and connections below the surface of presentations of Annapolis history that tend, on the surface, to appear fragmented.

Finally, in attempting to capture the ethos of Annapolis, its collective identity, I had two choices. I could have attempted a statistical, survey-based portrait of individually held attitudes within the city, a strategy that has already been attempted for Annapolis (Ives 1977), with results that are at best mixed. A second choice, and the one that I made, was to take seriously Annapolis's discussions of itself at the broad, popular level. In particular, I paid attention to the local newspapers, local radio, the speeches of politicians, and the city's own self-promotion. My concern was with the world of perceptions.

Furthermore, while I was studying Annapolis's present and its past and helping to create an archaeological interpretation of that past, I was at the same time a rent-paying, tax-paying, voting resident of the downtown Historic District. Not only did my experience as an Annapolitan shape my views of contemporary Annapolis, which is obvious, but it also influenced the way I looked at Annapolis's past. I looked for the histories of contemporary social issues, and not just several years back, or several decades, but several centuries.

So far, I have discussed my own point of view in researching and writing this book and the context in which I have done that work. There is one other point I want to discuss, namely what this book *is*. This is an experiment in the application of critical theory to historical archaeology, an attempt to create a critical archaeology for Annapolis.

Another way to think of this book is as an experiment in archaeological practice. By practice, I refer to the application of scientific techniques and methods to problems outside the laboratory. This definition is different from the usual archaeological definition that equates practice with technique.

The usual, narrow definition of archaeological practice probably results from an important difference between archaeology and the so-called hard sciences on which many archaeologists have tried to model their discipline. In most areas of science, there is a sharp distinction between theory and research on the one hand and practice on the other. In medicine, there are both researchers and clinicians (who use the results of medical research to make their patients healthy). The field of physics has physicists in labs and engineers in the field using physics to build things. But in archaeology the theoreticians and the practitioners are the same people. Except in rare cases, archaeology is not simulated in a laboratory setting, though archaeological simulation is becoming more common through experimental archaeology (Coles 1973; Ingersoll, Yellen, and Macdonald 1977) and the use of computers. Usually in archaeology, the lab *is* the field. The medical analog to this would be a family doctor using his or her patients for research. Further, inasmuch as many archaeologists are employed by universities, where creative thinking and scholarship are valued, the theoretical side of the discipline is often more highly valued than the practical side; rightly or wrongly, many academics *do* tend to feel superior to contract archaeologists. Discussions of archaeological practice usually end up being discussions of how to collect archaeological data, not discussions of how to apply archaeology.

This raises the question, to what nonarchaeological problems can archaeology be applied? There are at least two kinds. The first is demonstrated by the work of William Rathje, who applies archaeological techniques to contemporary materials, usually refuse, in an attempt to provide information useful for solving contemporary technical problems pertaining to trash disposal, for example (Rathje 1974, 1978, 1991; Rathje and McCarthy 1977; Rathje et al. 1992). Archaeology can also be used to address social and ideological problems, particularly those that result in inequality, coercion, and domination. This book is an experiment in using critical theory to create an archaeological practice of this second type.

Finally, there is the issue of the status of the practitioner, which brings us back to the "contract-versus-research" dichotomy I have already mentioned. Since the advent of cultural resource management (CRM) and contract archaeology, university-based researchers have generally been regarded as the "producers" of archaeology—or at least archaeological theory—and CRM archaeologists as the "consumers" of the latest versions of archaeology that have been provided for them by their more intellectual academic colleagues. It would be easy, or at least conventional, to view Archaeology in Annapolis as another large-scale, grant-funded, university-based research project with various aspects that could be scaled down and simplified for use by contract archaeologists. However, that would miss the point. While the funding for Archaeology in Annapolis has allowed me to conduct ethnographic research and has allowed Leone and me to mount an extensive public interpretive program, we have had to work hard to break out of the ivory tower and push our way into areas of contemporary life that are quite well understood by most contract archaeologists. There is no question that in American archaeology, the balance has shifted from grant-funded "pure" research to contract-funded survey and salvage. CRM archaeologists have the sites, the data, the experience, and the position not just to do a watered-down Archaeology in Annapolis every once in a while, but rather to take the next groundbreaking steps in expanding the concept of archaeological practice.

Organization

This experiment in archaeological practice and my report on it draw on ethnography, archaeology, and public interpretation. The ethnographic findings have guided the selection of archaeological problems, and both the ethnography and the archaeology have shaped the content of a program of public interpretation. Ideally, the experiment should have been organized so that the ethnographic component preceded the archaeological and interpretive components. However, for various logistical reasons, all three parts of the experiment have been carried out simultaneously in Annapolis. As a result, rather than being constant, my concern with the relevance of Archaeology in Annapolis to the contemporary life of the city has increased over the life of the project.

Structure

The discussion in this book falls into four parts. In chapters 2 and 3, I explain how contemporary archaeologists have accounted for the social context(s) in which they work. I suggest here that critical theory can be used to improve upon the discipline's ability to understand its relevance to modern life. In chapters 4–7, I describe my ethnographic and historical research into the use of the past in Annapolis and present the set of social and ideological problems to which Archaeology in Annapolis is relevant. My argument in this part of the book is organized around four topics:

Annapolis today (chapter 4), the history of Annapolis (chapter 5), the history of historical discourse in Annapolis (chapter 6), and the use of history in the city (chapter 7). Next, in chapter 8 I discuss the relationship between archaeological research in Annapolis and the ethnographic findings reported in the preceding chapters. Finally, in chapters 9–11, I present a record of Archaeology in Public, particularly of the ways in which archaeological interpretations were designed to address central issues in Annapolis today. The topics in these chapters include the relationship between Archaeology in Public and other forms of historical interpretation (chapter 9), the content of the Archaeology in Public tour program (chapter 10), and visitor responses to Archaeology in Public tours (chapter 11).

Substance

The structure just outlined provides the framework for the delineation of two central problems and suggested solutions. The first is a problem in American archaeology, for which I propose critical theory as a solution. The second is a problem in contemporary Annapolis, for which Archaeology in Annapolis constitutes a part of one possible solution.

The issue of relevance in American archaeology is addressed in chapters 2 and 3. This problem has two facets. First, despite wide claims that archaeology should be relevant to modern life, much of contemporary archaeology is, *on the surface*, irrelevant. Second, as a result of this perception, the relevance of scientific and historical research conclusions tends to be misunderstood. I contend that relevance/irrelevance is not the appropriate issue to examine. Following the mainstream of critical theory, I hold that all scientific and historical knowledge is relevant to and usable by some interest group or another. Thus, the issue the archaeologist needs to examine is not which findings are relevant and which are not, but what is the social usefulness of any particular set of findings. And the question that should be asked of any archaeological report is not whether its findings are relevant, but whether its author gave enough thought—and self-reflection—to the issue of relevance. This is the problem I set out in chapter 2. In chapter 3 I argue that critical theory can help archaeology achieve a more productive approach to relevance, thus showing how this theory can be used to solve a significant problem in American archaeology.

The remainder of the book is devoted to the thesis that all scientific and historical knowledge is relevant to some problem or another. In chapters 4–7, I discuss the set of problems in Annapolis that Archaeology in

Annapolis has attempted to start solving through the archaeology and interpretation I discuss in chapters 8–11.

Annapolis today is beset by an identity problem. For at least two centuries, Annapolis has had a difficult time creating an identity that connects residents with the local area through productive labor. For example, Annapolis is often called "Crabtown," but far more Annapolitans buy crabs in restaurants and seafood markets than harvest them from the Chesapeake Bay. Having a strong tie to the local environment has two benefits. First it gives rise to economic vitality. Second, it creates a basis for legitimizing political organization, on the assumption that those with the strongest claims to local identity have the strongest claims to authority. In Annapolis, the lack of a central productive activity has led the city to invite a succession of outsiders—including the state government, the U.S. Naval Academy, and affluent tourists—to help it achieve the economic vitality necessary to sustain the city. That the city has been able to survive through a combination of administration, education, and tourism makes a study of the city's survival a study of a problem in capitalism because all of these economic enterprises are based on a set of alienations or separations (for example, work time from leisure time) that are unique to capitalism. The city's mode of survival has solved one problem and created another. By inviting outsiders in, Annapolis has ensured its survival but has also been forced to negotiate with visitors for the right to local authority.

There is in Annapolis one solution to this second problem, embodied by the visible and vocal claims to localness made by the historic preservation movement, which is composed mainly of Annapolitans who are newcomers rather than natives. Many discussions of Annapolis history by what I call the "white historical elite" overlook (or deny) the fact that the city lacks a productive basis for establishing identity. Members of the preservation movement attempt to claim insider identity by curating the artifacts of Annapolis's past. This substitution of historical curation for productive activity constitutes an ideological misrepresentation of social reality. This misrepresentation is enhanced by the strategy of positing an inherent value in historic artifacts rather than acknowledging that historical value is established by contemporary actors seeking to achieve a variety of personal, social, political, and economic ends.

In chapter 8, I take up the use of archaeology to explore the roots of the ideas that have allowed Annapolis to thrive without a productive relationship with the local area. Chapters 9–11 examine Archaeology in Public, the part of the project that makes Archaeology in Annapolis an experiment in archaeological practice. The messages of Archaeology in

Public have been both general and specific but have grown more specific to Annapolis over time. At the general level, they have attempted to demonstrate the principle that history is often a tool used by those who control it to further their own particular interests. At the specific level, Archaeology in Public has attempted to illuminate the use of history and ideology by some residents in Annapolis to make a claim for localness and the right to control the behavior of various groups of visitors. The obvious question is, to what end do I wish to unmask this ideology in Annapolis?

Archaeology in Public does not propose a particular course of corrective action, but I believe that Annapolis as a whole—residents and visitors of all sorts—would benefit from an alternative mode of historical interpretation, one that abandons the inherency thesis and acknowledges that Annapolis is composed largely of outsiders. Archaeology in Public attempts to help Annapolis face the identity problem that nobody acknowledges in the hope that local residents might find a solution that is not based on denial. An assumption here is that an explicit bilateral solution is better than a unilateral ideological one. By acknowledging their own interests, those who write Annapolis history can produce a far more credible set of historical interpretations. Further, while there are some ways in which Annapolis's identity problems and its reliance on outsiders are unique, there are other aspects of the Annapolis situation that are found in many other places. By acknowledging its identity problems and using history to come to a less ideological solution, Annapolis could stake a claim for national importance by providing a model for other small towns dependent on powerful outsiders.

I would like to suggest that the readers of this book follow the text with a pencil in hand. I judge the books I read on the basis of how much they inspire me to take notes, and I would encourage you to read this book actively. Agree, disagree, and find your own examples. That way, when you are finished reading you will know something more than how to conduct Archaeology in Public in Annapolis—which is a good thing, because Archaeology in Annapolis has already been done! This book will have done something important if, at the end of it, readers feel more strongly— one way or the other—about the value of attempting such projects, or if they have a clearer idea of what lies behind the history on display in Annapolis and what kinds of tools they can use to understand the presentations of history elsewhere.

2

Archaeology and Relevance

One justification for the use of critical theory in this study is that the theory has been seldom applied in archaeology in a comprehensive fashion, even in historical archaeology, although Leone (1981a, 1981b) and Handsman (1980, 1981b, 1982) have laid much of the necessary groundwork. Also, Gero, Lacy, and Blakey (1983) and DeBoer (1982) have employed a critical perspective to derive what Wylie (1985: 134) calls "fragmentary insights" into the discipline of archaeology (see also Pinsky and Wylie 1989). Patterson (1986) has done the same. Trigger (1980, 1986) has cogently demonstrated that the archaeology of Native America has for nearly a century ignored the interests of Native Americans. And Schmidt's work in Tanzania (1977, 1981, 1983) enhances the historical image of Africans by overturning the myth of African technological inferiority. But I know of no attempts in American historical archaeology to use critical theory to link a long-term archaeological project with its contemporary social context in a specific local setting. Therefore, Archaeology in Annapolis and Archaeology in Public may have some value as a comprehensive experiment in conducting an archaeological research project based on critical theory. The steps in the experiment include determining whether the paradigm is workable in the field and evaluating the degree to which a critical archaeology in Annapolis is able to accomplish the basic goal of any critical theory: emancipatory understanding of the conditions of modern life. As explained in Chapter 3, Annapolis is an ideal place in which to conduct such an experiment. But before turning to Annapolis and its need for a critically informed archaeology, it is important to establish that archaeology also needs what critical theory has to offer.

The Mandate for Relevance

Many reasons can be given to suggest why archaeology should be relevant to modern life and to members of contemporary societies. To begin with, archaeology is costly and much of it is supported by public funds. It should be relevant, so the argument goes, to those who pay for it (Renfrew 1983: 8). Further, archaeology tends to be of widespread interest, often because of the attention it receives from the news media. In addition, the claim is often made that archaeologists, particularly those engaged in public archaeology, are serving society at large by protecting the artifacts of a common heritage. As a result, taxpayers who are also consumers of popular culture consider themselves enfranchised to ask what archaeology has to do with today (Lipe 1977: 21). In view of these claims (see also McGimsey 1972), it seems clear that archaeology bears the burden of proving its relevance to contemporary society.

When the concept of relevance is examined a little more closely, however, two important problems emerge, both highlighted by the question "Relevant to whom?" The notion that "archaeology should be relevant to those who pay for it" is not as clear-cut as it appears, because of the complex relationships between archaeological investigators and the objects of their study. As D. Miller (1980) and Trigger (1980) have pointed out, some archaeological investigations of colonized peoples conducted by representatives of the colonizing cultures have been detrimental to the colonized. Such archaeology may be relevant and useful to those who fund it, but in such cases its value lies in its justification and extension of colonial domination. Consequently, it is irrelevant or negatively relevant to the interests of the colonized. Although terms such as "colonizer" and "colonized" evoke images of Europeans in Africa, the British in India and Australia, and the Spanish in Central and South America, they apply equally well to the recent ancestors of many contemporary Americans. Trigger, for example, is concerned with archaeology that disfranchises Native Americans. Similarly, a growing number of archaeologists are studying the archaeology of a variety of historic ethnic groups as examples of the archaeology of colonization. The excavation and interpretation of

African-American sites by white archaeologists is not intrinsically an extension of colonial domination, but it is easier than we might think to perpetuate the structures of domination without intending to.

The relationships between the interests of archaeologists and those whose ancestors they study would seem to be more straightforward when the investigator and the objects of investigation are of the same culture, as in much of American historical archaeology. But this supposes an absence of sectional, class-based interests and conflicts within that shared culture, a condition that holds true for few modern societies. Thus the kind of vigilance Trigger, D. Miller, and Schmidt call for in postcolonial societies is equally necessary for American historical archaeology. Yet, it is fair to characterize historical archaeology as being among the least reflective branches of contemporary American archaeology. This book is an attempt to reverse that trend.

Archaeologists, on the whole, have not been shy about assuming the burden of relevance. As early as the turn of the century, Flinders-Petrie (1904: 167–93) expressed concern about the benefits of archaeology to society. More recently, Grahame Clark (1957: 251) responded strongly in the affirmative to his own question, "Does archaeology really mean enough to us today to support such large claims to social resources?" Since then, there has been little serious argument with Clark's position and considerable reaffirmation (Fritz and Plog 1970; Watson, Leblanc, and Redman 1971; Schiffer 1976; Dixon 1977; Grady 1977; Schiffer and Gummerman 1977; Renfrew 1983; Schmidt 1983). Some of this reaffirmation has been strident: "Unless we are prepared to argue convincingly that archaeology is more than just a game for the privileged few, we might as well check in our badges" (Lipe 1977: 21). My own case for critical archaeology rests on the same assumption—which is to say that archaeology must be relevant to contemporary life, and that the issue of relevance should have an explicit place in archaeological discourse.

A second problem has to do with how to achieve relevance. Archaeologists, it is often said, should strive to *make* archaeology relevant (Fritz and Plog 1970). Modern material culture studies are a good example of archaeology made to be relevant, or of archaeological techniques put to useful purposes. But many would argue that archaeological research and its results cannot help but be useful to some contemporary interest for some purpose or another (see Kohl 1981; Schmidt 1983; Wylie 1985; and Patterson 1986). Archaeology, like any procedure for producing (or acquiring) knowledge, is inevitably relevant. That is to say, there is no value-free knowledge. From this perspective, which is the view that informs my research, the basic task for the archaeologist is not to determine what is relevant, but rather, to assume the relevance of *any* finding and then to answer the question "Relevant *to what?*" Whether or not we choose to be advocates, there are partisans who will be able to put to use *any* results we produce. Thus, even when we decide not to use our work actively, we need to understand how that work could be used by others. Therefore, the first responsibility of the archaeologist is not to try to *make* his or her research relevant but rather, it is to be conscious of how that work *is* potentially relevant, what it is relevant to, and the uses to which such work could be put.

This rather abstract point can be clarified through an example. The archaeology of plantation slavery and Afro-American life have become popular topics for historical archaeologists, many of whom have begun thinking about the place of their results in contemporary American society. Singleton (1988), for example, has explicitly considered the use of archaeological materials in museum exhibitions on African-American life. In addition, Ferguson (1991, 1992) and Orser (1987, 1988a, 1988b, 1989) have examined plantation life and African-American material culture in terms of a complex discourse on power and empowerment that is still going on today. Singleton, Ferguson, and Orser all appreciate the need to consider the relationships between their work and contemporary African-Americans. However, a considerable body of plantation archaeology does not seem to acknowledge this kind of tie between past and present. Among others, Kelso (1984) and Otto (1975, 1984) have completed studies in plantation archaeology that seem disconnected from the present. But in reality, they are not (Leone and Potter 1988; Potter 1991).

In *Kingsmill Plantation*, Kelso divides his first chapter into three sections labeled "Land," "Things," and "People." By relegating his discussion of black people to the section on things, he reproduces eighteenth-century social relations of domination in the twentieth century. In *Cannon's Point Plantation*, Otto attempts to measure and evaluate the "quality of life" enjoyed by slaves at Cannon's Point. He measures quality of life in terms of square feet of living space, number of possessions, and the amount of protein in the slave diet. Using these categories allows Otto to measure the quality of slave life without confronting its central fact, namely bondage. A slave with a good diet is still a slave. Like Kelso, Otto chooses to understand slave life through the categories of the slave owners. Neither Kelso nor Otto attempts to make his book relevant to contemporary Americans, black or white. Yet both books *are* relevant because each reproduces domination by using, unreflectively, the conceptual categories of the dominant. This reproduction of domination was certainly not the intention of either Kelso or Otto, but it is undeniably a part of their books.

Relevance and Archaeological Theory

Several areas within American archaeology, such as modern material culture studies, explicitly take into account the relationship between archaeology (at least archaeological techniques) and contemporary life. The New Archaeology created by Binford and others in the 1960s laid some essential groundwork for the introduction of critical theory into American archaeology.

The New Archaeology enjoyed a decade of extremely vigorous fluorescence in the 1960s, beginning with the work of Binford (1962) and perhaps capped by the publication of *Contemporary Archaeology* (Leone 1972). (Renfrew [1983], however, takes *New Perspectives in Archaeology* [Binford and Binford 1968] as the capstone of the New Archaeology.) In any case, criticism of the New Archaeology had begun in earnest by the mid-1970s. Among other things some critics saw the New Archaeology as an invitation to explore the trivial fringes of the discipline (Price 1982: 714; Flannery 1982; Shanks and Tilley 1987: 32). Whatever the criticisms of the New Archaeology, what was once heresy became orthodoxy (Price 1982: 714; Renfrew 1983), and by the late 1970s the angry young men of the early 1960s had become elder statesmen. Shortly thereafter, a whole welter of new theoretical stances based on structuralism, symbolic analysis, and Marxism began to take the field, clearly signaling an era of paradigmatic pluralism, to use Deetz's (1983) term. Regardless of its success as an archaeological revolution (Schiffer 1976: 2; King, Hickman, and Berg 1977: 27; Renfrew 1983: 4; Patterson 1986: 19; Shanks and Tilley 1987: 30), and regardless of the esteem in which the various parts of it are now held, the New Archaeology has clearly been concerned with the question of relevance, either to "social science as a whole" (Fritz and Plog 1970: 411–12; see also Watson, Leblanc, and Redman 1971: 52; and Schiffer 1976: 3) or to both social science and contemporary life (Schiffer 1976: 3, 7–8).

To explore better the issue of relevance as expressed in the New Archaeology, it is helpful to consider separately two defining features of the New Archaeology: (1) its concern with the formulation and testing of laws of human behavior (Watson, Leblanc, and Redman 1971; Schiffer

1976), and (2) its emphasis on methodological sophistication and refine-ment. Its functionalist framework (Binford 1962, 1965; Flannery 1968; Watson, LeBlanc, and Redman 1971), which is based on general systems theory (von Bertalanffy 1962) and ecology, has played a less discernible role in the relevance or irrelevance of archaeology and is therefore not inte-gral to my argument (but see Potter 1991 on functionalism and plantation archaeology). The New Archaeology's greatest claims for relevance flow from its concern with laws, while its commitment to methodology may be seen both as a help and a hindrance to the discipline's quest for relevance.

Laws and Relevance

The orientation of the New Archaeology to the formulation and testing of laws of human behavior, coupled with the time-depth of the archaeologi-cal record, serves as the basis for the view that archaeology has a capacity and an obligation to produce findings relevant to social science or to con-temporary society. It has been said that this obligation to contribute to the knowledge of laws of human behavior can be met in the long run

> only by taking as explanations to be tested problems which are relevant not only to archaeologists but to social science as a whole. Archae-ologists claim to have a set of data which is of unique value in studying processes of long term change and development. Yet we have rarely used our data to do this. Given the freedom to choose explanations for testing, we have incurred the obligation to strive to be relevant. (Fritz and Plog 1970: 411–12)

The "haste" of many New Archaeologists to be relevant to both modern society and anthropology is understandable, according to Schiffer (1976: 3), because the laws arising from research guided by Schiffer's (1976: 7–8) "Strategy 3" for behavioral archaeology have the potential to shed light on modern social problems and issues (see also Reid, Schiffer, and Rathje 1975: 865). Schiffer also cites the early and continuous concern of Paul Martin with the social relevance of archaeology (Martin, Quimby, and Collier 1947; Martin 1954, 1971; Martin and Plog 1973). Despite promi-nent comments on the lack of published work "along these lines" (Watson, Leblanc, and Redman 1971: 52) and despite occasional attempts to carry out such work, with questionable success, the number of socially relevant archaeological projects remains notably small. Beyond any prac-tical constraints that have kept New Archaeologists from producing a large volume of relevant research results, there seems to be no mechanism within the well-documented procedures for archaeological law-making, law-testing, and law-using for distinguishing between important laws and trivial ones (Potter 1982: 92; Deetz 1983: 30). The unexamined underlying assumption seems to be that *any* law is important by virtue of the universality that flows from its being lawlike. Without a set of criteria for determining the significance of laws, or a procedure for creating criteria, nomothetic archaeology faces a severe challenge to its ability to produce relevant results.

Methodological Sophistication and Relevance

The other important aspect of the New Archaeology that has bearing on the question of relevance is its rigorous attention to methodology. However, the relationship between this concern with methodology and social relevance is complex.

On the one hand, a crucial contribution of the New Archaeology is the insight that how we collect the data is a part of the data we collect. This makes contemporary archaeological activity, and all of the things that can impinge upon that activity, legitimate and important objects of scholarly attention. In theory, a concern with the intellectual circumstances that surround archaeology should lead to a concern with relevance. On the other hand, some argue that a focus on the contemporary intellectual activity that constitutes, shapes, and interprets the archaeological record has made archaeology less rather than more relevant to today. This is especially true when intellectual activity is seen as disconnected from its social and political context.

Not only are we faced with deciding whether a concern with methodology leads toward or away from a concern with relevance, we must also assess the effects that a concern for a social relevance may have on methodology. Schiffer (1976: 3) argues that his program for behavioral archaeology is necessary because of a failure "to confront and resolve the complex problem of using archaeological data," a failure of methodology attributed to archaeologists' eagerness to make archaeology relevant to anthropology and to society.

Unlike Schiffer, who sees too little methodology, Price (1982: 714) sees a "preoccupation with methodology for its own sake" (see also Meltzer 1979) and a discomfort with "even middle-level theory" (Price 1982: 714), which together have served to divorce archaeology from social science and society. For Price, a view of the New Archaeology as methodology-rich and theory-poor argues for the use, in archaeology, of Harris's (1968, 1979) version of cultural materialism.

Leone (1986: 432) came to the same conclusion Price does, but has a different solution in mind, namely critical theory rather than cultural materialism. According to Leone (1986: 432), the New Archaeology "has become so rational it is dehumanized." By "dehumanized" he means that the New Archaeology is disconnected from human concerns, which is another way of saying that it is irrelevant or, more properly, that it is not self-consciously relevant. Further, "the unintended consequence of such heavy emphasis on a strict epistemology [an epistemology later termed 'deadening'] has been a deepening of the chasm between archaeology and its own society" (Leone 1986: 432). Both Wylie (1985) and Kohl (1981) note an interesting paradox here. Self-conscious or self-reflective archaeologists have been "motivated to reassess and overhaul their discipline by a deep concern to make it 'relevant'" (Wylie 1985: 133), hoping to put it in a position "to provide information of quite broad and even pragmatic value" (Wylie 1985: 133). Yet they have turned to logical positivism (discussed in greater detail in chapter 3) to develop that relevance, even though self-reflection in most other social sciences has led researchers to reject logical positivism, in recognition of the inevitable relevance of any scientific work.

A key element of logical positivism in this context is its emphasis on increasing the reliability of research results through methodological refinement, on "progressively eliminating error and . . . [on] assuring approximation to an ideal of objective and possibly useful [or relevant] knowledge claims about the past" (Wylie 1985: 133). It would seem that the hopes for relevance pinned on logical positivism were based on a faith in the usefulness of accurate results rather than on a demonstration of the ability of logical positivism to produce explicitly relevant results. Further, Wylie, along with Kohl (1981) and Handsman (1981a), believe that the self-reflection that leads away from a narrow focus on method is deeper or more comprehensive than the self-reflection that leads to an emphasis on method. But, leaving aside Wylie's immediate intention, which is to justify the use of critical theory, it is easy to see why overemphasis on the procedures by which knowledge is obtained can divert attention from the potential social uses of that knowledge.

In sum, it seems fair to attribute to some New Archaeologists a concern with the relevance of their discipline and their results. That concern has been a part of virtually every subsequent version of American archaeology from its structural (Schmidt 1977) to its critical wing (Leone, Potter, and

Shackel 1987). Yet, as already noted, very few products of the New Archaeology have successfully or explicitly addressed the issue of relevance. This is most likely a failure of both theory and practice.

Relevance and Archaeological Practice

I would now like to turn from archaeological theory to archaeological practice (defined here conventionally, as the conduct of the discipline) to discuss some of the ways in which American archaeology has dealt with the contemporary context in which it takes place. Context must be taken into account because the circumstances surrounding the discovery and creation of knowledge exert an influence on the knowledge produced. Further, many of the agents who compose the social context of archaeology have uses to which they may put the results of archaeological research. Although not all of the following examples are directly attributable to the New Archaeology or New Archaeologists, the New Archaeology was a dominant paradigm during the entire span of time from which these examples are drawn. Common to all these cases is the failure of American archaeologists to adequately take into account the context of their work, which is equivalent to saying that we have mishandled the issue of relevance.

The Lack of Anthropological Self-Reflection

In response to a wide range of activities, including cultural resource management (CRM) archaeology, pothunting (inside the United States), looting (outside the United States), and Indian–White relations, the attitude and the behavior of the archaeological community have been fairly uniform. The archaeological community, perhaps after some debate, forms an opinion—such as "CRM should be more research-oriented" or "dealing in antiquities is wrong"—and then the discipline's position is proclaimed and explained editorially, that is, outside the channels of normal scholarly discourse in the field. Most discussions of contemporary context appear in newsletters, bulletins, and editors' notes rather than in journal articles. This editorial discourse tends to lack self-reflection because it fails to use the analytical tools of anthropology to understand fully the stands taken by archaeologists. There are some exceptions, of course, but this trajectory is the standard course of events, and it has a fairly standard result: neither the premises behind the discipline's position nor those behind the situations archaeologists seek to correct are seen as worthy of examination or discussion and are not normally subject to scholarly attention and consideration. That "monument thievery is wrong" is taken as a proposition beyond challenge and therefore the activity is not considered worthy of scholarly study.

Exceptions to this unreflective stance can be found in the work of Trigger, D. Miller, and Schmidt, cited above, and in Heath's (1973) work on *huaquerismo*—archaeological looting—in Costa Rica, which, according to his estimates, accounts for approximately 1 percent of the Costa Rican economy. In referring to Heath's largely functionalist account of *huaquerismo*, I do not mean to suggest erroneously that the way things are is the way things must be, or that because huaquerismo can be seen as serving a purpose, it is right. Rather, I am suggesting that an anthropological account of any segment of contemporary context will help us better understand our own positions as well as those to which we are reacting. As well, once the discipline takes a position and decides on a course of action, we stand a far better chance of taking effective action if it is based on a comprehensive anthropological understanding of the situation rather than a poorly articulated reference to some moral or political high ground. In other words, if we want to stop looting or shut down the trade in illicitly obtained antiquities, then ethnography like Heath's is an ideal starting point.

However, the typical reaction to context is that of Clewlow, Hallihan, and Ambro (1971). They discuss two important sites that archaeologists were unable to study until after they were well picked-over by pothunters. Their principal concern is the bias introduced into the archaeological record by pothunters who prefer large artifacts to small ones. Although they deplore such biases, they seem to see no point in studying them. While we all can sympathize with their frustration, it is important to recognize what is lost by writing off hoards of hunted material, as Clewlow, Hallihan, and Ambro do. Such material may not prove adequate to answer these authors' immediate research questions, but it does speak volumes about those who collected it. By making a careful study of hunted material, and the people who collect it, we can learn about popular perceptions of archaeology and the prehistoric past. By learning about what people know of archaeology, we can learn what we need to teach them if we wish to use education as a tool for conserving the archaeological record. Used this way, sacks full of arrowheads, usually dismissed as nondata, can serve a purpose that any archaeologist would recognize as important. There is even a scholarly rubric for such studies. Pothunting and related activities may well produce a recognizable pattern. Schiffer (1976: 35) calls these activities "A-S processes," and several archaeologists have dealt with them (notably, Ford 1961: 156; Kelley 1963; Morse 1973, 1975; House and Schiffer 1975; Classen 1976; Price, Price, and Harris 1976; Schiffer and House 1975, cited in Schiffer and Gummerman 1977; Schiffer 1977, 1983; Schiffer and House 1977; and Wildesen 1982). However, this scattered work has had little impact.

As noted earlier, far too few archaeologists deal anthropologically with the social context of their work, and far too many treat context simply as a situation to be corrected or corrected for. Furthermore, editorializing about contemporary social context has the potential to backfire in an interesting way. One would think that stepping beyond the normal bounds of scholarly discourse would emphasize the timeliness of archaeological interpretations and their contingency on the context in which they are created. However, such editorializing is often based on reference to vaguely defined higher principles, which forecloses debate and helps obscure the relationship between the study of the past and the present.

Such editorializing also obscures the fact that there is no moral high ground, only a great deal of ambiguity. Consider, for example, that many archaeologists are working closely with Native Americans to see that human remains are treated properly. Yet some of the same archaeologists advocate stiff punishment for native looting in Central America. Why should one group of natives be mollified and another prosecuted when all each wants, from its own point of view, is to use its own past in the way it sees fit? Archaeological morality in these cases cannot be anything but relative, and to understand such relativity we should study context, including ourselves, rather than try to ignore it, factor it out, or claim to stand above or beyond it. We are, after all, scholars, and we deal with issues best by studying them, not by placing some of them beyond the realm of study. Is there really a danger in examining our own reasons for opposing pothunting or for choosing a side in the reburial issue? Academic archaeologists frequently give the impression of complete scholarly detachment from issues deeply touching other people, while they are unable to achieve the same kind of detachment from issues that affect their own scholarly livelihoods.

Archaeology as Reactive

In their approach to the contemporary context of archaeology, archaeologists have also been uniformly reactive (King, Hickman, and Berg 1977).

That is, they seldom consider the context of their work until that context has intruded on the practice of archaeology. For example, the scholarly value of CRM archaeology has received increasing attention over the past decade because more and more university-based archaeologists are being called to evaluate the work of CRM archaeologists in academic forums such as journals and in situations such as the reentry of CRM archaeologists into the academic world. Looting and pothunting are issues because they take data away from archaeologists. The relationship between white scholars and the Indian descendants of their research subjects never became an issue until Native Americans had developed the political voice to make themselves heard (Winter 1980). In each case, archaeologists have reacted to context, in an editorial mode, rather than taking context into account before it could no longer be ignored.

Why Take Context into Account?

One might ask, why take context into account at all, especially when it is not intruding on the practice of archaeology? As noted earlier, context is important because, acknowledged or not, the circumstances in which archaeological work takes place help shape the results produced. One need only think of the increasing body of archaeological data generated by CRM work. Leaving aside entirely the issue of the thoroughness and scholarly rigor of such work, there can be no argument with the fact that the body of data generated by CRM archaeology is geographically skewed toward locales targeted for contemporary construction activities. Such a skewing clearly shapes the data base and does so in a way that equally clearly has very little to do with the part of the past studied by using such data. Whether we like it or not, decisions made in Washington, D.C., by the Federal Highway Administration have helped in a measurable way to shape our understanding of North American prehistory. Dozens of aspects of contemporary context—from sources of funding to local reactions to archaeological work to scholarly feuds to tenure decisions—have a similar shaping effect on our data. Yet only rarely is context ever considered until it poses a "problem," and then, more rarely still, is context analyzed anthropologically; usually it is editorialized about in the hope that whatever problems it poses will go away so that archaeologists can go back to ignoring context.

I contend, however, that archaeology will become anthropology when and only when archaeologists treat the contexts in which they work with the same scholarly and analytical attention that they devote to their so-called data. I do not mean to lay all of this at the feet of the New Archaeology, but the kind of reactive, detached editorializing that has characterized archaeological considerations of context is just what one would expect of a highly objective research paradigm that at least in practice tends to deny the impact of the social and political situation of the investigator.

Without an explicit acknowledgement of context, archaeology cannot tie itself to the present. It gives the appearance of being unconnected while it is not at all; the assumptions and points of view that make the connections are simply unstated. This, in turn, makes it easier for archaeology and its results to be used by people in the present for a wide variety of purposes. The problem here is not that archaeology is being used for contemporary purposes; that is inevitable. Rather, the problem is that archaeological interpretations are being used for purposes not intended by their authors. This appropriation of historical interpretations is facilitated by a research perspective that claims impartiality.

In response, I suggest in chapter 3 that critical theory be used in archaeology—not to untie archaeology from contemporary interests, but rather to help archaeologists clarify their own interests and intentions regarding their own work and its implications. Critical theory can aid in the development of an archaeological practice, archaeology tied explicitly to needs and interests. And the more explicitly a piece of research or interpretation is tied by its author to a set of interests, the more difficult it is for others to appropriate that archaeological product for other purposes.

3

Critical Theory, Archaeology, and Annapolis

Critical theory is a political philosophy in the Western Marxist tradition, associated with the Institute for Social Research at the University of Frankfurt. Known as the Frankfurt school, this group of scholars came together in the 1920s and worked, together and separately, through the 1960s. Important early figures in the Frankfurt school include Max Horkheimer, Theodor Adorno, and Herbert Marcuse. The dominant figure in contemporary critical theory is Jurgen Habermas. In this chapter I examine the particular parts of critical theory that archaeologists may use to help them understand the relevance of their work.

First, though, I want to qualify my use of this philosophical perspective. To begin, I am borrowing from a philosophical school of thought that does not explicitly give consideration to archaeology. Thus, I use critical theory in ways not necessarily anticipated by its authors. In addition, my work embodies a specific relationship between philosophy and archaeology, one in which archaeological problems come first and parts of critical theory are applied to problems in archaeology. Thus, I am not acting as a philosopher attempting to import critical theory, intact, from philosophy to archaeology. Further, my knowledge of critical theory is limited and skewed in that I have learned about critical theory in the process of designing and mounting a program of archaeological interpretation. In sum, the view of critical theory presented in this chapter bears the stamp of my particular archaeological and interpretive needs.

This chapter consists of two main sections. The first deals with the parts of critical theory useful to archaeology. The second considers the applicability of critical archaeology to the history of Annapolis, Maryland.

Critical Theory for Archaeology

As pointed out in chapter 2, much of contemporary archaeology mishandles the problem of relevance by failing to recognize the potential of *all* archaeology to be relevant to some interest or another. Critical theory can lead to a better way of dealing with relevance in archaeology because of its concerns with (1) the particular, (2) self-reflection, (3) antipositivism, and (4) the integration of theory and practice.

Concern with the Particular

I have already discussed the general failure of American archaeology to take into account its contemporary social context. Understanding context is important because within that context, entangled in all kinds of relationships, are the various interests and concerns to which archaeology may be relevant. To understand relevance, it is essential to have a historical and particular appreciation for context. Particularism is central to critical theory: "Every thought, idea and particular is interwoven with the whole societal life process. Critical theory, in spite of its efforts to reflect the object in its manifold forms of development, depends in its every step on particular historical conditions" (Held 1980:182). Thus, an objective of critical social research is to "delve deeper and deeper into the particular and discover the universal law therein" (Held 1980: 189). That is why critical theory puts so much "emphasis on the uniqueness, importance, and complexity of the particular" (Held 1980: 207). It is out of particular understandings that specific historical moments and contexts are understood and affected.

Early critical theorists—such as Horkheimer, Adorno, and Benjamin—developed critical theory as a rejection of "identity thinking," the idea that every particular phenomenon can be identified with, or subsumed under, some general concept—which was a key tenet of German idealism. According to Horkheimer, the proper subject of critical theory is the "irreducible tension between concept and object" (see Held 1980: 180). Adorno (in Held 1980: 212) adds that "objects do not go into their concepts without leaving a remainder." The question is what to do with this remainder. Idealists do not acknowledge any remainder and thus focus on the points of correspondence between particular and concept. Their rejection of the particular is similar to the New Archaeology's concern with general laws, a concern that has inhibited the development of an adequate concept of relevance within the New Archaeology. Adorno holds that the idealist failure to confront the remainder leads to a false identity that violates the integrity of the object and ignores "the matters of true philosophical interest" (Adorno in Held 1980: 206). In his view, anyone who sees individual cases *only* as expressions of broader concepts *cannot* accurately see the individual case; identity thinking is simply bad science.

Adorno's solution to the problem of identity thinking is to attend to the "remainder" in a procedure he calls nonidentity thinking or "negative dialectics," a procedure that operates "within the 'force-field' between concept . . . and object, idea and material world" (Held 1980: 214). The value of nonidentity thinking for critical theory is the fact that many of the ideologies that critical theories challenge misrepresent the interests of one segment of society as universal interests. By attending to particular circumstances and detecting their particularities, critical theorists are better able to recognize threats to local interests.

One value of nonidentity thinking for archaeology is that it preserves the particularity of local contexts. This preservation of the particular, in turn, facilitates the identification of interests, which contributes to a consciousness of relevance. Adorno sees identity thinking as an expression of the desire to control knowledge. In the case of archaeology, to subsume the particular into conceptual categories, artifacts into classes, and sites into complexes and phases is to take archaeology out of local history (or local history out of archaeology) and make it the exclusive property of the professionals who create and manipulate the categories. When this happens, any particular archaeology is relevant to discourses within the discipline, but not necessarily to the community that constitutes its context. Nonidentity thinking is a conceptual tool that can guide an archaeological practice that is conscious of the context in which it takes place.

Self-Reflection

As explained in chapter 2, many American archaeologists ignore, or do not consider fully, the contexts in which they work. They do this by exempting themselves and their work from systematic self-reflection.

Self-reflection has a central place in critical theory, for, as Horkheimer says, "the social theorist is at every moment a part of the societal process analyzed as well as 'its potential critical self-awareness'" (Horkheimer in Held 1980: 191). Note, too, that Adorno's "negative dialectics seeks to be the self-consciousness of the context of ideology" (Held 1980: 222). Habermas, meanwhile, "examines the way the significance of the epistemologic subject—the capacity for reflection by the subject on his or her activities—has been gradually eclipsed" and, "he argues, if emancipation from domination is to remain a project of humanity, it is essential to counter this tendency and to reaffirm the necessity of self-reflection for self-understanding" (Held 1980: 254). According to Geuss (1981: 2), "one goal of the Frankfurt School is . . . the rehabilitation of 'reflection' as a category of valid knowledge."

Critical theorists put considerable emphasis on self-reflection for two reasons. I have already suggested the first: self-reflection is a form of vigilance against domination. Adorno seeks "to prevent an unreflected affirmation of society typical of bourgeois ideology" (Held 1980: 211). It is precisely the lack of this kind of self-reflection that allowed Kelso and Otto to perform studies of plantation slavery that use, and thus reaffirm, the conceptual categories of domination. Had either Kelso or Otto thought that their archaeological work made them active participants in the negotiation of contemporary race relations, they may not have used the categories they did, in the ways they did. Further, when society is affirmed through a lack of reflection, domination often ensues through the misidentification of interests. Typically, the specific interests of a dominant class are made to appear as general interests. In this way, the lack of self-reflection among the dominated makes them the agents of their own domination; "the masses, by means of their own work 'produce a reality which enslaves them to an increasing degree and threatens them with every kind of suffering'" (Held 1980: 184). As for remediation, Geuss (1981: 2) says, "A critical theory, then, is a reflective theory which gives agents a kind of knowledge inherently productive of enlightenment and emancipation." I will have more to say about the issues of enlightenment and emancipation later in this section.

The second reason for critical theorists to embrace self-reflection has to do with the relationship between subject and object. Critical theory charts a middle course between the idealist's "absolute subject" (Held 1980: 204), each of whom produces his or her own world, and positivist attempts to legislate away the subject in a world of absolute objects. "Horkheimer contended that a critique of knowledge, presented as a dialectical critique of

ideology, must locate all thought in historical context, uncover its rooted-
ness in human interests and yet (itself) avoid relativism and be distinguished
from skepticism" (Held 1980: 176). Further, Horkheimer rejects Hegel's
goal of the "transcendence of all subject-object differentiation" (Held
1980: 178). Instead, he follows Marx in "a rejection of objectivism and
subjectivism [seeing instead] social reality [as] neither something wholly
'outside' of the subject nor . . . simply a creation of human thought" (Held
1980: 190). According to Adorno, "most philosophies . . . fail to provide
an adequate account of the relation between subject and object" (Held
1980: 202), a relation which is "neither an ultimate duality nor a screen
hiding ultimate unity" (Adorno in Held 1980: 202). Rather, "subject and
object are constituted by one another but are irreducible to each other—
neither can be wholly subsumed by the other" (Held 1980: 202). To sum
up, critical theory strongly asserts that social science research should com-
bine equal parts of objectivity and subjectivity.

Thus, self-reflection, as an examination of the active subject, is an
essential complement to the traditional scientific attempt to examine and
understand the object world. If subject and object are constituted by each
other, then to understand either, one must examine both. Examination of
the subject by the subject is self-reflection. Without self-reflection, archaeologists cannot understand the relationships between their work and contemporary life.

Antipositivism

A third key element of critical theory is its sharp critique of positivism, a
school of philosophical thought that originated with Comte in the mid-
nineteenth century and that found its greatest advocates among the members of the Vienna circle. Positivism here is taken to be a set of ideas based
on the assumption that knowledge arises from observation and experience
and the mathematization of nature. In addition, positivism holds that
social science should be modeled on the natural sciences, that human
behavior is governed by natural laws, and that social science should be a
value-free search for those laws. Positivism also maintains a strict separation between fact and value, and a strong commitment to objectivity. The
Frankfurt school challenges these positions on the grounds that positivism
has no capacity for self-reflection, that it constitutes an affirmation of society, and that it can be used to support domination.

To understand why self-reflection is essential for creating a relevant archaeology, it is necessary to examine the ways in which "the internal connections between science and life practice remain unacknowledged by modern science and positivist philosophy." Positivism's "denial of reflection" is the result of value-neutrality and objectivity, which make it "impossible for [positivist] science to assess its own objectives, or the purposes for which it is employed . . . it cannot even comprehend or assess itself; for it cannot reflect upon itself" (Held 1980: 167). The positivist bent of the New Archaeology is no doubt responsible for the general lack of self-reflection in contemporary archaeology.

Beyond claiming neutrality, positivism inhibits its capacity for self-reflection in at least three ways: (1) by limiting knowledge to what can be observed or experienced, (2) by confining investigation to the use of a verifiability theory of meaning, and (3) by granting no status to knowledge inaccessible to experience. According to Held (1980: 171), these stipulations ensure "positivism's inability to account for itself, let alone justify itself [as well as its ability] to elucidate neither the conditions and limits of its own validity and method nor those of modern science." This happens because, "with positivism, science is no longer understood as one possible form of knowledge but is identified with knowledge as such" (Held 1980: 172). If there is only one valid way to think, then there is little reason to think about thinking (see Richard Watson's [1991] diatribe against philosophy in archaeology); positivism discourages self-reflection by claiming that it serves no purpose.

Of the flaws arising from this lack of self-reflection, the tendency to affirm society and to permit domination is particularly dangerous because it assumes "what is is what ought to be" (Held 1980: 162) without putting this notion to a test. Positivist social science is an inquiry into how things got to be the way they are, not an inquiry into how things could have turned out differently. As Held points out, in most positivist inquiry "the existing order is taken to exhaust all possible alternatives" (Held 1980: 169). If there are no alternatives, society is affirmed. Alternatives are difficult for positivism to accommodate for several reasons. Primary among them is the radical objectivity of positivism. The status quo is not challenged because there is no active subject to undertake such challenge. The world is seen as containing nothing but objects that operate under the sway of rules that exist beyond the agency of individual actors. Further, positivism supports the current order because to do anything else, to challenge society, would imply value judgment, and as I have already noted, positivism places values beyond the realm of discussion and consideration.

Is the affirmation of the status quo the same thing as domination? The answer is that it can be in certain instances. First, when positivism affirms a social formation that contains inequality, it contributes to domination. Second, since positivism assumes that both the natural and social world are governed by laws, domination is inevitable. Third, positivist science is predisposed to seeking "knowledge of a particular type and form, namely knowledge suitable for prediction and, therefore, technical control" (Held 1980: 167). Even when this technical control is intended only to apply to the natural world, it is easily extended to the social world by virtue of the positivist insistence that the social world is analogous to the natural world. And fourth, positivism can lead to domination because it is a closed system of thought. Its belief in closure and completeness, a by-product of radical objectivity, makes knowledge a zero-sum game. The transformation of knowledge into power has increased consequences when knowledge is considered to be finite.

This is not to say that the Frankfurt School completely rejects positivism. Critical theory does not say that positivist empiricism should be thrown out, only that *by itself* positivism produces a distorted and inadequate view of the world. Within this understanding, critical theory places a high value on empirical research.

In addition to having a multidisciplinary character, the Frankfurt school was committed from the beginning to augmenting its philosophical work with empirical research. In a discussion of a study on the psychological basis for susceptibility to fascist propaganda conducted by Adorno and R. Nevitt Sanford, Held (1980: 141) notes that "despite Adorno's very critical attitude toward the use of quantitative methods, he felt that given a suitable theoretical framework, they could be employed fruitfully." Specifically, Horkheimer advocated a two-step procedure in which "concrete research conducted by relatively traditional sociological techniques" (Jay 1984: 199) should be followed, and framed by "the totalizing 'representation' of that work in a new theoretical synthesis" (Jay 1984: 200). Horkheimer drew the inspiration for this procedure from Marx, who referred to the two parts as *forschung* and *darstellungsweise*.

The Frankfurt school's position on empirical research is the basis for Wylie's statement that "critical self consciousness . . . is then a necessary extension of the New Archaeological revolution" (Wylie 1985: 144), rather than a rejection of the New Archaeology. Wylie suggests that the logical procedures developed within the New Archaeology can simply be turned to the study of the context in which archaeology takes place and the contemporary interests that surround archaeology. Such a strategy

> amounts to a recommendation that the New Archaeological revolution should simply be extended, not abandoned. The practice of systematically testing knowledge claims about the past, advocated by the New Archaeology should be used, self-consciously, to expose and test the underlying category assumptions that structure un-self-critical approaches of the past. (Wylie 1985: 143)

Wylie (1985: 141) sees this approach in the work of Leone and Handsman, who "typically build a case for rejecting or revising entrenched views of the past as distorted ideological constructs by exploiting the very empirical—analytic methods and standards of validity that unreflective researchers would normally use to establish the 'accuracy of their reconstructions.'" In Leone's view (1986: 418–19), critical archaeology is a continuation from, rather than a break with, the New Archaeology. Like Wylie, Leone would graft self-reflection onto the empiricism of the New Archaeology and call the result a critical archaeology.

To restate, critical theory takes issue with positivism, rejecting in particular the lack of self-reflection it often entails. However, when used with self-reflection, the same research techniques that affirm society and underpin domination if they are used *unreflectively*, can be used to question society and challenge the domination associated with it.

Theory and Practice

According to Shanks and Tilley (1987: 32), "divorcing theory from practice is one of the fundamental features of positivism." In contrast, critical theory holds that theory and practice are inseparable because "the social theorist is at every moment a part of the societal process analysed" (Held 1980: 191). That is to say, any theoretically directed program of inquiry has practical applications, regardless of whether they are acknowledged by the investigator. Questions of practice are worthy of attention here in light of my suggestion in chapter 1 that contemporary archaeology contains no real conception of archaeological practice.

George Lukacs's discussion of theory and practice in historical materialism is a useful introduction to the position of critical theory on this matter:

> The most important function of historical materialism is to deliver precise judgments on the capitalist social system. . . . For this reason, the chief function of historical materialism did not lie in the elucidation of

pure scientific knowledge, but in the field of action. Historical materialism did not exist for its own sake, it existed so that the proletariat could understand a situation and so that, armed with this knowledge, it could act accordingly. (Lukacs 1968: 224)

At the same time, Lukacs (1968: 225) argues that it would be detrimental to the interests of the proletariat "to remain satisfied with the scientific value of historical materialism and to see in it nothing more than an instrument of knowledge. The essence of the class struggle of the proletariat can in fact be defined by its union of theory and practice so that knowledge leads to action without transition." Lukacs's statements, representing a relatively mainstream Marxist position, are parallel with the position of critical theory on this matter.

To reiterate the Frankfurt school position, critical theory follows Marx in claiming that "all thought and theory is tied to human interests" (Held 1980: 192). This is another way of stating that theory and practice are inseparable. Given this, a real danger in unreflective research is that by not acknowledging contemporary interests, unreflective researchers risk producing results that may be appropriated for practical applications they never intended. Kelso certainly did not intend *Kingsmill Plantation* as an apology for either eighteenth-century slaveholding or twentieth-century racism. I do not claim that self-reflection is a complete safeguard against such misappropriation, only that it is a necessary first step. By recognizing and constructing the links between theory and practice, critical theorists intend to take control of the practical application of the research they produce. Alternative applications are still possible. However, when the originator of a body of knowledge explicitly links that knowledge to a particular use, any secondary user must acknowledge the original use. Then the secondary user must explicitly disconnect the knowledge in question from that initial use. Forcing these discussions to the surface allows broader participation in judging their legitimacy. If critical theorists produce knowledge for specific purposes, then the next question is: What does critical theory try to do?

As Geuss (1981: 2) says, "a critical theory is a reflective theory which gives agents a kind of knowledge inherently productive of enlightenment and emancipation." Enlightenment here refers to the piercing of ideology, and emancipation is taken to mean gaining freedom from the coercion or domination facilitated by ideology. Ideology is the misrepresentation of social reality, typically the masking or the naturalizing of social inequality. Individuals are said to be suffering from domination when they are persuaded by ideology to act in ways counter to their own interests, ways they would not act if not for the distortion of ideology. Critical practice is the production and presentation of research results that contribute to enlightenment and emancipation. Thus, the kind of misappropriation of knowledge to which I referred in the previous paragraph is any use of knowledge that works for domination and against freedom. Critical theory calls for control over the use of knowledge only to the extent necessary to keep knowledge from being used to curtail freedom.

One form of archaeological practice informed by critical theory consists of research into the origins of modern ideology and the presentation of that research to an appropriate public. Following critical theory's acknowledgment of the particular, the specific issues that require illumination will vary from place to place. In American historical archaeology, significant critical archaeologies will be critiques of capitalism or some part of capitalism. Such research, "directed to explore how people, their social relations, and their object world have developed as they have" (Held 1980: 235), is illuminating and emancipatory because, unlike positivist historical inquiry, critical historical scholarship does not assume that the way things are today is inevitable. Different decisions could have been made in the past; thus choice and freedom are possible today. Critical theory claims that the presentation of the present as an inevitable outcome of the past is ideology that removes an important basis for challenges to the contemporary social order.

A definition of ideology as the misrepresentation of social reality raises one important problem. To call something misrepresentation requires a standard for judgment. This in turn suggests an ability to know the truth about particular pieces of misrepresented reality. However, claims to have such an ability would seem to be at odds with the antipositivist thrust of critical theory and its rejection of the idea of knowledge as finite and based on absolute timeless truths.

Critical theorists have devised standards for judgment that do not require the positivist concept of absolute truth. Following Hegel and Marx, Marcuse defines truth as freedom from contradiction and "a society in which all [human] potentialities are fulfilled" (Held 1980: 240) when both of these conditions are realized through the process of labor. This is an interesting concept but difficult to use. More useful is Horkheimer's idea of immanent critique, which consists of two steps. First, the analyst studies a social formation to determine the explicit claims and promises it makes. An example would be the various guarantees of social equality in the U.S. Constitution. After establishing the claims made by a social formation, the analyst judges social practice against those ideals or standards. Such an analysis avoids "the charge that its concepts impose irrelevant criteria of evaluation on the object" (Held 1980: 184) because it uses criteria defined by the object itself. When a social formation is found lacking by an immanent critique, it is because it "fails by its own standards" (Held 1980: 185). Referring to Adorno's understanding of immanent critique, Held (1980: 220) suggests that "the truth and falsity of capitalist society can be assessed according to whether or not it is adequate to its concept." Not only does immanent critique provide a theoretically acceptable way of dealing with the idea of truth, it serves as a method for critical research.

The idea of immanent critique could be applied to historical archaeology in several ways in an attempt to create an archaeological practice. For example, for many of the kinds of material culture recovered by historical archaeologists, it is possible to use the documentary record to locate claims made by manufacturers. Archaeological analysis can play a role in determining whether various classes of material culture performed as their makers claimed they would. To take but one case, Josiah Wedgwood strongly implied that common people could be more like their social superiors by using Wedgwood's creamware and other ceramic wares (McKendrick 1982). This claim has yet to be fully examined (or refuted) and is thus potentially both a historical and a living ideology, the ideology of emulation. A historical archaeology that puts Wedgwood to the test would be an immanent critique of one of the important bases of modern consumerism. Presenting an archaeologically based critique of this ideology to contemporary victims of it would constitute a critically informed archaeological practice.

However, to the extent that most ceramic analyses are highly dependent on Wedgwood's categories, current approaches can only affirm the intentions of Wedgwood. Employing the same argument I made for the work of Kelso and Otto, using Wedgwood's categories puts twentieth-century archaeologists in the same position as eighteenth-century consumers. Critical theory at least forces us to ask ourselves whether we are well served by this.

Critical Archaeologies

Critical archaeologies are programs for archaeological practice based on self-reflection and the idea that all knowledge serves interests. These two ideas, combined in a self-reflection on the interests served by any particular application of archaeology, provide critical archaeologists with an answer to the problems of archaeological relevance raised in chapter 2. Because twenty-five years of positivist-inspired New Archaeology has failed to produce a significant body of archaeological interpretation that fulfills the New Archaeology's self-imposed mandate for relevance, it is time to turn to other approaches. The main objective of this book is to determine whether critical theory, with its powerful tools for dealing with the issue of relevance, can be used to produce archaeological interpretations that are more explicitly relevant than those produced under the New Archaeology. The appropriate standard of evaluation will be whether the products of this particular critical archaeology take into account their relationships to specific audiences. In chapter 2, I argued that trying to *make* archaeology relevant is beside the point, since archaeology cannot help but be relevant to some interest or another. Here I go one step further by suggesting that if archaeological interpretations are going to serve interests, archaeologists should use the tools of critical theory to retain some measure of control over the uses of their research and results.

A consideration of interests may be a fruitful way to sort out an important issue left unaddressed so far, the relationship between critical archaeology and Marxist social theory. Critical theories, of which my critical archaeology in Annapolis is one, often work to uncover the roots of domination and to examine the exercise of power. They *assume* that domination is a central element of modern capitalist societies. Furthermore, critical theories actively oppose such domination and attempt to provide those who are dominated with a way of understanding their condition. Ideally, this is knowledge that may be used by agents to overcome their domination. Critical theories attempt to replace domination with freedom and strongly oppose the creation of new, authoritarian orthodoxies. Similarly, critical theories do not tell people what to think; they show people a new way of thinking and invite people to think for themselves. In these ways, critical theories are clearly allied with a particular set of social interests, those of the dominated. Critical theories claim to be able to pierce the ideologies that support domination only because they *assume* that domination exists. If one chooses to believe that modern capitalist societies are free from coercion and domination, then there is no need for critical theories, including critical archaeologies.

In some circumstances, critical archaeologies would focus on classic Marxist issues like class conflict and the subordination of the proletariat. However, and as I will demonstrate in chapters 4 through 7, this is not the most productive way to view Annapolis. Annapolis certainly has social classes in the Marxist sense, but because the city is much more an administrative center than an industrial place, the most productive foci for critical attention are institutions and social groups. Even without a traditional Marxist class analysis, issues of power and domination may be identified in Annapolis. As I will discuss in chapters 4 through 7, one key venue for the exercise of power in Annapolis is the determination of just who is and is not an Annapolitan. Thus, the key conflict in Annapolis is not over the rights to labor, raw materials, or the means of production; the central conflict is over rights to identity.

At this point, it is fair to ask how critical archaeologists can claim to speak for the interests of subordinate classes and groups. My position is that the New Archaeology amounts to an *implicit* attempt to do science for the benefit of humanity as a whole. As I have argued repeatedly, this attempt has yet to bear fruit. Because positivist science assumes that the accumulation of information is inherently and universally advantageous, positivists do not consider the idea that knowledge may serve sectional or individual interests. Critical theory does recognize the existence of social classes and the possibility that the interests of subordinate groups may be different from the interests of dominant groups. This is the basis for the claim that critical theories, and critical archaeologies, can address the interests of the dominated.

The procedure for critical archaeology that I advocate consists of three steps. The first is historical and ethnographic research to determine the ideological uses of the past in an area where archaeological work is to be undertaken. Second, once the ideology has been identified, archaeological fieldwork is conducted. This research is directed toward elucidating the roots of elements of that ideology. The third step is archaeological practice, which in Annapolis has taken the form of presenting archaeological information and insights to the public. This public interpretation constitutes an archaeological practice to the extent that its goal is to provide people with information they can use to challenge an ideology that inhibits their freedom. (When public archaeological interpretation is impossible, critical archaeologies can still be produced by archaeologists who attempt to operate with the interests of a defined audience in mind.) The goal of this kind of archaeological education is enlightenment and emancipation from ideological constraints.

One question raised by this third step is just how far a critical archaeology can go and just what kinds of effects it can have on its audience. The work of Marcuse suggests that any endeavor as completely bourgeois as archaeology would be socially and institutionally inhibited from producing critical insights. But if Marcuse is wrong, then it is necessary to ask whether a critical archaeology needs to fully enlighten and emancipate to be successful or whether some partial movement toward these goals is adequate.

I am willing to accept enlightenment as an adequate result. Further, I am going to suggest a rather liberal definition of enlightenment. I think it is appropriate to use that term to denote any instance in which a member of an audience for a critical archaeology is inspired to think in a broader, more open way. Breaking a closed system of thought must be counted as a critical success. Critical archaeologists can demonstrate some of the ways in which a particular body of knowledge serves certain particular interests but it is up to individual actors to determine whether those interests are their own (Geuss 1981: 78). Action is yet another matter. Most critical archaeologies advocate no particular steps toward emancipation. Interestingly, this rather conservative stance is precisely the position maintained by most members of the Frankfurt school. While Lukacs submitted to pressure from the Second Communist International and renounced most of *History and Class Consciousness* in the name of correct practice, Horkheimer, Adorno, and Habermas all stood apart from politics after the Second World War, particularly during the late 1960s, and were criticized for doing so by those committed to radical politics. Because of his stronger commitment to political involvement and the unity of theory and practice, Marcuse was a particular favorite of the New Left in the 1960s, while most other critical theorists were faulted for their conservativism. Nevertheless, I follow the lead of Horkheimer, Adorno, and Habermas; I stop short of insisting that a critical archaeology must contain a concrete plan for social action.

Criticisms of Critical Approaches

Archaeological applications of critical theory have themselves been challenged and here I will deal with three specific criticisms of critical archaeology: namely, that it politicizes archaeology, abandons scientific standards of judgment, and assumes the same kind of privileged epistemological position it denies positivist archaeologists.

Turning first to the charge of politicizing archaeology, Hodder suggests, with some sarcasm, that to conduct a critical archaeology one should "choose any political stance he or she likes as a member of society and . . .

write the past so as to further that political viewpoint" (Hodder 1986: 168). Washburn makes this same point more strongly in his response to "Toward a Critical Archaeology" (Leone, Potter, and Shackel 1987):

> The insulation from the present that some archaeologists would consider an advantage, however, has been deemed by others a defect. Archaeologists missed out on the turmoil and excitement of the 1960s and 1970s when cultural anthropologists became activists in behalf of the "oppressed" people they studied against their "oppressors." . . . But the call to "critical," "radical," and "reflexive" anthropology was too strong to be put off forever. . . . [C]ritical archaeologists, when pressed, are usually willing to concede that liberation of the oppressed from the "capitalist roots of alienation"—to choose just one favorite phrase— takes precedence over a politically neutral search for factual evidence. . . . [some] cultural anthropologists were quite frank in choosing their political ideals over their scholarly responsibility to truth. . . . They have, I would assert, set anthropology back in many ways. (Washburn 1987: 544–45).

Schiffer makes the same mistake when he worries "that some investigators, wishing to use archaeology as a means to further unspecified political ends, will subvert the scientific process" (Schiffer 1988: 469). On this point Hodder, Washburn, and Schiffer have all misunderstood critical theory, or at least archaeological applications of critical theory. As I have already noted, critical theory is not a tool for politicizing archaeology, but is instead a tool for recognizing the political implications and ramifications of *any* archaeological undertaking. One does not *make* archaeology political; archaeology *is* political. Critical theory simply allows archaeologists to identify the interests served by their work, whatever those interests are, and then decide whether those interests are interests they care to support. Speaking for the critical position, Gebhardt (1982: 372) says, "Science . . . must know why it is doing what it is doing" in order to overcome the usual situation in which "social scientists especially tend to investigate problems without considering who those problems are *for*" (Gebhardt 1982: 372, 384).

Another objection to critical archaeology is the claim that its critique of positivism precludes the application of scientific standards to research activities. Critical theory, it is argued, reduces archaeology to an interpretive free-for-all in which "anyone's interpretation is as good as anyone else's" (Hodder 1986: 168). Again, this is a criticism based on a misunderstanding of critical theory. Says Gebhardt (1982: 371, 372), "It is sheer nonsense to assert that critical theorists were antiscientific. Quite to the contrary, the group relentlessly defended the sciences" in the process calling for "unconditional empirical stringency." The early critical theorists, especially Adorno and Horkheimer, were quite explicit on two relevant points: (1) that critical theory is an extension not a rejection of positivism (as I have noted above, both Leone and Wylie have concurred on this point, for critical archaeology); and (2) that empirical research is an essential element of critical theories. Not only does critical theory call for empirical research, critical theorists nowhere reject the logic that if things are going to be counted and measured, it is reasonable to have rules for conducting these activities and standards for judging their results.

Although critical theory does not object to the use of standards for the judgment of empirical research, it objects strenuously to overemphasizing the importance of those standards. Stated another way, critical theory does not oppose science, only scientism. There is clearly a place, within critical archaeologies, for checking calculations and arguing over which statistical test to use. However, getting the statistics correct is *not* the last word; the quality of the counting we give to our data is only a part of the meaning that adheres to those data. As Marcuse remarks, "scientific procedure is never itself a guarantee of truth" (in Gebhardt 1982: 372). Critical theory opposes the use of so-called scientific standards only when such standards are given more weight than they should be, and are, therefore, used inappropriately. The phenomenon critical theorists find particularly unacceptable, which could be termed the tyranny of technique, is the use of technical criteria to reject an entire piece of empirical research and not just its technical aspects. Too often, the selection of the "wrong" statistical test is taken to disprove not just the statistical analysis contained in a report but also the premises and assumptions on which that research project is based. Critical theorists would argue that both assumptions and the manipulation of empirical data can be questioned and challenged, but that it is simply bad science to challenge premises with chi-squares.

The third criticism I want to deal with has been made by several commentators and is clearly expressed by Hodder (1986: 164): "Critical Theorists claim on the one hand that all knowledge is historically conditioned, but at the same time suggest that truth can be evaluated and criticism can be conducted independently of social interests—in short, that Critical Theory has a privileged position in relation to theory." To paraphrase, Hodder's concern is that critical theorists make the case for relativity and then claim that their own knowledge is more accurate than other knowledge. This problem is both complex and serious. It is in part a problem with critical theory and in part a problem with our standard modes of scholarly discourse.

The problem with scholarly discourse is that virtually all the communicative acts we use in our academic lives—including books, museum exhibits, newspaper interviews, scholarly papers, *and* dissertations—are structured to be expressions of authority. Furthermore, one of the most accepted ways of introducing new knowledge is to claim that it is a necessary replacement for old, flawed knowledge. As a result, there are almost no recognized techniques in contemporary academic circles for expressing and presenting multiple pasts or a multifocal past. *Any* statement is an act of authority that is based on the speaker presuming to know more than the listener. My point here is that few if any accepted modes of scholarly discourse today allow for the expression of (as opposed to the argument for) a version of the past offered by a nonauthoritative historian.

Even beyond this structural limitation, however, critical theories do seem to place themselves beyond ideology by claiming the power to create more truthful versions of reality than their positivist counterparts. Although it can easily seem self-contradictory for critical theorists to make such a claim, and regardless of whether this claim is fully warranted, there are several reasonable grounds for making it. Among them are the critical definition of truth and the technique of immanent critique, both of which I have already discussed. To those I would add the following argument.

A central tenet of critical theory is self-reflection, and one important use of self-reflection is to examine and discuss the assumptions that underlie any attempt at critical research. I have attempted, in chapter 1, to shed light on the biases and assumptions that guide my study of Annapolis. Critical theorists contrast their attention to assumptions with the positivist approach, which is to ignore or hide premises, assumptions, and biases. To the extent that these characterizations of critical theory and positivism are accurate, critical research can claim superiority on the basis of being more inclusive than positivist research. Critical theory is better science than positivism, critical theorists argue, because critical theory studies more than positivism does. Critical theories constantly scrutinize their own assumptions in addition to considering traditional objects of research. This broadening of the focus of scholarly attention is one important basis for claiming that the knowledge produced by critical theories is superior to the knowledge produced by positivism.

Critical Archaeology and Annapolis

The remaining task in this chapter is to explain why critical archaeology is an appropriate method for Annapolis, Maryland. One reason is that Annapolis has a long history of historical thinking. As I will argue over the next four chapters, that history has been used as an ideological tool by various factions in Annapolis to create and strengthen their relative positions. In particular, the historic preservation movement, and the part of Annapolis for which it speaks, has found in the curation of eighteenth-century relics a way of making a claim to preeminent localness. I propose that critical archaeology is an effective tool for examining, in public, this use of history in Annapolis. Second, Annapolis has a number of house museums and other historic sites that attract a considerable visiting public from the city itself, from Maryland, and from beyond. This large potential audience for archaeological interpretation in Annapolis makes the city a good place to construct and test a critical archaeology, on an experimental basis. It seems reasonable to conduct such an experiment in a place like Annapolis, under favorable conditions. In chapters 9 and 10, I will discuss the creation of critical archaeologies under the conditions that characterize most American archaeology; there are a variety of ways to create an archaeological practice without doing site tours for eight hours a day, six days a week. Annapolis's history of history is the reason why a critical archaeology *should* be done there, and the city's large visiting public is why an experiment in critical archaeology, with an interpretive component, *can* be done in Annapolis.

Summary

In chapters 2 and 3 I have attempted to build a case for my application of critical theory to historical archaeology. In chapter 2, I suggested that one long-standing goal of American archaeology is to be relevant to contemporary society but that it has by and large failed to meet this goal. I have suggested that critical theory as a way of dealing with the issue of archaeological relevance. Thus, one test of my particular critical archaeology is whether my interpretations are relevant to contemporary life in Annapolis.

As I have noted several times, my point is not that archaeology should struggle to be relevant, but rather that archaeologists need a systematic way to understand and control the relevance that already adheres to archaeological versions of the past. This is based on the understanding that knowledge is not simply a collection of objective facts but can only exist in the context of interests. This introduces the second test of my critical archaeology for Annapolis: Does it enlighten Annapolitans with regard to their interests and help them emancipate themselves from domination?

Most American archaeology fails to understand its context because of its rigid objectivism. By considering the subject and its relation to the object, through self-reflection, critical theory contains the methods necessary to understand the contemporary social context of archaeology.

I have suggested that critical theory not only solves a significant problem in contemporary archaeological practice, but further, that critical archaeology is an approach well suited to Annapolis, Maryland. With these arguments made, the balance of this book will be devoted to a discussion of my data and interpretations from Annapolis.

4

Annapolis Today

This chapter is about Annapolis, Maryland, in the mid-1980s, which is the "today" of this study. Although a consideration of contemporary social context is not normally a part of archaeological discourse, it is essential here because critical archaeologies are particularly sensitive to context. Archaeological investigations of the eighteenth century in places other than Annapolis, if conducted from a critical perspective, would probably examine and explicate issues different from those chosen by Archaeology in Annapolis. Furthermore, critical archaeologies different from Archaeology in Annapolis could be developed for Annapolis, on the basis of a different reading of the local context; I claim no omniscience for my ethnographic observations and analysis. This makes it all the more important to describe my particular reading of the local context as a prelude to showing how Archaeology in Annapolis, as a critical archaeology, is based on and responds to the social, political, and economic circumstances in which it is conducted. So, this book is not a set of substantive instructions for critical archaeology but is, instead, an example of a critical archaeology. And, as I have suggested already, I do not intend this example to be useful only to archaeological projects funded in the same ways as Archaeology in Annapolis; a large and growing number of public archaeologists, both in government and in the private sector, are in a position to develop the kinds of local knowledge I present in the next four chapters.

This chapter opens with a discussion of six key elements of Annapolis's identity: Annapolis is (1) the home of the United States Naval Academy, (2) the capital of Maryland, (3) a yachting center, (4) a tourist destination, (5) a historical place, and (6) a small town. Interestingly, in each of the first five of these "roles," Annapolis draws identity primarily from transient individuals and institutions composed of transients. The remainder of the chapter focuses on dynamics, on major issues in the life of the city as they have been articulated by and to the public during the mid-1980s. In particular, I examine conflicts that have resulted from Annapolis's economic reliance on outsiders.

Elements of Identity

Although Annapolis is a small town (its population is about 32,000), it has a complex identity, as noted above. Since Annapolis is probably best known as the home of the U.S. Naval Academy, perhaps that is the most appropriate place to begin discussing the city's various sources of identity.

Annapolis as Home of the U.S. Naval Academy

Beyond a radius of about 30 miles or so, the terms "Annapolis" and "Naval Academy" are virtually synonymous: "Ask the first ten people you meet on the streets of Fort Wayne, Penobscot, Orlando, or Amarillo where Annapolis is and at least nine out of every ten will give you some such answer as, 'Oh, Annapolis—why that's the United States Naval Academy—down there somewhere near Washington and Baltimore'" (Emery 1948: 7).

It is therefore surprising that the academy is nearly invisible inside the city. One can see midshipmen walking the streets of the town; one can eat a "middyburger" at a local lunch counter; several shops sell Naval Academy hats, T-shirts, and other souvenirs; traffic is heavy when the Navy football team plays at home. *But* for all of these relatively minor reminders, one can walk through the downtown Historic District of Annapolis and be only vaguely aware that the eighteenth-century city shares a small peninsula with the Naval Academy and its approximately 4,500 midshipmen. Two academy buildings, the chapel and the gymnasium, do loom over the lower residential and commercial neighborhoods adjacent to them. Even so, the city does not have the appearance of a sub-

The Maryland State House in the mid-nineteenth century. (Photograph courtesy of M. E. Warren, Annapolis, Maryland)

urb of the academy. Despite the fact—pointed out in the standard tour of the academy grounds—that the campus is visited by more than a million people a year, Annapolis rarely tells *itself* that it is the home of the Naval Academy.

Annapolis as the State Capital

Since Annapolis is the capital of Maryland, every day hundreds of people commute into the city to work in various state offices. The influx is even greater during the ninety-day session of the Maryland General Assembly. The legislative session fills the best downtown hotels, and, along with the lobbying activities that accompany it, enlivens the local nightlife. This activity, however, helps conceal the fact that Annapolis is an unusual, if not unique, state capital.

It is said that Annapolis is the only state capital in the nation with no state museum and no railroad service. Annapolis was once served by several railroad lines connecting it with Washington and Baltimore, but, as the title of a popular local book of historical photographs says, *The Train's Done Been and Gone* (Warren and Warren 1981). Train service itself is not so important; the relative isolation of Annapolis is. For example, until the late 1980s, the most direct overland route from Annapolis to Baltimore, less than 40 miles away, involved three state highways, a parkway, and an interstate.

Another unusual feature of this state capital is that many parts of the state bureaucracy are headquartered elsewhere. Of the fourteen departments that make up the executive branch of Maryland's state government, eight are located in Baltimore and two more are located in nearby suburbs. Legislative and ceremonial components of the state government are located in Annapolis along with four relatively small departments: Agriculture, Budget and Fiscal Planning, Economic and Community Development, and Natural Resources. Thus, it is reasonable to think of Baltimore as a co-capital of Maryland. But whatever kind of capital Annapolis is, that identity is important and it brings many people into the city.

Annapolis as a Port of Call for Pleasure Boaters

Annapolis is also a busy and nationally known pleasure-boating port, one of the busiest on the East Coast. Results of the local Wednesday and Friday night sailboat races are reported in the local daily newspaper, the *Capital*, and the local semimonthly tabloid, the *Publick Enterprise*. A popular social activity is to spend a summer evening at the city dock watching the fleet come in. During the 1987 America's Cup yacht races, at least one local pub stayed open all night to provide live, big-screen television coverage from Australia. Several annual ocean races begin or end in Annapolis, including one to Bermuda and another to Newport, Rhode Island. Each fall, Annapolis hosts two boat shows, the U.S. Powerboat Show and the U.S. Sailboat Show. The sailboat show, the larger of the two, is the largest in-water sailboat show in the United States, perhaps in the world. It draws more than 100,000 visitors over a three day-weekend, pays the city upward of $250,000 in rent for the use of the city dock, and is reputed to add $14 million to the economy of the city. Both Annapolis proper and Eastport, a section of the city located across Spa Creek on a neighboring peninsula, are ringed with yacht clubs, yacht yards, sailmaking lofts, and other businesses serving the hundreds of pleasure boats docked in the creeks that surround Annapolis.

The Annapolis city dock in the late 1980s, a port of call for pleasure boats. Note the dome of the Naval Academy chapel barely peeking over the row of low waterfront buildings. (Photograph courtesy of M. E. Warren, Annapolis, Maryland)

Annapolis as a Tourist Town

Allied with Annapolis's pleasure boating, but not completely encompassed by it, is tourism. Visitors are attracted by the Naval Academy, by the buildings associated with state government, by water sports, and by history. Annapolis is a tourist destination for school children, museum and university groups, spouses of people attending conventions in Washington and Baltimore, and busloads of retired people, to name just a few categories of Annapolis tourists. Annapolis has the appearance visitors have come to expect of an upscale tourist town; its waterfront dock area is lined with moderately expensive bars and restaurants, specialty shops (including one that sells nothing but sunglasses), and local outlets for regional or national clothing store chains such as Banana Republic and Britches Great Outdoors. In addition, there is an Irish shop, a Welsh shop, and a Scottish-Irish shop, each stocked with fine woolens. Add to these shops and restau-

rants several ice-cream parlors, souvenir stands, and a market house full
of stalls selling inexpensive prepared food, and the picture of Annapolis as
a tourist town comes into focus.

Annapolis as a Historical Place

The historic character of the city attracts many visitors. Its eighteenth-century heritage is evident almost anywhere in the one-third-of-a-square-mile
Historic District. Small reminders such as Daughters of the American
Revolution plaques appear on some buildings and Historic Annapolis
plaques on others. Street signs in the Historic District indicate the year a
street was laid out and named (usually 1695), as well as the original name
for a street if it has been changed since 1695. Middleton Tavern, on the
city dock, reminds potential patrons, via a sign, that it was established in
1750.

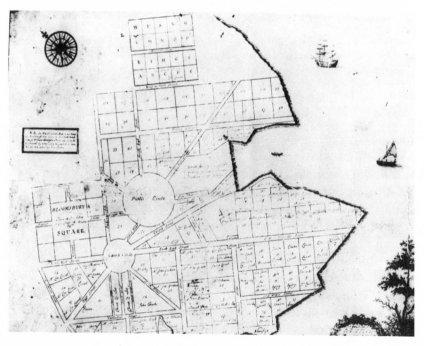

The 1743 redrafting of the 1718 Stoddert survey of Annapolis, clearly showing
Nicholson's plan for the town. (Photograph courtesy of M. E. Warren,
Annapolis, Maryland)

A contemporary view up Main Street to St. Anne's Church (on the left) and up Francis Street to the State House (on the right) showing the continuing presence of Nicholson's town plan. (Photograph courtesy of M. E. Warren, Annapolis, Maryland)

At a more substantive level, Annapolis still uses its 1695 baroque town plan, as laid out by Governor Francis Nicholson. Even to those without specific knowledge of the plan's history, casual observation suggests its antiquity. This is especially true of those unfortunate enough to be confused by the city's two main circles with their sets of radiating streets. Along its seventeenth-century roadways, Annapolis boasts over 50 eighteenth-century buildings or building fragments and over 1,500 historic buildings. In addition to authentic eighteenth-century buildings, Annapolis maintains its eighteenth-century proportions. It is a walking city with a human scale. Most of its nineteenth- and twentieth-century buildings are two or three stories tall, their height and mass sympathetic with the scale of most of the city's eighteenth-century architecture. In addition, there are at least seven late eighteenth- or early nineteenth-century buildings in the city that serve museum purposes as at least a part of their overall function.

Many other historic buildings, although not museums per se, contain shops, restaurants, inns, or offices that are open to the public.

History in Annapolis is not just buildings; history is an activity created, studied, curated, and presented by a wide variety of individuals and groups in the city. Two different groups—Historic Annapolis and a commercial enterprise, Three Centuries Tours of Annapolis—present walking tours of the historic district. The Naval Academy operates a small historical museum, and the Maryland Commission on Afro-American History and Culture has a small museum in Annapolis, the Banneker-Douglass. Annapolis is the home of the Maryland Historical Trust, which includes the State Historic Preservation Office. The Maryland State Archives are also located in Annapolis and constitute an important scholarly resource, as well as a center for genealogical research by the public. The archives are housed in a new building, built to commemorate the 350th anniversary of the founding of the colony of Maryland. Interestingly, this new building replaced the previous Hall of Records building, which was erected in 1934 to commemorate the 300th anniversary of the founding of Maryland.

Historical celebrations have been a part of the life of Annapolis at least since the turn of the century. Notable celebrations include the 200th anniversary of the city's charter in 1908, the 200th anniversary of the birth of Charles Carroll of Carrollton (one of Maryland's signers of the Declaration of Independence) and the 150th anniversary of the Constitution, celebrated jointly in 1937, and the city's tricentennial in 1949. Such celebrations have become even more frequent in recent years, probably as a result of the American bicentennial. Since 1983 Annapolis has celebrated a variety of events with parades, balls, reenactments, and fireworks. Celebrations in 1983 included the 200th anniversary of the signing of the Treaty of Paris, which ended the American Revolution (September), the 275th anniversary of the granting of a charter to Annapolis by Queen Anne (December), and the 200th anniversary of George Washington's resigning his commission in the Continental Army (December). In 1984 the city celebrated the 200th anniversary of the ratification of the Treaty of Paris (January) and the 350th anniversary of the founding of Maryland (over the entire year). In 1986 there was a celebration of the 200th anniversary of the Annapolis convention, a largely unsuccessful meeting to discuss trade between states which called for the Philadelphia convention, which then replaced the Articles of Confederation with our current Constitution. Finally, in 1987 there was a commemoration of the 250th anniversary of the birth of Charles Carroll of Carrollton, a celebration that included archaeology at Carroll's Annapolis home, undertaken by Archaeology in Annapolis.

The historical character of Annapolis owes a great deal to the local preservation movement spearheaded by Historic Annapolis, which calls itself the preservation organization for Annapolis and Anne Arundel County. Historic Annapolis, founded in 1952, is a state-chartered, private, nonprofit organization with a membership of more than 3,000. It relies on several hundred volunteers per year, has a paid staff of fifteen, and has an annual operating budget of nearly $1 million. Historic Annapolis sponsors research, has a vigorous educational program that includes outreach to schools and school tours in Annapolis, and sponsors special educational events for adults. All of this activity is in service of the organization's primary function which is preservation. Historic Annapolis claims full or partial credit, with reasonable justification, for the preservation of 350 buildings in the city. Among its preservation tools are the advice it provides to local property owners, its purchasing of easements on properties, its use of a revolving fund to purchase properties for restoration and resale, and legal action. Historic Annapolis's goal is authenticity rooted in research, and this commitment to authenticity informs its conviction that new buildings in the Historic District should be well-designed and explicitly modern, while compatible with the sizes and shapes of the old ones around them, rather than copies of old buildings.

Historic Annapolis is not shy about standing up for its convictions publicly, even if doing so means taking highly unpopular stands. The organization has unapologetically taken actions that have resulted in long-term antagonisms and adversarial relations between itself and various segments of the local community. However, even many of its detractors grudgingly acknowledge the role the organization has played in the city's recent revitalization. In addition, and partly making up for periodic or episodic lapses of public support, a close relationship has developed over the years between Historic Annapolis and powerful members of the legislative and executive branches of state government. Superficial products of this relationship are the dozen or so certificates of commendation for exemplary public service that have been awarded Historic Annapolis and several of its officers. More significant are several contracts under which Historic Annapolis manages four state-owned museum facilities, for an annually negotiated fee. Furthermore, the 1987 session of the state legislature committed well over $500,000 to the Preservation Keep, a city history museum proposed by Historic Annapolis.

A colonial-dress event from the 1950s. Costumes like these have appeared on the streets of Annapolis throughout the twentieth century. (Photograph courtesy of M. E. Warren, Annapolis, Maryland)

Annapolis as a Small Town

As a residential place, Annapolis retains some small-town characteristics. The Historic District itself contains several pockets of residential blocks filled with wooden houses 80 to 120 years old on narrow, deep lots. One need only live in the Historic District a short time to experience this aspect of the life of the city. The friendliness among neighbors and between residents and merchants is the epitome of Norman Rockwell's small-town America. However, businesses oriented to a local clientele seem to be decreasing in number in the Historic District, a phenomenon about which more will be said later. This set of observations is based not only on my own experience but is reinforced by the work of Sallie Middleton Ives (1977). In an in-depth study of the attitudes of Historic District residents, Ives concluded that the historical qualities of the city played a small role in most residents' appreciation of Annapolis. More significant was the "quality of life," as measured by things like shady streets, friendly neighbors, helpful merchants, and the like. It should be noted, however, that many long-time Annapolitans who remember the 1930s, 1940s, and even the 1950s would argue that the Annapolis neighborhoods they knew then are a thing of the past, done in by the dramatic increases in property values in recent years.

Annapolis has a population of about 32,000 people, and approximately one-third are African-Americans. Many African-Americans in Annapolis are employed as laborers by the Naval Academy or in other blue-collar or service jobs. There is almost no manufacturing in the city or the surrounding area. Many white Annapolitans, and most who live in the Historic District, are white-collar professionals. A significant number are lawyers practicing locally. The opening of U.S. Route 50 in the 1950s provided a quick route to Washington and has contributed to the transformation of Annapolis into a bedroom community for professional people employed in the nation's capital. The Naval Academy employs hundreds of Annapolitans and the brigade of midshipmen numbers about 4,500. St. John's College, also located in Annapolis, has an enrollment of about 400 students. A significant, though seemingly unorganized segment of the Annapolis population is composed of retired naval personnel, some of whom are employed by high-tech, defense-related engineering and computer firms located in or near Annapolis.

In addition to the many different kinds of Annapolis newcomers, Annapolis has some old-timers and even members of ancient Annapolis families who still live in the city. I once attended a dinner held in Annapolis, prior to a lecture on Annapolis history, and asked my dinner companions whether they were life-long Annapolitans. They laughed and said that there was no such thing as a life-long Annapolitan. By and large, Annapolis old-timers tend to be a rather quiet group and only rarely do they advance the argument that "progress" should be slowed down or halted because some innovation is "not how things were in the old days." (Proposals for change are challenged on many other grounds, but not that one.) The more typical response among long-time Annapolitans is to reminisce about the 1950s, about how half the stores on Main Street were empty and the sidewalks rolled up at 6 p.m. Beyond these observations generally lies an ambivalence toward contemporary Annapolis; local residents cite both advantages and disadvantages of Annapolis's new-found popularity and prosperity. To distinguish between newcomers and old-timers, one needs to consider length of residence and how long it takes to become an Annapolitan. However, the value Annapolitans place on length of residence is difficult to determine. In the 1985 mayoral election, a relative newcomer to the area defeated an incumbent with deep local roots whose father had been a popular alderman for many years until his retirement in the early 1970s. This episode may suggest that in Annapolis localness does not matter much; the city council has some born-and-bred Annapolitans but certainly is not dominated by them.

Although localness may be coming to mean less in Annapolis politics, in both the 1986 Fourth District congressional race (Robert Neall, Republican, versus Tom McMillan, Democrat) and the 1986 race for the U.S. Senate (Linda Chavez, Republican, versus Barbara Mikulski, Democrat) localness was an explicit issue. Both McMillan and Chavez were characterized by the local press and in letters to the editor as "carpetbaggers" for being comparative newcomers to the area and for not having "paid their dues" on the local political scene. As it turned out, McMillan defeated Neall and Mikulski defeated Chavez. So, while localness was an issue in these elections, it was obviously not the sole determinant.

Annapolis is unquestionably a politically oriented city. Annapolis politics may have been overstated by one local wit: "Natural evolution develops . . . in [Annapolitans] a taste for oysters, as they need no carving, and a phosphorus diet swells the brain; they talk politics continually" (Riley 1887: 145). But Annapolis is a political place. Just one of the city's eight wards, the ward containing the downtown Historic District, is home to at least two business associations (the Inner West Street Association and the Maryland Avenue/State Circle Association) and at least two residents' associations (the Pinkney Street Residents' Association and the Murray Hill Residents' Association) in addition to the Ward One Residents' Association. Many other residents' associations—complete with officers and newsletters—are scattered throughout the city. Beyond this level of microorganization is the city government with an elected mayor, whose job became full-time only in the mid-1960s, and eight aldermen. (The city council elected in 1985 included two African-Americans and two women.) In addition to its elected officials, Annapolis city government has a large, effective, professional component. Further, Annapolis is both the seat of Anne Arundel County and, as already noted, the capital of Maryland. If we add to this mix two federal installations, the Naval Academy and a small naval research station directly across the Severn River from the academy, the full complexity of Annapolis becomes apparent: in this city of 32,000 people four levels of government come together.

Dynamics

The foregoing represents a static portrait of Annapolis, composed from the point of view I acknowledged in chapter 1. Most of the significant parts are included, although other observers certainly would have selected or arranged them differently. It is time now to look at Annapolis in motion. The motion I deal with here consists of two sets of conflicts between Annapolis insiders and outsiders of various sorts. The conflicts in the first set are those that arise between several of the various units of government that come together in Annapolis. These conflicts were easy to predict and locate and are similar to those that arise in any city in which different levels of government are forced to interact. The second set of conflicts, between various segments of the resident population, are more specific to Annapolis. The issues in this second category were somewhat less predictable than the intergovernmental conflicts and were identified from local popular discourse.

Annapolis and the State of Maryland

Because Annapolis has county, state, and federal property within its borders, it has a severely diminished tax base. This is but one of several problems that result from Annapolis's status as the state capital.

In particular, the city seeks financial compensation from the state for the services it provides that are directly related to "hosting" state government. Conversely, the state seeks from the city assistance in making Annapolis as "convenient" as possible for legislators and other state officials. The context for the city's requests from the state is a line-item allotment to the city in the state's annual budget. The state's requests of the city are less routinized but pertain to matters such as parking spaces on the circular roadway surrounding the State House. Mayor Dennis Callahan, in one of his first official acts, changed the traffic pattern on a street near a parking facility used by many state workers in the interest of city–state relations. He did not, however, get nearly as large an increase in the state's allotment to the city as he asked for in his first year in office.

On occasion, the city government or other Annapolis-based organizations will lobby the state for funds for some particular special project. One such project, as yet only partly completed, is the burial of overhead utility lines throughout the Historic District. The city and Historic Annapolis have made this request for reasons of both safety and aesthetics, but the city says that it cannot afford the full cost of the project. In 1987 the state provided partial funding, dependent on matching funds. There have been attempts to fund this project for well over ten years, and although it is still unfinished, the burial of these lines is likely to be completed sooner or later.

All in all, conflict between the city and the state on both general and specific issues is likely to continue into the distant future. Put simply, Annapolis knows it benefits from being the state capital and the city wants to maximize those benefits while giving up as little authority as possible. And while Annapolis is developing sources of identity and income beyond those it derives from its status as capital, it cannot afford to become too independent because with so much of state government already located in Baltimore, it would not be difficult to mount a cogent argument for moving the entire state government to Baltimore in the name of "efficiency" or perhaps "modernization." Annapolis has been threatened with losing the state capital before, and while its removal to Baltimore is unlikely, it is a possibility that cannot be dismissed.

Annapolis and the U.S. Naval Academy

Perhaps in Nebraska the phrase "Annapolis and the Naval Academy" might be as redundant as the phrase "cattle and bovines," but it is surely not redundant in Annapolis. Relations between the city and the federal installation it seems to host are complex but outwardly cordial.

The academy has more than enough midshipmen from Anne Arundel County to protect itself from claims of discrimination against local applicants. All midshipmen have local "host families" with whom they can relax during off-duty hours. From time to time, the local newspaper runs a feature story sympathetically describing the difficult life of midshipmen, particularly the plebes or first-year students. The following story exemplifies the town's attitudes toward midshipmen.

It is a custom at Navy football home games for midshipmen to run out of the stands after a Navy score and do push-ups equaling the Navy team's total score up to that point in the game. During the game between Navy and the University of Virginia in 1986, the Virginia pep band, a small, relatively disorganized group of students, approached the midshipmen doing push-ups after a Navy score. At what appeared to be slight provocation, hundreds of midshipmen swarmed after the pep band, chasing it back to its own side of the field, wrestling its members to the ground, and grabbing hats and other items of the band members' attire. This free-for-all was ultimately brought under control by a group of midshipmen acting as military policemen, but not before some members of the Virginia band received minor injuries. Several days later, a letter to the editor appeared in the *Capital* condemning the midshipmen's behavior as undisciplined, uncivil, and worthy of punishment. This letter was followed by at least two in support of the midshipmen, arguing that such hijinks are a Navy tradition, that midshipmen are good, hardworking, all-American boys (and girls), that letting off a little steam is perfectly OK, and that the first letter writer was naive and "unenculturated."

Reaction to the academy at the institutional level is another thing. Again, cordiality prevails on the surface, but there are other, deeper currents as well. In the fall of 1986, downtown businesses began flying windsock kites in the Navy colors (navy blue and gold) on occasions like parents' weekend and home football games. This was a way, merchants say, of welcoming to Annapolis people connected with the academy. More to the point, some merchants see the influx of visitors associated with the academy as an opportunity to make money. At the same time, many local residents feel forced out of their downtown by these same visitors and resent having to compete with out-of-towners for parking spaces near their homes. Many of these same residents do, on occasion, take advantage of the situation, renting out their homes for upward of $1,000 during the Academy's Commissioning Week in May.

Beyond the inconveniences associated with being the home of a well-visited college, there are larger issues, or issues that are specific and acute rather than chronic. Two confrontations between the Navy and local residents are instructive.

In the first case, the Navy announced a plan to build a McDonald's restaurant on its small base directly across the Severn River from the academy. The first plan called for placing the restaurant just outside the gate of the base, near a narrow road leading to Providence, an exclusive subdivision. Many neighbors, including retired naval personnel, complained about the placement, fearing increased traffic, noise, and litter. The Navy held a public meeting, collected neighborhood opinions, and reversed its decision, opting to put the McDonald's just *inside* the gate, making it inaccessible to anyone without access to the base.

The same pattern of events characterized a confrontation over the location of mooring buoys. The Navy decided that it needed a set of mooring buoys in the Severn River to provide safe anchorage for certain midsized ships during hurricane conditions on the Chesapeake Bay. It proposed a system of twenty or so independent buoys to be located in Little Round Bay, just upriver from the academy. The people who lived around Little Round Bay objected to the plan, claiming that it would make the area unsafe or unusable for pleasure boaters and people fishing in the area. The Navy quickly came up with a compromise plan that entailed attaching the twenty anchor lines to a single, large buoy.

In both instances, the Navy proposed a plan, listened to local objections, and enacted a modified plan with local support. In each case, the Navy appeared quite accommodating and willing to compromise, although the simplicity of each compromise, which consisted of only small concessions on the Navy's part, suggests that the Navy's strategy was to *seem* quite sensitive to the needs and desires of its neighbors while implementing a predefined fall-back position. What the Navy really gained was positive publicity on which it could draw in the future in a situation in which it was *not* prepared to compromise.

Behind all the levels of cordiality lie two realities: the Naval Academy is a part of the Department of Defense, one of the largest arms of the federal government, and as a consequence, there is no real basis for negotiation between the "host" (the city) and the "guest" (the academy) other than the willingness of the Navy to allow such relations, and the appearance of equality they imply. In addition, as government property, the academy grounds—an area at least one-quarter the size of the city's downtown Historic District—are *not* on the local property tax rolls. This means that virtually the entire contribution the academy makes to the local economy falls under the heading of "discretionary spending," money that the academy and its visitors spend as they like and wherever they choose. That both puts Annapolis under the thumb of the academy and forms the basis for pitting local merchants against each other, competing for academy-related business.

Two other examples demonstrate the unequal relationship between the city and the academy and the speed and strength with which the academy can and will act to protect its own interests. In the fall of 1986, an intoxicated midshipman died behind the wheel of an automobile. Several days later, the lead story in the *Capital* attributed to an academy official a threat to make some or all Annapolis bars "off-limits" to *all* naval personnel, not just midshipmen, because some bars had been known to serve underage or intoxicated midshipmen. As the story went on to note, the academy's alcohol awareness officer had routinely visited Annapolis bars undercover, in civilian clothes, and had observed illegal sales to midshipmen. Rather than, or in addition to, punishing the underage midshipmen who had requested service, the academy chose to make a public threat to punish the local bars. This reaction was particularly interesting when contrasted with the aftermath of another incident reported in the *Capital* in which two midshipmen were apprehended by Annapolis police in a public park while in the act of providing champagne to a pair of Annapolis girls aged sixteen and seventeen. In the newspaper account, a spokesperson for the academy simply said that alcohol consumption is a serious matter and that the incident was under investigation, all this in a small story buried inside the *Capital*. As is frequently the case when midshipmen break the law in Annapolis, the police pressed no charges and considered the case closed. The point is that in two cases involving alcohol and midshipmen rather different standards were applied by academy officials and by others, with the result that in each case, the interests of the academy were served before all others.

A Brief Segue

The previous sections contain examples of local issues that have developed along the lines that divide the various government entities with interests in Annapolis. The specific issues may change, but conflicts between Annapolis and the county, the state, and the Naval Academy are likely to continue. There will also be periods of cooperation. But at least in the cases of the state and the Naval Academy, it is important to keep in mind the essential inequality that is a part of any current relationships between those two institutions and the city. Other issues in contemporary Annapolis are, or appear to be, independent of these particular political relationships. Unlike the first set of issues, which could have been predicted from a reading of the Annapolis telephone directory, this second set of issues consists of concerns and conflicts that emerged during my residence in Annapolis. These issues are just as grounded in political and economic structures as the ones discussed above, except that the relationship is not as obvious.

In Annapolis in the mid-1980s, one read and heard a great deal about tourism, development, and public housing. To these I add a fourth issue, gentrification. Gentrification, as defined by Wallace (1986: 179–81), refers to the displacement of poor residents from downtown neighborhoods by more affluent professionals intent on restoring old houses. Although gentrification is not mentioned much in Annapolis, the process has certainly been enacted in the downtown Historic District. One could consider each of these four issues separately, but it is far more productive

Cornhill Street, between the city dock and State Circle, midway through the process of its gentrification. (Photograph courtesy of M. E. Warren, Annapolis, Maryland)

to consider them in two pairs, gentrification and public housing, tourism and development.

Gentrification and Public Housing

The downtown Historic District is about 75 percent gentrified. Many small vernacular houses have been purchased and rehabilitated by and for professionals from Annapolis or Washington. This has forced African-American renters out of the center city to either another African-American neighborhood near the edge of the Historic District or to the edges of the city itself. There is no question that the cost of the revitalization of the downtown was the displacement and reconfiguration of a community of African-American tradesmen and watermen, and their families, who lived in the small houses on East, Cornhill, Fleet, and Pinkney streets, between the State House and the city dock. This area has contained an African-American community since at least the 1870s (Ives 1979). Some of the men who lived in this neighborhood worked the bay and sold their catch on the dock. These watermen have been replaced by "urban homesteaders." The harbor is filled with yachts, and any fresh produce sold in the Market House on the city dock is trucked in. Pizza, Perrier, and ice cream have successfully displaced fresh-off-the-boat seafood.

The kind of displacement that took place in Annapolis, involving dozens of families, has been a tense issue in many other cities. I was not surprised to hear members of the white preservation community argue that moving African-Americans out of rundown, substandard housing was doing them a favor. However, I *was* surprised to hear these sentiments echoed by virtually all of the African-Americans with whom I spoke. They, too, suggested that displacement from downtown had been a good thing. People can regroup and keep in touch, I was told, and a house with a yard near the edge of town is better than a smaller house without a yard in town.

This does not mean that the demise of one of Annapolis's two long-time African-American communities has been without consequences. One of the consequences has been public housing, the flip side of gentrification. If people are forced out of one place, they must move somewhere else. In Annapolis, one-sixth of all housing units are publicly subsidized, the highest ratio of any municipality in Maryland, and in 1987 the city had more than 700 families on a five-year waiting list for public housing. Not all public housing residents were displaced from downtown. And not all those displaced from downtown ended up in public housing. But taking the broad view, it is helpful to think of the two issues as parts of the same process.

The issue of public housing is complex. Public housing became highly visible and political in early 1986. At that time, newly elected Mayor Callahan called for the resignation of all five members of the Annapolis Housing Authority (AHA) Board of Commissioners. The AHA solicits and administers federal housing funds. The members of its Board of Commissioners are appointed by the mayor to terms that are staggered, to keep the authority from becoming politicized. In asking for the resignation of the board, Callahan's real goal was to remove the authority's executive director, Arthur Strissel.

Since the executive director is appointed by the board, with a cooperative board in place, Callahan would have been able to install his own candidate in this position. This was necessary, Callahan claimed, because the

AHA had grown insensitive toward tenant concerns and had allowed the city's public housing units to fall into disrepair. The conflict between Callahan and Strissel was long and complicated. Only one of the five commissioners resigned, and Callahan ultimately withdrew his request for the other resignations. Subsequently, Callahan brought charges of misconduct against the four remaining commissioners, only to drop them when they could not be substantiated. In response, the board brought suit against Callahan for bringing charges he could not prove. At about this time, Callahan was able to add another one of his people to the board, since the term of one of Strissel's supporters had expired. Then, in early 1987, Callahan persuaded the Annapolis delegation to the state legislature to sponsor legislation that would expand the AHA Board of Commissioners, allowing Callahan to gain control by making two new appointments. These legislative initiatives never made it out of committee, and when I left Annapolis Callahan and Strissel were still at an impasse, although Callahan was within months of gaining control over the board upon the expiration of the term of another Strissel supporter.

This fight over the AHA is more complicated and far more acrimonious than I have indicated here, but the intricacy and tone of those debates is beside my point. Much more important is the broader discussion of public housing in Annapolis initiated by the political battles between Callahan and Strissel. A key factor in that discussion was the high concentration of public housing in Annapolis, the level of subsidization, and the long waiting list. It was on this point that Callahan's anti-Strissel coalition began to split. Callahan had the support of Carl Snowden, the alderman from Ward 5. Snowden, an African-American, was first elected to City Council from a ward designed to have an African-American majority. For fifteen years prior to his election, Snowden had been an activist for various civil rights causes in Annapolis. While both Callahan and Snowden opposed Strissel, Snowden favored expanding public housing and affordable housing in the city, while Callahan felt that Annapolis had enough public housing and that Anne Arundel County should shoulder more of the burden. Many residents of public housing in Annapolis are African-Americans, and public housing became a contentious racial issue when the city's chief of police commented that public housing encouraged criminal activity. In response, Alderman Snowden accused the chief of racism.

The public housing issue in Annapolis, and in particular the 700-family waiting list, points up an increasing gap between rich and poor in the city. Also evident is the effectiveness with which African-Americans in Annapolis have been "hidden" in housing projects like Newtowne 20, far off the beaten track and without easy access to places of employment. This is at least in part a product of the process of gentrification, which is itself based on the commodification of people and property and an ideology that condones the movement of poor or African-Americans around Annapolis as if they were pieces in a board game, as if they were not "real" Annapolitans.

Public housing is only the most visible of a number of black–white issues in Annapolis today. As a baseline for my discussion of these issues, it is important to understand that Annapolis, like most of the South, was segregated until the 1950s. During my stay in Annapolis, the city saw legislation or legal action dealing with discrimination in the police department, discrimination in hiring and promotion at Anne Arundel General Hospital, segregation in private clubs, and the creation of a redistricting plan that would provide proportional representation of African-Americans on the City Council. Reports on these various issues in the local press kept racial discrimination a perpetual topic of discussion during the mid-1980s. Furthermore, official findings of one sort or another in almost all of these areas confirm a long-standing pattern of subtle, institutionalized racism in Annapolis.

Tourism and Development

The discussion that concludes this chapter flows out of an observation I made earlier, that Annapolis's major sources of income—the Naval Academy, state government, yachting, and tourism—all have a similar structure: Annapolis depends heavily on transient individuals and on institutions made up largely of transient individuals. In abstract terms, the issue for Annapolis is how to maximize its profits from such visitation while protecting itself and limiting the costs. The town has articulated this concern with regard to tourism, and I would contend that arguments about tourism apply equally to the state government and the Naval Academy.

Tourism was a major issue in the 1985 mayoral election, and to the best of my knowledge the term "quality tourist" first entered the Annapolis lexicon during that campaign. Annapolis has lived with intensive tourism for twenty to twenty-five years and understands it fairly well. From time to time, the *Capital* runs what can only be called "pep-talks" in print, articles commiserating with local residents over the inconveniences associated with being a tourist destination. These articles also remind Annapolitans of the millions of tourist dollars spent in Annapolis every year, including $14 million, by some estimates, during the boat shows alone. This "We've got to live with it" attitude was supplanted by a vigorous effort on the part of the Callahan administration to control tourism by attracting "quality tourists," and by strongly discouraging unacceptable tourist behavior. The quality tourist is a doctor, lawyer, or other professional, who visits Annapolis with his or her family, spends a night or two in a local hotel, patronizes local restaurants, buys from local shops, and generally enjoys the historical and maritime pleasures of Annapolis quietly. To be discouraged are loud, bare-chested, beer drinkers who raft-up power boats at the city dock, harass passers-by, and urinate in public. Weekend bar-hoppers, night-trippers as opposed to day-trippers, are also considered relatively undesirable. They are loud, have weak bladders, and contribute to what Mayor Callahan once termed the "Georgetowning" of Annapolis, in reference to the popular Washington, D.C., party spot.

Before Callahan's arrival, there was a tourism council for Annapolis and Anne Arundel County. In addition, Historic Annapolis and Three Centuries Tours of Annapolis did what they could to attract and entertain serious, historically minded tourists, but there was no city official or department with jurisdiction over tourism. That changed with Callahan's appointment of a director of tourism and public information as one of his first official acts in early 1986. The appointment was initially challenged on procedural grounds, but most people in Annapolis hailed the move as necessary and overdue. The job of the tourism director is to market the city to appropriate target populations of potential visitors and to coordinate the activities of groups and institutions within the city serving the needs of tourists.

Another part of Callahan's tourism initiative was to initiate police foot patrols and a police cadet program, both with jurisdiction over the heart of tourist Annapolis, the city dock. In addition to putting more officers on the street in areas with heavy tourist traffic, the mayor used legislation to help them enforce polite behavior at the dock. Until recently, urinating in public was classified as indecent exposure, a sex crime, and a felony. Police officers were reluctant to arrest people on such a serious charge, so many violators went unpunished. In response, the city council separated indecent exposure from urinating in public, creating a new misdemeanor, in the hope that the availability of a lesser charge would encourage officers to be quicker to make arrests for public urination. On the face of it, this would seem a superfluous bit of legislation, but the structure that lies behind it validates its importance. In a further move to exercise control over the dock, Callahan arranged the acquisition of a police boat, to help officers enforce noise restrictions and other regulations. All of these moves were intended to strengthen the city's control over visitors, an important move, considering the small size of the city and the large number of visitors it serves annually. The effect of Annapolis's decision has been to increase its ability to protect those aspects of the city that attract the kinds of tourists the city wants, so that the city may continue to attract them.

Attracting visitors, however, has been recognized as a two-edged sword. Once attracted, visitors must be controlled and then sent on their way. This is where development becomes an issue. Just as public housing may be considered the other side of gentrification, development may be seen as connected to tourism. Although attracting "quality tourists" is an important and much-discussed issue at the city level, controlling land development is a key issue at the level of county politics.

For example, in the 1986 Democratic primary election for the District 7 seat on the County Council (Annapolis is in District 7), Brad Davidson, a politically ambitious young Annapolis alderman, ran against a popular, two-term incumbent with a single issue: the need for tight controls on development. That the incumbent won handily was due at least in part to her having already built a solid record of working for controlled development. Development is so key an issue that it even figured in the smear tactics on both sides; at one point backers of each candidate accused the other of owning recently developed property or rental units. In the climate of local issues, this was far worse than accusing them of sexual indiscretions.

Development, less explicitly a political issue in Annapolis proper, owing to the lack of open property that can be built on, is tied to the issue of tourism. For tourism to work to the greatest possible benefit of the tourist destination, the tourists have to go home. From the point of view of a tourist destination, the ideal tourist is the most disfranchised tourist, and the ultimate act of deference to local authority is to return home at the end of a visit. However, tourism is not the only way to make a living from outsiders to an area. In contrast to true tourists, developers—or more properly the people to whom they cater—are the outsiders who do not go home. There are probably hundreds of current Annapolitans who, not so long ago, drove or sailed into the city for a day or two, fell in love with the narrow streets, and bought a house on one of them. The potential danger in tourists who do not go home is twofold: they increase pressure on local facilities and services, and they pose a threat to local authority. That is to say, outsiders may come to Annapolis, stay, and become insiders with whom authority must be shared. More than a few Annapolitans have experienced this process themselves. Many Annapolis insiders are former outsiders, and a big joke in the city is that every newcomer wants to be the last one in. More broadly, Annapolis insiders have lost enough of their authority to the state of Maryland and the Naval Academy to understand the need to monitor and regulate the activities of outsiders.

Summary

The foregoing is a sketch of Annapolis in the mid-1980s. Annapolis is a small but complex place, politically active, relatively self-conscious, and concerned with image and identity, as well as with its relationships with other governmental entities. The city is best understood through the dynamics of tourism, broadly defined. Annapolis is a place largely dependent on outsiders, but not just tourists. The relationship between locals and outsiders that is clearly defined in the context of tourism is the same kind of relationship that surrounds many of Annapolis's most important "industries"—yachting, state government, and the Naval Academy.

Of necessity, much has been left out of this portrait. However, most of the issues identified in this chapter are dealt with, directly or indirectly, in the next several chapters. They also play an important role in the concluding chapters dealing with Archaeology in Public. Archaeology in Public has focused on some of these issues more than on others, but any of them could serve as the focus of an archaeological site tour in Annapolis, as could entirely different aspects of the contemporary life of the city. Again, this chapter is not the final word on Annapolis, only my particular impression.

5

An Outline History of Annapolis

As explained in chapter 4, Annapolis is a historical place. The city's historical character, as identified by a variety of Annapolitans, has both advantages and disadvantages. For example, history attracts tourists, but it also is the basis for local regulations that constrain property owners from radically altering the external appearance of buildings within the Historic District.

This chapter provides a brief review of Annapolis history and outlines several key themes I have abstracted from that history for further consideration. These themes are (1) the city's long-standing and seemingly conscious drive for gentility with a connection to the water, (2) its weak urban identity or ambiguous urbanism, and (3) its economic reliance on outsiders and transients.

A Chronological History of Annapolis

A chronological history can be constructed in at least two ways: by dealing with the past as a series of discrete events or by considering the past as a series of time periods. I take the latter approach in this chapter, although there is no particular justification—past or present—for my periodization of Annapolis history other than convention and convenience. That is to say, I am following no particular "native taxonomy" in my construction of the chronology in this chapter.

Seventeenth-Century Beginnings

The settlement that eventually became Annapolis was founded in 1649. The area around the mouth of the Severn River was originally settled by Puritans fleeing from religious persecution in Virginia. They arrived in the area fifteen years after the colony of Maryland was established by the Calvert family in 1634. The Calverts had been granted Maryland and the hereditary title "Lord Baltimore" by Charles I of England. From 1634 until the American Revolution (except for the period 1689–1715), the holder of the lordship was also known as the proprietor of Maryland. Events in Maryland in the 1650s were largely colonial versions of the English Civil War and represent the first of many expressions of English politics in the colony. The most important of these events, particularly for the history of Annapolis, was a small naval engagement in 1655 between a group of Puritans and the largely Catholic forces of the proprietor (Riley 1887: 19; Radoff 1971: 15–16). Called the Battle of the Severn, this engagement took place near what is now Horn Point in Eastport and was the first and last military engagement ever to take place in the immediate vicinity of Annapolis.

Between its initial settlement and 1695, the city now called Annapolis went by a number of names, including Providence (Riley 1887: 19), the Town Land at Proctor's (Riley 1887: 52), Arundelton (Radoff 1971: 177), and Anne Arundel Town (Riley 1887: 62), to cite the main ones. The town was a part of a larger colonial system devoted to making a profit for the Calvert family, based primarily on tobacco and secondarily on the land speculation attendant on an agricultural economy in a frontier area. The town remained small during the second half of the seventeenth century, growing to perhaps forty dwellings by the 1690s (Papenfuse 1975: 9). To encourage growth, the authorities issued a series of acts making the town a port of entry and therefore giving it an important legal function. Unlike New England, however, the Chesapeake region, with its hundreds of navigable rivers and creeks, did not favor or require the development of port cities with large populations (Papenfuse 1975: 5). Since only the paperwork and not the ships themselves had to pass through a port of entry, Annapolis's legal status did not automatically dictate urban development parallel with that of cities such as New York, Philadelphia, and Boston.

Moreover, unlike cities such as Baltimore, Annapolis was not geographically situated to command a large hinterland.

Toward the end of the seventeenth century, events in England again had a major impact on Maryland and Annapolis. In the Glorious Revolution of 1688, two Protestants, William and Mary of the House of Orange, ascended the throne of England, with the result that in 1689 Maryland shifted from proprietary government (headed by a Catholic family) to royal government (Radoff 1971: 178). From then until 1715 Maryland was governed by five royal governors, but the proprietorship was reinstated upon the conversion to Protestantism by Benedict Leonard Calvert, the fourth Lord Baltimore (Eareckson 1980: 3–16). However, the impact of the ascension of the House of Orange was profound. In 1694 the city of Annapolis took its name from Princess Anne, second daughter of James II and sister of Queen Mary, who became Queen Anne in 1702 (Ramirez 1975: 48). More important, under the leadership of Sir Francis Nicholson, Maryland's second royal governor, Annapolis became the capital of Maryland in 1694, replacing St. Mary's City. Modern scholars attribute Nicholson's decision to a mixture of economic and religious reasons. For one thing, Annapolis had a central location in seventeenth-century Maryland, in contrast to St. Mary's City, located at the southern tip of the colony (Radoff 1971: 178–79). For another, Nicholson, a Protestant appointed by a Protestant monarch, is thought to have moved the capital to a part of the colony inhabited by Protestants and away from an area considered to be a Catholic stronghold (Riley 1887: 58). Also noteworthy is the fact that as early as 1674 citizens of Providence had called for just such a shift (Riley 1887: 57). Therefore it seems fair to suggest that the local citizenry welcomed their town's new status.

Nicholson, who served as governor or deputy governor for Virginia, Nova Scotia, New York, and South Carolina in addition to his service in Maryland (Norris 1925: 38), is generally considered to have been an able colonial administrator. The biggest mark he left on Annapolis is its baroque town plan, still called the Nicholson plan. Upon making Annapolis the capital, Nicholson attempted to transform the little settlement into a truly urban place by introducing circles, radiating streets, and vistas adapted to the topography of the Annapolis peninsula—including two prominent hills—and to a rudimentary and unfinished street plan in existence at least as early as Richard Beard's survey in 1683 (Ramirez 1975: 38). Nicholson's plan used vistas up the radiating streets to the two central circles, to highlight the two linked sources of authority in colonial Annapolis and Maryland, church and state; the smaller circle contained St.

Anne's Church, the larger one the State House (Ramirez 1975: 45). It is widely accepted (Reps 1972; Ramirez 1975: 69–75) that Nicholson knew the work of John Evelyn and Sir Christopher Wren, both of whom designed baroque plans for the rebuilding of London after the great fire of 1666, and St. Mary's City is also said to have had a Baroque plan (Miller 1988). After leaving Annapolis, Nicholson continued to use baroque principles for town planning. As governor of Virginia, he laid out Williamsburg along an axial plan that used several streets to form the initials "W" and "M" (Reps 1972; Ramirez 1975: 75), a first-class baroque fillip. Contemporary Annapolis bears at least three marks of Nicholson's brief tenure. The city is still the capital of Maryland. The street plan remains largely intact. And both Williamsburg and Annapolis have a Francis Street, named for the governor by the governor.

The Early Eighteenth Century

In 1708 Queen Anne granted Annapolis a charter, despite several less than favorable appraisals of living conditions there. John Oldmixon (1708, cited in Papenfuse 1975: 9) claimed that Annapolis would never amount to much and Ebenezer Cook's description of Annapolis in *The Sot-Weed Factor* (1708) refers to

> A City Situate on a Plain
> Where scarce a House will keep out Rain
> The Buildings fram'd with Cypress rare,
> Resembles much our Southwark Fair;
> But Stranger here will scarcely meet
> With Market-place, Exchange, or Streets;
> And if the Truth I may report,
> 'Tis not so large as Tottenham Court.

Annapolis remained a small and physically unimpressive town through much of the first half of the eighteenth century. Estimates place its population at 252 in 1699, 469 in 1720, and 832 in 1740 (Papenfuse 1975: 14). Few dwellings were bigger than 18 by 30 feet (Ramirez 1975: 106), and most buildings from this period were probably of frame construction. Only in the 1740s did significant numbers of private citizens begin building substantial brick structures.

Many other important trends of the first half of the eighteenth century are not necessarily represented architecturally. Annapolis, and Annapolis

The backyard of the Hammond-Harwood House with the State House dome in the background, showing the continuing presence of Nicholson's plan from yet another angle. (Photograph courtesy of M. E. Warren, Annapolis, Maryland)

merchants in particular, began learning how to profit from the tobacco trade. Annapolis grew into its role as capital of the colony. Several important Annapolis families—the Bordleys, the Carrolls, and the Dulanys—established themselves early in the century. In addition, this was the time of a dramatic shift in wealthholding (Leone and Shackel 1987, 1990; and

Shackel 1987; Leone 1988). By the 1730s a once substantial middle class had been almost obliterated, while a few people at the top of the economic scale had augmented their wealth considerably. Historical work attests to this transformation (see Baker 1983, 1986; Russo 1983; Walsh 1983a, 1983b; and Carr 1983), and archaeological techniques are being developed by Leone and Shackel for studying it further. This work suggests that the economic shift was responsible for Annapolis's short-lived "golden age" in the third quarter of the eighteenth century.

The early eighteenth century in Annapolis probably ends with the founding of the Tuesday Club in 1745. Modeled on English and Scottish clubs of the early eighteenth century, this club's membership consisted of the leading members of Annapolis society, including mayors, vestrymen, businessmen, and Jonas Green, printer to the colony and the publisher of the *Maryland Gazette*. The club often hosted distinguished visitors such as Benjamin Franklin (Breslaw 1975a, 1975b). The club was noted for its witty and sophisticated, usually satirical, repartee. Club meetings featured debates, mock trials, the singing of odes, and a variety of "clubbical" rituals, all governed by the "gelastic rule." Under this rule, anyone who made any kind of serious remark about politics, current events, business, religion, or the like was roundly laughed down by the rest of the club. Members *did* discuss the issues of the day but only in a veiled, roundabout way, characterized by "wit, whimsey, and satire" (Breslaw 1975b). The club is also known today for its music; several members wrote music and most played musical instruments. The urbanity of the Tuesday Club, which disbanded in 1756, upon the death of its founder, Dr. Alexander Hamilton, was a portent of things to come in Annapolis.

The Late Eighteenth-Century Golden Age

Toward the end of the eighteenth century, Annapolis experienced a brief "golden age" of culture and sophistication (Norris 1925: 42–224; Stevens 1937: 46–65; Wertenbaker 1942: 85–104). Because it was the colonial capital, the city attracted wealthy and important people from all over Maryland, and among the refinements they discovered there was one of the earliest theaters in the colonies (Riley 1887: 146–48; Ward 1975), along with the wares of a wide range of luxury craftsmen. The more permanent product of this golden age may still be seen in Annapolis today in the form of the Georgian mansions that seem to fill the city. Four of the greatest—the Wm. Paca House, the Chase-Lloyd House, the James Brice

A view of Annapolis in 1797 with the State House in the right center and St. Anne's to the far right. (Photograph courtesy of M. E. Warren, Annapolis, Maryland)

House, and the Hammond-Harwood House—were all constructed within a span of eleven years, from 1763 to 1774. Politically, this period saw a hearty dispute in Annapolis between the Court Party (loyalists) and the Country Party (patriots). Annapolis had a local group of Sons of Liberty, and the Annapolis Liberty Tree still stands today on the campus of St. John's College. Annapolis patriots mounted a vigorous opposition to the Stamp Act and held their own Tea Party. The city still contains houses owned by all four of Maryland's signers of the Declaration of Independence. Although there were no military engagements in or near Annapolis, the city did act as a supply center and a staging area for troops.

Annapolis served briefly as the capital of the United States when the Continental Congress met in the Maryland State House from November 26, 1783, through August 19, 1784 (Fortenbaugh 1973). During this session of Congress, George Washington resigned his commission in the Continental Army, and the Treaty of Paris was ratified by Congress. Two-and-one-half years later, Annapolis hosted a national convention (attended by delegates from only five states) that led to the Philadelphia

Constitutional Convention, which drew up a replacement for the Articles of Confederation. In all, during its brief heyday, Annapolis was the social, economic, and political center of the Chesapeake Bay area, despite having a population of no more than 1,300 (Papenfuse 1975: 14). During the 1780s, at the end of Annapolis's period of ascendancy, and as the government of the new United States was attempting to find a permanent home, Annapolis offered itself as the national capital, promising to build thirteen governor's mansions along the circular roadway around the State House, which was to be used as the national Capitol (Riley 1887: 198–200; Norris 1925: 227–28). The city's offer, needless to say, was turned down.

The Nineteenth Century

By the end of the Revolution, and certainly by 1790, Annapolis had entered a period of what one writer has termed "genteel eclipse" (Norris 1925: 225–44). Less euphemistically, Annapolis lost its preeminent position in the Chesapeake economy to the growing commercial and industrial port of Baltimore (Riley 1887: 319; Radoff 1971: 188; Papenfuse 1975: 169–223). Many people, particularly apologists for Annapolis, have suggested that Baltimore overtook Annapolis because the principal cash-crop in the region had shifted from tobacco to grain and because Baltimore had a larger and deeper natural harbor. As a consequence, Annapolis lost much of its commerce after the Revolution and its wealthiest residents moved to Baltimore, presumably followed by the merchants and craftsmen who had dealt in luxury goods in eighteenth-century Annapolis. The city suddenly became a small, local market town (Papenfuse 1975: 225–36). In the nineteenth century, the City Dock, once an anchorage for ocean-going ships traveling to and from New England, the Caribbean, Europe, and Africa, came to be used for bay-going boats with cargoes of lumber and produce, and by Annapolis-based watermen.

However, this economic eclipse may not have been as profound as suggested by an unnamed member of late nineteenth-century naval commission:

A polar expedition is useless to determine the Earth's Axis. Go to Annapolis rather. It should be called the pivot-city. It is the centre of the universe, for while all the world around it revolves it remains stationary. One advantage is that you always know where to find it. To get to Annapolis you have but to cultivate a colossal calmness and the force of

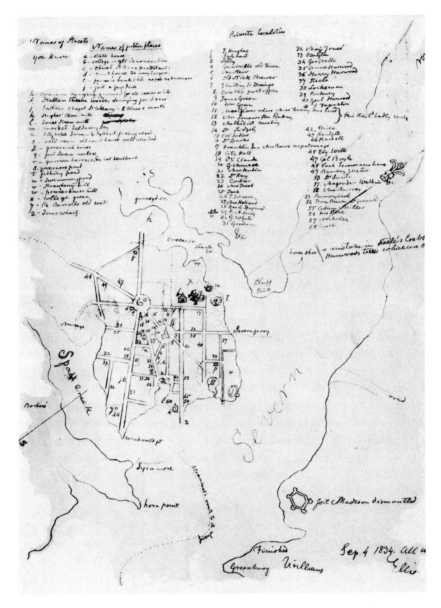

Ellie's 1834 map of Annapolis. Note the relative lack of buildings on the eastern part of the peninsula, the section of town that was given over to the Naval Academy shortly after this map was made. (Photograph courtesy of M. E. Warren, Annapolis, Maryland)

gravity will draw you towards the great centre—once there, there is no centrifugal force to displace you and you stay. By natural evolution your hands disappear in your breeches pockets and you assume the most marked characteristic of the indigenous Annapolitan. No glove merchant ever flourished there. Annapolitans in heaven have heads and wings, their hands disappear. On old tombstones you may see them as Angels, on earth they resemble exclamation points, all heads and tails, like the fish they eat. Natural evolution develops itself in a taste for oysters, as they need no carving, and a phosphorous diet swells the brain; they talk politics continually. Annapolis keeps the Severn River in its place. This will be useful when the harbour of Baltimore dries up. Annapolitans are waiting for this. They are in no hurry, they don't mind waiting. Two or three centennials will do it. (Quoted in Riley 1887: 145)

Although it was the capital of Maryland and the nautical entrance to Washington D.C., and was visited by several important personages such as President James Madison in 1818 (Riley 1887: 255) and LaFayette in 1824 (Riley 1887: 239–43), Annapolis was no longer the premier city of Maryland. Annapolitans understood this and fought political skirmishes in a two-front battle to keep what claims to importance the city had and to acquire new ones. On at least three occasions—in 1786 (Ramirez 1975: 178), 1817 (Riley 1887: 254), and 1864 (Radoff 1971: 189)—Baltimore attempted to have the state government relocated from Annapolis to Baltimore and was rebuffed in the Maryland Legislature, once by a single vote. Alarmed by the threat from Baltimore, Annapolis worked to entice the federal government to establish a naval school in Annapolis (Riley 1887: 264). This campaign eventually succeeded, in 1845, but only after twenty years of perseverance.

The date of the establishment of the U.S. Naval Academy is often taken as a turning point, the dawning of a new era for Annapolis (Riley 1887: 268; Radoff 1971: 189), but throughout the nineteenth century the academy was relatively small and physically unimpressive, housed partly in decaying remnants of Annapolis's colonial golden age. At the time of the Civil War, the academy was so small that most of its students and instructors were easily packed up on a boat and sent off to Newport, Rhode Island, to wait out the war safely removed from the fighting. Despite the small size of the academy, the city recognized its potential for growth and economic benefit and grew concerned that the academy would not come back after the war.

Even with the academy, and its contribution to the economy of

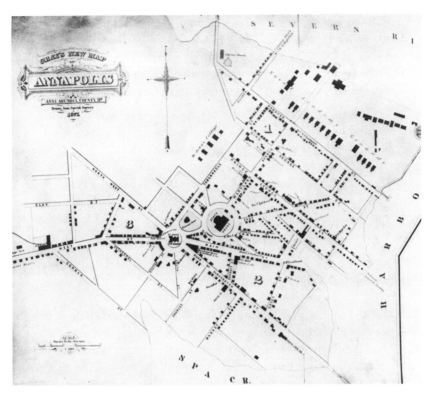

Gray's New Map of Annapolis, 1877. Note all the buildings on the Naval Academy grounds, and the filling of the governor's pond. (Photograph courtesy of M. E. Warren, Annapolis, Maryland)

Annapolis, some Annapolitans still felt the need, around the turn of the century, to try to attract industry to the former queen of the Chesapeake. In a chapter entitled "Annapolis as a Trade, Manufacturing, Commercial, and Residential City," Phillip Porter, City Clerk of Annapolis, wrote the following in Riley's (1906) *Pictorial Annapolis*: "The business of Annapolis is constantly increasing. The country about Annapolis is most productive of fruits, berries, and vegetables, suitable for canning. Farmers are ready to enter into arrangements to grow the vegetables that packers may need for their business. The very name of Anne Arundel is a commendation to berries, fruits, and vegetables." In an earlier book, Riley (1897) remarked:

> It is true that the business of Annapolis has declined in past years from the former glory of the colonial period, yet the oyster trade has given an

impulse to its commercial affairs. During normal seasons of trade from five to seven thousand dollars weekly are paid by the oyster packers of this city to [African-American] oystermen, shuckers and workmen in their houses. This goes into the hands of men who cannot hold the money and it passes from hand to hand to the great benefit of all trades.

Riley also states that "the harbor of Annapolis is unsurpassed on the bay or coast and its practical use for commerce should have long since been established." In his initial historical work (Riley 1887: 323), he had cited the value of a new railroad for "bringing to the attention of capitalists the magnificent harbor of Annapolis." This invitation, issued by Porter, Riley, and the Businessman's Association of Annapolis, had virtually no response. Annapolis was not able to lure back what it had lost a century earlier.

The Twentieth Century

Annapolis's "slumber" continued virtually unabated through the 1950s. It was punctuated early in the twentieth century by a massive rebuilding of the Naval Academy campus, which changed the face of Annapolis in two ways. First, the new campus obliterated parts of the eighteenth-century street pattern and some eighteenth-century buildings, replacing them with a set of modern, large, granite, beaux-arts buildings designed by Earnest Flagg. These new buildings were situated on a plan with an inward focus and sightlines to the Severn River. Second, to create housing for the workers involved in the rebuilding, the city had to further subdivide many of its lots and fill in Nicholson's plan for the city. Nicholson almost certainly intended the city to be three-dimensional; buildings along the roadways were supposed to frame the views of prominent landmarks. The relative calm of the early twentieth century was also punctuated, from time to time, by the construction of new facilities for the state government. However, none of this construction was extensive enough to destroy the eighteenth-century character of the city, although many eighteenth-century buildings were destroyed in the process. One positive result of Annapolis's 150-year eclipse, from the viewpoint of the twentieth-century preservationist, is that the lack of large-scale commercial and industrial development served to preserve many eighteenth-century buildings. In the nineteenth century it was not generally profitable to tear down eighteenth-century buildings. As a result, the city has, by Historic Annapolis's count, about fifty-five eighteenth-century buildings, a collection larger than that of any other American city along the eastern seaboard, with the exception of Williamsburg. In short, none of the twentieth-century government-sponsored development of Annapolis did much to alter the essential slowness and sleepiness of the city. There can be no better evidence for that than the discontinuation of rail service between Annapolis and both Baltimore and Washington by the late 1930s (Stevens 1937; Warren and Warren 1981).

Annapolis's period of economic eclipse began abating in the 1950s and 1960s. One factor contributing to the city's renaissance was the opening, in the early 1950s, of U.S. Route 50, a four-lane divided highway linking Annapolis to Washington. Up to that point, Annapolis had made do with an out-of-date land entrance to the city, its eighteenth-century "back door," the narrow and crowded West Street corridor that linked Annapolis to Washington through a series of two-lane roads. Little attention was ever given to the eighteenth-century land approach to the city because its principal eighteenth-century entryway, its "front door," was the harbor and the city dock. West Street was not intended to be anything more than a back way, and when the harbor contracted to serve only local boat traffic, Annapolis was truly cut off. This isolation was eased by the railroads, but after they ceased serving the city, the completion of Route 50 constituted a major reopening of Annapolis. Easy access to Washington paved the way for Annapolis to become a suburb, a tourist destination, and a nightspot to rival Georgetown.

The city's commercial rebirth has been fueled by historic preservation, gentrification, tourism, and yachting. The historic preservation movement, which had several building-specific beginnings in the early twentieth century, began in earnest, throughout the city, with the founding of Historic Annapolis in 1952. Historic preservation made Annapolis an appealing place to live and attracted historically minded tourists. In yachting, Annapolis finally found, after 150 years, a purpose for which its much maligned harbor was admirably suited. Like the results of historic preservation, yachting has attracted its own wave of tourists.

Summary of the Chronology

The preceding discussion provides merely a thumbnail sketch of Annapolis history. It presents major events and suggests trends. It is not intended to be exhaustive. It is a presentation of events abstracted and synthesized from a wide variety of sources and from a point of view I began to develop in Chapter 1. I will continue to develop that point of view in the remainder of this chapter and in the two that follow. While no collection or presentation of historical information is fully objective or without a bias or an analytical intent, my purpose in this discussion has been to provide the reader with something of a consensus view of Annapolis history derived from a variety of sources in order to ground the analyses that follow. Furthermore, this collection of information does not in and of itself constitute a history of Annapolis. In this context I use the term "history" to refer to a coherent and comprehensive telling of the past from a discernible and consistent point of view. According to this strict definition, there currently exists no true history of Annapolis. This is largely because the city's past is presented in a highly fragmented way, an issue that is critical to an argument I develop later. At best, the history of Annapolis is composed of histories of parts of the city. The basic incoherence that characterizes the currently available discussions of Annapolis history may be remedied by this book, but not by the first half of this chapter. To reiterate, the first half of this chapter is intended simply to provide a basic framework for understanding Annapolis's use of history and to serve as an inventory of elements from which discussions of Annapolis's past have been—and can be—created.

A Thematic History of Annapolis

The remainder of this chapter is devoted to a discussion of three themes that I have abstracted from the basic history of Annapolis: (1) the city has always prized institutions and activities that link gentility and the water, (2) Annapolis is characterized by ambiguous urbanism, and (3) transience has helped shape the character of the city. None of these themes has been expressed coherently by any of the historians who have written about Annapolis, but I think that I have been able to derive them without violating the data.

Gentility and the Water

The three significant episodes in the city's history—the golden age, the establishment and ascendancy of the Naval Academy, and the yachting/tourist boom—have all allowed Annapolis to consider itself genteel and connected to the water. Annapolis in its golden age was unquestionably a maritime place, filled with nautical industries and connected to the rest of the world far better by water than by land. Not coincidentally, many of Annapolis's most important eighteenth-century buildings were sited so as to have water views. The city's gentility was also clearly evident in this period. Commentators from both sides of the Atlantic complimented Annapolis on its sophistication, culture, and learning (Eddis 1969; Ramirez 1975: 161–62). At least during the nineteenth century, the Naval Academy offered Annapolis some of these qualities. The connection of a naval school to the water is obvious; as Wright (1977a: 146) observes, "The founding of the Naval Academy in 1845 reaffirmed a long association with maritime affairs." And during the nineteenth century a military career was certainly considered genteel: "The coming of the Naval Academy in the middle of the last century did not destroy Colonial Annapolis but merely enabled it to achieve sufficient material prosperity to maintain its gentility" (Norris 1925: 1). And in later years: "The Naval atmosphere which at present dominates the life and thought of Annapolis does not really obliterate the chief qualities of the earlier period. In its emphasis on formality and its generally aristocratic tone, the Navy fits perfectly into the picture of the past" (Norris 1925: 6). Today, yachting has everything to do with the water, and it is probably safe to assume that most yachtsmen and yachtswomen would be considered culturally sophisticated by almost any measure. In three successive centuries, three identities Annapolis has chosen for itself each entail gentility and a connection with the water.

This point becomes clearer if one examines things Annapolis has *not* become—or more properly, has not chosen to celebrate becoming. For much of the nineteenth and twentieth centuries, Annapolis was home to a community and a fleet of Chesapeake Bay watermen. In making Annapolis into a yachting center, it was easy to justify pushing the watermen aside. While they offered a connection to the water, they offered little in the way of high-style cultural sophistication. Conversely, Annapolis has come to have less use for the Naval Academy as its naval mission has become less visible. With the academy's current emphasis on science, engineering, and computers, it is easy to walk through its campus and forget that the students there are being trained to become naval officers. The academy has a large fleet of recreational sailboats, but it is nearly impossible for most naval warships to dock at the academy. So while the academy does offer some degree of gentility (a dress parade is a dress parade) it no longer offers a vital, visible link to the water. It seems clear that a connection to the water and gentility are two elements Annapolis insists on in its perception and presentation of itself.

An Ambiguous Urban Identity

My identification of gentility and a concern with the sea as intertwined themes in Annapolis history is straightforward; it occurred to me during my first weeks in the city. Less obvious is this second theme, the city's ambiguous urban character. Here I define urban character in basically demographic terms. Even though it had been chartered as a city since 1708, Annapolis was not a fully urban place in the eighteenth century. By the Revolution, its population was barely 1,300, which was significantly smaller than New York's 25,000, Philadelphia's 24,000, Boston's 16,000, Charleston's 12,000, Newport, Rhode Island's 11,000 (Chudacoff 1981: 4), or even Baltimore's 6,755 (Caton 1971: 192). Annapolis's small population is a result of the geography of the Chesapeake, with its hundreds of tributaries, and the ease of packing and shipping tobacco from a small, local wharf. These factors decidedly inhibited the development of large, urban places throughout the region. Further, the population of Annapolis had a diminished middle class and a larger than normal share of luxury craftsmen. Generally speaking, the city was populated by people associated primarily with the city's governmental functions but only distantly with any aspect of the area's natural or productive environment.

Thus, while Annapolis was the scene of considerable patriotic activity during the American Revolution, Annapolis was not an "urban crucible." Like Williamsburg to the south, Annapolis did not see the kind of revolutionary ferment that took place in true urban centers such as Boston (Nash 1986). Boston itself—or masses of Bostonians working out urban issues— made a measurable contribution to the American Revolution. By contrast, specific Annapolitans, but not Annapolis as an urban place, played a role in the Revolution, contrary to the impression given by some contemporary popular historical interpretations. The distinction is an important one.

To cite two telling examples, Annapolis served briefly as the capital of the United States in 1783 and 1784, and in 1786 the city hosted a national meeting to discuss trade issues, known today as the Annapolis Convention. In the first case, although Annapolis did serve as the capital of the United States for about nine months, between 1774 and 1800 the First Continental Congress and its successors met in fifteen buildings in eight cities, including Philadelphia, Baltimore, Lancaster (Pennsylvania), York (Pennsylvania), Princeton, Trenton, and New York. The probable intention of celebrating Annapolis's stint as the U.S. capital is to link Annapolis to Washington, D.C., but the reality is that references to Annapolis as capital point up its similarities to Trenton, New Jersey, and

York, Pennsylvania. Annapolis was not a national capital in any institutional sense, and nothing uniquely Annapolitan played a significant part in what Congress did while it met there; the city was a backdrop—as it was in the case of the Annapolis Convention. Invitations were issued to representatives of all thirteen states. Only five states sent representatives (and, ironically, Maryland was not among them). The convention has been celebrated in Annapolis for its one meaningful piece of business: it issued the call that led to the Philadelphia Constitutional Convention. But, as with the previous example, Annapolis did not really play a role in the creation of the Constitution; events that took place in Annapolis did. Annapolis as an urban place did not function in eighteenth-century colonial politics in the same way that places like Boston did.

To restate, my second theme is that despite being chartered in 1708, electing its first mayor in that year, and having other urban characteristics, Annapolis has been for much of its history only incompletely citylike. In its colonial golden age, the city was not a fully urban place, even by colonial standards of scale. Thus contemporary discussions of Annapolis history that talk of the city playing a role in revolutionary or early American politics overstate the urban aspect of Annapolis' eighteenth-century identity.

Transience

My understanding of transience in Annapolis arises from the observation that most of the important figures in Annapolis history are people who passed through it, and that the major institutions in the city with historical origins are composed of transients.

Annapolis contains houses owned by all four of Maryland's signers of the Declaration of Independence: Charles Carroll of Carrollton, Samuel Chase, William Paca, and Thomas Stone. However, the only claim that popular versions of Annapolis history can make is that these men owned houses in Annapolis, *not* that Annapolis was their home (Anderson 1984: 18). Carroll was the closest to being a native Annapolitan; his Annapolis home was one of several he lived in before moving to Baltimore shortly after the Revolution. Paca built his house between 1763 and 1765 and had sold it by 1780 (Stiverson and Jacobsen 1976). Chase did not even finish building his house before running out of money and selling it. During the eighteenth-century colonial golden age, many influential Marylanders came to Annapolis to transact business associated with the city's function

A 1905 postcard of the Hammond-Harwood House; this card was sold after Chase-Lloyd was opened to the public but before Hammond-Harwood was. (Photograph courtesy of M. E. Warren, Annapolis, Maryland)

as state capital, and some built townhouses. These houses were not residences in the usual sense, and many who came to the city during the legislative season, also the social season, left at the conclusion of the public times (Norris 1925; Ramirez 1975).

Given the essentially transient nature of many important figures in Annapolis's past, it is interesting to note that two important American families from the eighteenth century may be considered Annapolis families, the family of Charles Carroll of Carrollton and the Dulanys. Both, however, existed outside the mainstream; the Carrolls were Roman Catholic and the Dulanys were loyalists during the Revolution. This may explain why neither family is celebrated nearly as conspicuously in contemporary Annapolis as are the Protestant patriots, such as Paca and Chase, whose houses are today museums. In contrast, one of the several Dulany houses was demolished by the Naval Academy in the 1890s (Ramirez 1975: 256) and the family's loyalist stance could well have eased the decision to destroy an important eighteenth-century house.

Beyond the individuals in Annapolis history, many of the big events in the city's history amount to business transacted in Annapolis by people passing through. The meetings of the Continental Congress and the Annapolis convention are clear examples. So, too, is an event that took place during the Congress's session in Annapolis: George Washington's resignation of his commission in the Continental Army in December of 1783. Washington rode in, resigned the commission, and rode back out again. Nonetheless, Annapolis relishes having played such an important part in the history of the United States. Again, Annapolis did not play a part; people passing through Annapolis did.

Not only are Annapolis and Annapolis history filled with nonnatives, but Annapolis has promoted this transience. Since the seventeenth century, Annapolis has almost continuously invited individuals and institutions to relocate in Annapolis. The state government, the Naval Academy, yachters, and tourists have come. The federal government (in the form of the national capital) and heavy industry have stayed away. The recipients of the invitation have changed through time but the invitation has remained open for no less than 300 years. This perpetually open invitation appears to have had two motives.

The first is economic. Annapolitans appear to have targeted groups, institutions, or industries expected to bring the greatest revenue at the lowest cost to the city itself. At the same time, this invitation may have been—and may be—an attempt to augment the identity of the city. Any city that has worked so hard to be "capital of Maryland," "capital of the United States," and "home of the United States Naval Academy" is a city that has been unable to find within itself a basis for creating a satisfactory identity.

Evidence of a search for identity can be found in Annapolis's long and impressive list of nicknames: "the ancient city" (Riley 1887), "the finished city" (Stevens 1937), "the city of chimneys" (Stevens 1937),"the Athens of America" (Riley 1887), "the Bath of America" (Stevens 1937: 50), "the Paris of America" (Riley 1906), and "the Venice of America." Interestingly, none of these nicknames identifies Annapolis with the local area and many go rather far afield. I would suggest that these invitations to outsiders constitute a step toward establishing identity by importing it. Annapolis decides what it wants to be and then invites the kind of people and institutions capable of bringing about the desired transformation.

But in issuing any invitation there is a risk that the invitation will be accepted. That is to say, a large problem for Annapolis has been how to manage to its advantage the institutions and individuals who have responded to its invitation. Invitees who stay may grow too powerful and threaten the authority of the host. By depending on outsiders for so much, Annapolis places itself in a vulnerable position. A certain amount of graciousness is expected of any host, and this complicates the delicate matter of staying on the tolerable and profitable side of the line between the city serving its guests and the guests serving the needs of the city. This line is, of course, continually changing. It is pushed from one side by aggressive local residents looking to capitalize on tourist interest in the city and from the other by residents more concerned with preserving the city's residential qualities. The challenge will be to keep the line just this side of the point at which potential visitors will be put off by what they perceive as a hostile attitude toward outsiders. This tension has been an integral part of Annapolis life for generations and continues to be a major political issue.

Summary

The purpose of this chapter has been to present a useful history of Annapolis. I began with a simple chronological presentation, but the important points for interpretation and analysis concern the city's genteel connections with the water, the city's ambiguous urbanism, and the transient nature of many of Annapolis's most celebrated individuals and institutions. Furthermore, these three trends in Annapolis history are closely intertwined.

I believe that Annapolis has understood for some time its ambiguous or partial urbanism. The town never developed an internally based life of its own. Perhaps this is because it has relied on "industries" like the state government and thus has not endeavored to develop true, productive industries. Or it may be the case that Annapolis is simply unsuited environmentally to be the locus of any kind of industrial development. Whatever the cause, it is the result that matters. Annapolitans have devoted considerable energy to determining just what their city should be. Failing to find a local basis for establishing an identity, Annapolitans have turned to the world beyond, inviting various groups or institutions to visit or settle in Annapolis. In issuing these invitations Annapolis seems to have insisted on only two things, gentility and a connection to the water. Annapolis has been willing for 300 years to reinvent itself in order to survive and prosper, so long as it has been able to reinvent itself as a genteel, maritime place.

6

The History of History in Annapolis

This chapter is about the history of history in Annapolis, an interesting and complex subject, given the fact that Annapolis has considered itself a historical place for more than 100 years. The discussion bridges the gap between the historical facts presented in chapter 5 and the various uses of those facts that are the topic of chapter 7. In other words, this chapter explores Annapolis's historical thinking and historical consciousness, and, more specifically, the origins of Annapolis's current attempts to solve its identity problems through the creation and curation of a usable past. Annapolis's long history of historical thinking gives credence to the idea that the city tries to use history today. Like chapter 5, this one opens with a chronological narrative, followed by a more analytical discussion.

A Chronological View

Since the eighteenth century, Annapolis has experienced several episodes of sustained, public historical discourse. Among the products of these discussions are the late nineteenth- and early twentieth-century works of Elihu Riley, the most important and prolific historian Annapolis has ever had, several other influential twentieth-century history books, and the preservation of three Georgian mansions.

An Eighteenth-Century View of the Past

Annapolis's understanding of itself as a historical entity, or as the subject of historical treatment can be traced back to Dr. Alexander Hamilton, the leader of the Tuesday Club, mentioned in Chapter 5. Dr. Hamilton was responsible for the first recorded instance of a sustained historical consciousness in Annapolis. The meetings of the Tuesday Club are known today through the detailed minutes recorded by Dr. Hamilton and illustrated by his cartoon-like pen-and-ink drawings. In addition, Dr. Hamilton wrote a fanciful history of the club that traces its pedigree back through various Scottish clubs, and eventually back to Roman times.

What is significant here is the pattern of thought, which rationalizes the past and turns it into a sequence of segments that may be traced backward, like the links of a chain. This is by no means a universal way of characterizing past time, but rather a specific cultural construct. Although it is much like our modern Western way of thinking about the past and writing history, it was a relatively new way of thinking about the past in the mid-eighteenth century. This move to rationalize and segment past time is one element of the larger cultural phenomenon called the "Georgian worldview" by Deetz, Leone, and scholars who have followed their lead. This set of ideas is discussed more fully later, but note for the time being that historical thinking of a kind we would term "modern" was taking place in Annapolis in the 1750s. Note, too, that members of the Continental Congress who met in Annapolis in 1783 and 1784 referred to it as the ancient city (Wright 1977a: 146). Whether that designation was intended to suggest that Annapolis was historical or just old is, of course, an open question.

Nineteenth-Century Approaches to Annapolis History

The first history of the city was written by David Ridgley and published in 1841. Ridgley's book, *Annals of Annapolis*, is a chronicle filling about 200 pages. It contains reports of events, lists of office holders, and other facts drawn from the *Maryland Gazette* and other primary sources, all flatly presented with no theme, no explicit point of view, and no interpretation. Owen Taylor's (1872) history of Annapolis is of a piece with Ridgley's.

Shortly after the publication of Taylor's book and before Riley's appeared, Annapolis experienced its first preservation crisis. In 1876, the year of the nation's centennial, state officials gutted the Old Senate Chamber in the Maryland State House (Tilghman 1925: 20–21; Radoff

1972; Handsman and Leone 1990). This is the room in which Washington resigned his commission, an act many considered to be among the most significant in Washington's career (McKeldin 1957). The resignation is depicted in two famous paintings, one painted by Edwin White in 1857 and now hanging in the Maryland State House, the other painted by John Trumbell in 1817 and now in the Rotunda of the U.S. Capitol. Despite this graphic proof of the importance of the events that transpired in the Old Senate Chamber, it was gutted just seven years before the 100th anniversary of Washington's resignation—an event vigorously celebrated in Annapolis on its 200th anniversary. The room was emptied of its furniture, some dating to the eighteenth century and made by John Shaw, an important local cabinetmaker. Cornices were removed, the mantlepiece dismantled, and the spectators' gallery taken down, all as part of a renovation program for the State House.

Many commentators were critical of the state's action, including Dugan (1902); Riley (1887: 162), who called it "a profanation"; and both Tilghman (1925: 20) and Duval (1926), who called it "a mutilation." Perhaps the most notable protester was Frank B. Mayer, an Annapolis artist known for his historical paintings, several of which hang in the Maryland State House. Mayer's campaign to restore the Old Senate Chamber was joined by many historically minded Annapolitans. It took more than twenty-five years, but the room was eventually restored to its eighteenth-century appearance in the early twentieth century, thus resolving Annapolis's first preservation controversy in favor of preservation. Although the battle to restore the room was long, loud, and public, it is not included in most recent and contemporary presentations of the history of the room, which exists today as a museum room or shrine, containing among other things a mannequin of Washington, and is visited by hundreds of people every day. Rather than discuss how aspects of the past are preserved by contemporary social and political action, most guides and guidebooks perpetuate the myth of continuity in the Old Senate Chamber and the underlying myth that historical value is inherent in objects and places, which sometimes speak for and perpetuate or preserve themselves. This may have been the first instance of this attitude toward material culture in Annapolis, but it was by no means the last.

Elihu Riley

After the beginning, but well before the end of the Old Senate Chamber preservation controversy, Elihu Riley began writing and publishing his histories of Annapolis. Riley, a nephew of David Ridgley, author of the *Annals of Annapolis* (1841), was the city clerk of Annapolis, published a local newspaper (the *Annapolis Republican*), and was active in local civic and business affairs. His major work, published in 1887, was *"The Ancient City": The History of Annapolis in Maryland, 1649–1887*. The book is drawn largely from his uncle's work—some sections are repeated verbatim—and it contains an update covering the period from 1842 until 1887. The book is both chronicle and mosaic, organized principally along chronological lines with sections on local institutions inserted throughout. It is fair to say that the presentation does not even reach the level of narrative. Nonetheless, *"The Ancient City"* was, and is, a much-used reference work. It is the book that people turn to first when they are trying to locate a historical fact about Annapolis. Regardless of appraisals of its theoretical orientation or even its overall organization, everyone acknowledges that it is filled with basic data. As evidence of the esteem in which Riley's work is still held, the book was reprinted in 1976 as a part of the local celebration of the American bicentennial by the Annapolis and Anne Arundel County Bicentennial Celebration Commission.

Between 1887 and 1906 Riley published at least four more books on Annapolis and one on Anne Arundel County. Each of the Annapolis volumes is much shorter than *"The Ancient City"* and incorporates passages from the older book in a new format. The 1906 volume is basically a picture book, and another, published in 1897, was a souvenir for a statewide convention of firemen held in Annapolis. A 1901 publication is essentially a guidebook, and during this period Riley also published a historical map of Annapolis. In all, Riley produced virtually every kind of historical book that has ever been written about the city. All of Riley's books, including the first one, contain a section at the end celebrating Annapolis as an ideal place to live and do business. Riley the civic leader and Riley the historian came together as he attempted to use his books as a tool for Annapolis's late nineteenth-century boosterism, making history a part of the attractiveness of the city. Whereas the campaign to industrialize Annapolis failed, Riley's books still stand as a source of historical information and as a record of the shape of some of Annapolis's earliest sustained historical thinking.

Historical Consciousness: 1895—1910

With the publication of *"The Ancient City"*, Annapolis entered a period of intense historicism, the first of three. Riley wrote throughout this period and at its start, the restoration of the Old Senate Chamber was still unsettled. A great deal of other historical activity took place during this period as well. The city celebrated the 200th anniversary of becoming the capital of Maryland (Riley 1906). The first of its three Georgian-period historic house museums, the Chase-Lloyd House, was opened to the public in the 1890s (Ramirez 1975). The Farmers National Bank, founded in Annapolis, celebrated its centennial in 1906, with the publication of an anniversary volume (Randall 1905). Two years later, the city celebrated the 200th anniversary of its charter, granted by Queen Anne in 1708. The festivities included a service at St. Anne's Episcopal Church inside Church Circle.

Much of the historical activity initiated in Annapolis during this time is similar to historical activity elsewhere in the United States during the colonial revival, which coincided with the birth of the American preservation movement. Annapolis's earliest preservation action was patriotic and site-specific, and thus similar to other early preservation projects like Mount Vernon. Even so, little is gained, at least in terms of understanding this first period, by thinking of events in Annapolis as expressions of national preservation trends.

In 1899 Winston Churchill, a former midshipman (*not* the prime minister of Great Britain), published a historical novel set in colonial Annapolis, *Richard Carvel of Carvel Hall*. The novel features actual historical figures—both John Paul Jones and George Washington appear—and it makes fairly detailed and accurate references to famous historical houses in Annapolis. At one time, a popular local guessing game involved linking the homes of characters in the book to actual houses in Annapolis. The book was a runaway success in Annapolis and beyond. It went through more than a dozen printings and was the most popular of Churchill's many novels, and also the most popular of the half dozen or so historical novels set in colonial Annapolis. *Richard Carvel*, published in New York and sold nationally, put Annapolis on the map, and the city was quick to understand this. In about 1905, the 38-room mansion of William Paca and the 2-acre piece of ground on which it was built were purchased by a company that built a 200-room hotel onto the back of Paca's house and on top of Paca's formal, terraced pleasure garden. The hotel, completed in about 1907, was named Carvel Hall. In Annapolis the name of a fictional character was considered more attractive to visitors, hence more economically prudent, than the name of an American patriot and signer of the Declaration of Independence. At the very least, this suggests an approach to history far more romantic than scholarly or intellectual.

In 1901 a new post office was built in Annapolis. The building, which still stands at One Church Circle, is an appropriately scaled and ornamented example of neo-Georgian architecture and was praised as such in Thruston's (1916) guidebook. The 1901 Post Office is one of several thousand nationwide expressions of the colonial revival. At the local level, it demonstrates that people in Annapolis were paying attention to architectural history at the turn of the century, if not earlier. The architecture of the Post Office exhibits an understanding of the quality of Annapolis's surviving Georgian architecture and expresses a desire to achieve architectural sympathy in contemporary construction. The problem addressed successfully by this building, balancing the need for new construction with a commitment to protecting architecturally significant old buildings and their environments, has been an issue in Annapolis throughout the twentieth century.

In the middle of the first decade of the twentieth century, the Naval Academy undertook a massive construction project, literally rebuilding itself, following a plan drawn up by Earnest Flagg and featuring massively scaled beaux-arts buildings. As a part of the rebuilding, the academy constructed a new chapel, one of the last buildings to be completed. At the time the academy rebuilding project was taking place, the U.S. ambassador to France was engaged in a search for the remains of John Paul Jones (Norris 1925: 289–90), which took the better part of six years. The remains were finally located in a long-abandoned Paris cemetery, underneath a building (Stevens 1937: 271) and eventually were recovered and sent off to the academy for reburial. The body was stored in a makeshift building until a crypt below the chapel was ready to receive it. When the crypt was finished in 1912, the body of John Paul Jones was reburied, with full military honors, in a crypt similar to Napoleon's at Les Invalides in Paris.

This elaborate reburial of John Paul Jones could have been, at least in part, the academy's reaction to Annapolis's increasing interest in the past. The reburial could also have indicated a recognition that in building its explicitly new and modern campus, the academy obliterated several eighteenth-century roadways and destroyed several eighteenth-century buildings, including a home of one member of the Dulany family and a former governor's mansion. To return to the first point, Annapolis was, by the first decade of the twentieth century, celebrating its colonial history. The audience for this celebration was nationwide, at least in terms of the readership for *Richard Carvel*, and Annapolis appeared likely to benefit from this interest in history. As things probably looked in 1905, Annapolis was poised to outshine the academy in *any* historical comparison. In 1908 Annapolis celebrated the 200th anniversary of its charter. The city was 259 years old and had been a backdrop to the birth of the nation. By contrast, the academy was only 53 years old and seemed to be turning its back on the past, at least architecturally. How better to compete historically with Annapolis than by securing the remains of a genuine Revolutionary War hero, the father of the American Navy, John Paul Jones? The reburial of his remains extended the history of the academy by 70 years, more than doubling it. The reburial gave the academy a connection to the birth of the nation as solid as that claimed by the city, and created the illusion of continuity by manipulating powerful symbolic ties to the past. What is even more interesting is that the reburial of John Paul Jones seems to be one of the academy's last institutional attempts at historicism. It seems never to have followed up on this brilliant opening salvo.

Historical Consciousness: 1925—37

Annapolis's second major period of historical activity began in 1925 with the publication of *Annapolis: Its Colonial and Naval Story* by Walter B. Norris, a historian at the Naval Academy. This period ends with the publication in 1937 of *Annapolis: Anne Arundel's Town* by William Oliver Stevens, also a Naval Academy professor.

In addition to his major Annapolis book and several small books of humorous verse on Annapolis (1906, 1907), Stevens wrote a series of historical travel books, which included volumes on the Shenandoah Valley (1941), Long Island (1939), Williamsburg (1938), and Nantucket (1936). These books were intended to supply tourists with historical background on various popular vacation spots. Unlike most of the previously published books on Annapolis (with the exception of *Richard Carvel*, published by Macmillan) Norris's book and Stevens's were both published by New York publishing houses, Thomas Crowell and Dodd, Mead, respectively. Both books are rich, thick narratives long on romance and the colonial golden age, and short on analysis, interpretation, and an explicit point of view. Nonetheless, some scholars of today regard Norris's book as the best available history of Annapolis (Middleton, personal communication; Ramirez 1975: 302).

One aspect of Norris's book relevant to this discussion is demonstrated by its subtitle. In referring to the "colonial" and the "naval" parts of Annapolis's history, Norris mixes semantic categories. In standard con-

A 1930s map of Annapolis, demonstrating the city's growing sense of its history over the twentieth century. (Photograph courtesy of M. E. Warren, Annapolis, Maryland)

temporary American discourse, "colonial" refers to a time period in American history, whereas the term "naval" refers to maritime military activities and says nothing about time. To avoid mixing categories, Norris could have called his book either *Annapolis: Its Eighteenth- and Nineteenth-Century History* or *Annapolis: The History of the City and the Naval Academy*. But by mixing categories as he does, Norris sets up an association between "nineteenth/twentieth century" and "Naval Academy" and another association between "eighteenth century" and the rest of the city. Norris's title was probably intended only to indicate that he was writing a comprehensive history of Annapolis, covering all aspects of the city's past, but it has deeper implications. The association between "eighteenth century" and the non–Naval Academy part of the city implies that Annapolis had no significant nineteenth- or twentieth-century history, that the most important thing in town after the Revolution was the academy. This argument is important because it states the strongest of a series of oppositions between the city and the academy set up in most versions of Annapolis history, Norris's and Stevens's included. These oppositions will be discussed in greater detail later in this chapter.

Many developments during this second period of historical activity paralleled those in the first. The first steps were taken leading to the preservation and opening of Annapolis's second major historic house museum, the Hammond-Harwood House (c. 1774), designed by William Buckland and considered to be one of the finest examples of Georgian architecture in the United States. There is a story that in the 1920s Henry Ford wanted to buy the Hammond-Harwood House and move it, brick by brick, to Greenfield Village. It is also said that John D. Rockefeller came to Annapolis before he went to Williamsburg but was discouraged from focusing his philanthropic and historical interests on the former by Annapolitans who were too proud to see their living city turned into a museum village. Accurate or not, the number of times these stories are retold is ample evidence of their contemporary value in establishing, for Annapolitans, the superiority of their city over Colonial Williamsburg:

> Ask . . . ten people what Williamsburg is and you'd probably get the reply,—"That's the Colonial Virginia city which Rockefeller built over." Annapolis and Williamsburg were colonial contemporaries—centers of learning, of culture, of wealth, of entertainment and of colonial society. But no one has ever attempted to "build over" Annapolis; those that remain of her old colonial houses (about thirty in all) are still serving as family dwellings. . . . Annapolis has never felt the touch of the magic monied hand of wholesale restoration. (Emery 1948: 7–8)

Developments occurred in the architectural realm as well. In 1934 a neo-Georgian building was erected in Annapolis to house the Maryland State Archives and Hall of Records and to commemorate the 300th anniversary of the founding of the colony of Maryland in 1634. Government House, the Maryland executive mansion, built in 1867, stands on State Circle, less than 200 feet from the 1901 neo-Georgian Post Office. Built as a typical, mansard-roofed, Victorian mansion, the house was redone in the 1930s in the manner of a Georgian five-part mansion, like the city's architectural gems, the Paca, Brice, and Hammond-Harwood houses. This approach to creating architecture compatible with the eighteenth-century scale and flavor of Annapolis, different from that taken with the Post Office, also differs from the approach taken in constructing the earliest of the large state office buildings in Annapolis. Directly behind Government House and virtually next door to the Post

Office stands a large building containing offices for legislators, built in the 1930s. The building is as symmetrical and segmented as any Georgian building, but it is out of scale, far larger than any Georgian building in eighteenth-century Annapolis ever would have been. Equally significantly, a number of small, authentic, eighteenth- and nineteenth-century wooden vernacular houses were destroyed in order to make room for this over-sized, neo- or pseudo-Georgian building.

Also during the 1930s in the course of planning for a new state office building, considerable public debate ensued over its location in view of the building's potential impacts on structures of historical significance and architectural value. In this debate three different sites—all on State Circle—were considered. This preservation crisis led to the creation of the Company for the Preservation of Colonial Annapolis, a local preservation and restoration organization interested in the city's historical and archi-tectural heritage. The group's efforts paid off. The site selected for the

In the foreground, the 1930s "colonial" governor's mansion, mirrored by a neo-Georgian state office building directly behind. To the left is the 1901 Post Office. (Photograph courtesy of M. E. Warren, Annapolis, Maryland)

The Wm. Paca House as it appeared in the early 1950s, when it was still a part of Carvel Hall Hotel. (Photograph courtesy of M. E. Warren, Annapolis, Maryland)

office building was their choice. Each of the other two sites contained relatively large, early eighteenth-century buildings, one occupied by members of the Calvert family during the eighteenth century, whereas the parcel selected contained mostly smaller, more recent buildings. The company itself was essentially defunct by 1938 (Ramirez 1975: 300), but it did achieve specific successes and is generally considered to have been an important forerunner of Historic Annapolis.

Historical Consciousness: 1952—87

The founding of Historic Annapolis in 1952 marks the beginning of the third major period of historical interest in Annapolis. The 1940s, like the 1910s, were characterized by a relatively low level of local historical activity and few publications, events, or preservation initiatives with the exception of a large-scale celebration in 1949 of the 300th anniversary of the settlement of Annapolis. Committees were set up to plan the celebration, a play was produced, and the *Capital* ran a special edition.

Historic Annapolis was founded in 1952, in much the same way as the Company for the Preservation of Colonial Annapolis, in response to a specific preservation question. The particular issue was whether the city's first comprehensive zoning ordinance should include provisions for a historic district. A coalition of concerned citizens was formed, and this group wrote a Historic District ordinance, lobbied for it, and ultimately incorporated itself as Historic Annapolis, Inc. (Ramirez 1975: 310–11; Symonds 1977: 146). Unlike the Company for the Preservation of Colonial Annapolis, Historic Annapolis did not fade out of existence after its inception, but its greatest impact was not felt until the 1960s.

In 1966, the eighteenth-century core of Annapolis, covering approximately one-third of a square mile, was made a National Historic Landmark District by the U.S. Department of the Interior. In 1969 Annapolis passed a Historic District ordinance that placed in the hands of a five-member citizen's board—known as the Historic District Commission (HDC)—the responsibility for approving any new construction or alteration to standing buildings in the Historic District visible from a public right of way. The ordinance was submitted to a City Council vote in 1968 and was defeated. Subsequently, Historic Annapolis coordinated a campaign to call a referendum on the issue. Put to a popular vote, the measure passed with a two-thirds majority in every ward (Symonds 1977: 147). Another of Historic Annapolis's major accomplishments was the purchase and restoration, between 1965 and 1975, of the Wm. Paca House and Garden (c. 1765), the third of the Georgian historic house museums opened to the public in Annapolis. One of the costs of the restoration of the garden was the demolition of Carvel Hall.

Historic Annapolis prides itself, with justification, on taking a sophisticated and research-based approach to preservation. Historical accuracy is a paramount virtue to Historic Annapolis, hence the need for research. In this context, the organization's commitment to Archaeology in Annapolis flows directly from its understanding of the usefulness of scholarly research for legitimizing their particular historic preservation decisions. The sophistication of Historic Annapolis's approach is evident in several areas. It strives to acknowledge that Annapolis is a living city and is in favor of adaptive reuse, finding ways to use buildings while preserving their historic character. The organization attempts to look beyond individual buildings to consider blocks, streetscapes, the environment and setting of buildings, and the city as a whole. The organization also has a keen sense of precedent with regard to political issues that affect preservation. Further, Historic Annapolis attempts not to focus on any particular time period or architectural style to which the entire city should be changed. Rather, it attempts to recognize *and* preserve well-designed buildings of *any* period, including modern ones. For new construction, Historic Annapolis's recommendation is not to build a copy of an eighteenth-century building, but to build a clearly modern building that is well designed and compatible with its older neighbors in terms of height, bulk, and material. This is simply the logical extension of the organization's concern with authenticity; buildings should represent their own times and not pass themselves off as something they are not.

Historic Annapolis is only one of a number of local agencies concerned with the presentation of history in Annapolis. Both Historic Annapolis and Three Centuries Tours of Annapolis, a commercial tour operation that split from Historic Annapolis in the mid-1970s, present walking tours of the Historic District. This is in addition to a wide range of public lectures on historical topics offered by a number of institutions, special Christmas (and other) celebrations at the various historic houses, and the full menu of 200th, 275th, and 350th anniversary celebrations held in Annapolis during the mid-1980s. The *Capital* does its share to satisfy local interest in history. In addition to both local and wire-service stories on archaeology, the *Capital* runs two historical columns each Thursday, "Arundel Vignettes" and "10, 50, and 210 Years Ago." The former is a highly fragmented collection of historical information about the Civil War, railroads, steamships, place names, ephemera, and local industries. The latter is just what its name implies, a listing of interesting items culled from Annapolis newspapers from 10, 50, and 210 years ago. (Ten years ago the column was called "10, 50, and 200 Years Ago" but was changed so that material from the 1770s could still be used through the 1980s.) Needless to say, this column is as fragmented as the "Arundel Vignettes," and this theme of fragmentation will be discussed at greater length later in the chapter.

Parallel with, but not necessarily a product of, Historic Annapolis's commitment to research and accuracy is the first sustained and comprehensive scholarly interest in Annapolis history, which came in the 1970s. In the early twentieth century, the *Maryland Historical Magazine* began publishing sections of the letters or other papers of prominent Annapolitans such as Charles Carroll of Carrollton. These presentations are primarily documentation and contain virtually no analysis or interpretation. The 1970s saw a spate of popular picture books and guidebooks

(Mitchell 1969; Taliaferro 1971; M. Warren and M. E. Warren 1981; M. E. Warren and M. Warren 1981), modern examples of an idiom of historical expression used nearly continuously for at least 80 years (Riley 1906; Stevens and Alden 1910; Thruston 1916; Tilghman 1925; Duval 1926; Stieff 1935; Anderson 1984; Leone and Potter 1984). But the 1970s also saw the publication of *In Pursuit of Profit* (Papenfuse 1975) and two dissertations, *A Symbolic Interaction Approach to the Place Meanings in a Historic District* (Ives 1977) and *Urban History for Preservation Planning: The Annapolis Experience* (Ramirez 1975).

Papenfuse's book is a study of Annapolis merchants in the era of the American Revolution. His approach is that of the New Social History. *In Pursuit of Profit* deals with individual merchants but looks more at the aggregate and is highly statistical. Papenfuse's work is one of the first applications of this approach to Annapolis data. Even more data from Annapolis could be treated in this way. By considering a broad issue or segment of society, Papenfuse was one of the first commentators on Annapolis history to go beyond individual houses, persons, families, or institutions to gain an understanding of Annapolis as a city.

Sallie Ives's dissertation is a sociological and statistical attempt to understand what characteristics of Annapolis are important to residents of the Historic District, a study undertaken with the local historic preservation movement in mind. Ives began with an acknowledgement of the work of Historic Annapolis and others, and attempted to find out whether local attitudes helped or hindered preservation and whether the preservation movement reflected the interests of local residents. Using a symbolic-interaction approach, she mailed a complex, six-page questionnaire to hundreds of households in the Historic District and received responses to nearly 50 percent of the questionnaires she sent out. Ives posed several kinds of questions: standard ones requesting demographic and residential data, and a variety of questions soliciting attitudes about self and about perceptions and uses of the Historic District. The immediate product of the questionnaire was an extremely detailed body of multivariable data. The interpretive results were largely inconclusive but suggest that historicity is not particularly important to residents of the Historic District: "In general, the residents of the Historic District tend to rate as more important those place attributes that deal with the Historic District as a residential experience rather than those which deal with the physical uniqueness of the place which we associate with an historic meaning" (Ives 1977: 74). What Ives terms the "residential experience" of living in the Historic District is a constellation of factors usually called "quality of life," which refers to things

The Historic Annapolis plaque, which adorns many buildings in the historic district, indicates periods of primary construction and significant alteration through a color code. (Photograph courtesy of M. E. Warren, Annapolis, Maryland)

like safety, neighborliness, and shady streets. Her study does not suggest the degree to which the desirable "quality of life" was, or was perceived as, an indirect product of the historic preservation movement.

Constance Ramirez was a student of John Reps, the most influential historian of American town planning and the author of *The Making of*

Urban America (1965) and *Tidewater Towns: City Planning in Colonial Virginia and Maryland* (1972), among other works. Reps was largely concerned with the context of the creation and layout of the "modern" plan of cities and his work tends toward the synchronic. In her dissertation, Ramirez attempts to do for Annapolis what Whitehill did for Boston in *Boston: A Topographic History* (1968). Ramirez works diachronically, tracing the physical development of Annapolis from the 1640s through the 1970s, paying attention to natural environmental constraints, to the relations between changes and antecedent conditions, and to the social and political context of physical changes to the city. Her understanding of physical changes in Annapolis as the work of various individuals, groups, and institutions both supercedes a view that urban change is some sort of self-generating process that can only be described and also creates a framework for a critical appraisal of the historic preservation movement as a part of, rather than outside, the historical flow of physical development in Annapolis. Like Ives, Ramirez writes with an understanding of, and sympathy for, the preservation movement and with the intention of providing a useful document for historic preservation.

Over the past twenty years, Annapolis has captured the attention of other scholars as well. Both Elaine Breslaw and Barry Talley have written dissertations on the Tuesday Club (Talley concentrating on the Tuesday Club music). A number of scholarly biographies are now available on eighteenth-century Annapolitans, including the Dulany family (Land 1955), Charles Carroll of Carrollton (Hanley 1982, 1983), and William Paca (Stiverson and Jacobson 1976). Beyond that, there is a considerable body of largely unpublished social history on Annapolis (Baker 1983, 1986; Carr 1983; Russo 1983; and Walsh 1983a, 1983b). In addition, there is the growing body of work published by the participants in Archaeology in Annapolis. Taken together, this scholarship represents a quantum leap in serious historical interest in Annapolis over the past twenty years or so. What is particularly significant about this recent scholarship is that it considers Annapolis as a place rather than as a set of parts, individuals, and institutions.

Thematic and Analytical Views

One prominent theme in past discussions of Annapolis history is that things from the past, particularly architecture, have an inherent "quality" and the power to communicate directly to visitors and residents today.

Another theme is that the period from about 1760 through about 1775—a time when many African-Americans in Annapolis were slaves, the Naval Academy had not yet been founded, and tourism had not yet been invented—was its golden age. In addition to expressing these themes, most histories of Annapolis—both individually and in the aggregate—give a strong sense of fragmentation.

The "Inherentness" of Historical Qualities

An attitude that lies behind both the large number of Annapolis picture-books and much of the historic preservation movement is that high-quality historical materials can virtually speak for themselves. This is clearly the idea behind picture-books, and while it is not an inevitable characteristic of historic preservation, it does seem to be the idea that has guided preservation in Annapolis. Historic Annapolis officials, like virtually all previous Annapolis preservation activists, either believe that they do not create or establish historical value, or instead just act as if that were the case. In short, they simply claim to be particularly adept at knowing how to see historical value and make it more visible to others.

A further assumption behind Historic Annapolis's work is that any thinking person would evaluate buildings the same way Historic Annapolis does, once the obstacles to doing so were removed. This is the attitude exhibited when a tour guide or someone testifying before the Historic District Commission refers to some structure as a "good building" without specifying what it is good for or the standards by which it was so judged. Without explicit standards, the only conclusion one can draw is that "goodness" is inherent in buildings, self-evident to trained eyes, and not negotiated in the present. A further conclusion is that the job of preservation is simply to help people see more clearly the quality inherent in some old building.

The second clue to this attitude is what Historic Annapolis calls the "key to interpretation" on the first page of its guide-training manual. The reason for all Historic Annapolis interpretive and educational programs is the 1966 designation of the Annapolis Historic District as a National Historic Landmark District. This designation is taken as recognition, from the highest possible authority, of the intrinsic value of Annapolis, and Historic Annapolis tours of the city are intended to further the goals of preservation.

While Historic Annapolis takes the scholarly high road in its identification of and response to the innate qualities of Annapolis, there are other responses. The more low-brow approach to appreciating Annapolis's historical character is a call to experience the city's charm simply by being exposed to it. Such suggestions are at the heart of many guidebooks like those of Schaun and Schaun (1955) and Thruston (1916), as well as the longer works of Stevens and Norris. As Taliaferro (1971: 7) points out: "The smell of old boxwood, the sound of the bells from St. John's College or from the spire of St. Anne's Church, the old vine covered houses, and the uneven cobblestones beneath the feet, all cast a spell of the past." Stevens (1937: 6) expresses a similar sentiment: "Much that is ugly and modern has driven off the streets the beauty of the old, but there are still so many relics of the eighteenth century that one has the sensation of having slipped back, like the hero of the play, 'Berkeley Square,' right into the heart of an eighteenth-century English town." Stevens goes on to say:

> Here [across from the Hammond-Harwood House], in a long, quiet June twilight, facing one of the most beautiful mansions of the eighteenth century, one need not be a "psychic" to conjure up a procession of ghostly memories, shades of the past. (p. 328)

> As you gaze at that doorway [of the Hammond-Harwood House], . . . you will have no difficulties in seeing on that deserted street a return of the spirits who long ago walked this way. (p. 328)

> Few streets in America can call back such an array of ghosts. They are easy to see if you look for them on such a June night as this, with the soft breeze from the bay stirring the leaves, and the moonlight shining down on the old houses of the Golden Age. (p. 330)

Norris (1925: 1) claims that the charm of Annapolis is not that "it contains houses and survivals of Colonial times" but that "it has retained something of the rollicking days before the Revolution. As it has never expanded commercially it has never changed its character and has preserved its old buildings, streets, alleys, and general air of cultivated aristocratic complacency." Its "ghostly shadows of an aristocratic past" and "charming relics" have given it a varied store of "historical interest," says Norris. "Like Bruges and Perugia, Warwick and Nuremberg, its charm lies in its actual preservation of the atmosphere of the past in everything except flesh and blood, not mere sites where famous actions took place but the very houses, streets, and drawing rooms in all their character." Thus he concludes: "It ought, therefore, to be worth the while of every American who venerates the historic foundations of the nation to-day, and the men who laid those foundations so well, to trace the growth of one town where these facts are so evident" (1925: 8). These approaches to Annapolis' historicity are very different in tone from Historic Annapolis's much more scholarly approach, but the two are structurally similar, for each assumes that what is important about Annapolis history is inherent in the physical aspect of the city.

So, a first theme in the presentation of history in Annapolis is the impression that history is to be breathed in, walked through, experienced, reacted to, but *not* interpreted, created, used, or challenged. History is a feeling, not an activity.

The Colonial Golden Age

Most presentations of Annapolis history tend to focus on the colonial golden age, which began about 1760, and to consider the entire period before that, going back to 1708, the year when Annapolis was granted a charter by Queen Anne, of little historical interest. Annapolis's nineteenth- and early twentieth-century history is also bypassed, except for the founding of the Naval Academy in 1845. Norris, for example, devotes 178 of the 301 pages of his book to the quarter century that constitutes the golden age. The golden age is given 4.2 pages per year, compared with 3.6 pages per year for the Civil War and about half a page per year or less for any other time period. Further, Norris's use of the term "genteel eclipse" to refer to the post-Revolutionary period is a strong indication of the importance he assigns to the golden age.

Not only do most written histories devote a disproportionate amount of space to the golden age, but the city's historical bias toward the eighteenth century is evident in the contemporary names given to most of the eighteenth-century buildings in Annapolis. A small gambrel-roofed structure on Prince George Street, dating to the early eighteenth century, is named the Patrick Creagh House by most commentators, for an eighteenth-century occupant, as opposed to being named for Lucy Smith (or Aunt Lucy), a nineteenth-century, free-black woman who ran a bake shop there. Reynolds Tavern, on Church Circle, now one of the Historic Inns of Annapolis, was built in 1747 and was used by its builder, William Reynolds, as a tavern for only *10* of the 240 years it has been standing. The building is named Reynolds Tavern, despite the fact that it was used as the home of the cashier of the Farmers National Bank and as a branch of the Anne Arundel County Library for far longer periods of time than the 10 years it spent as William Reynolds's tavern. Either of these uses could have provided a marketable motif for a contemporary inn and restaurant, but the eighteenth-century identity was chosen.

That was also the case with the Governor Calvert House, another of the Historic Inns of Annapolis. The building was owned and lived in by members of Maryland's proprietary family, the Calverts, for most of the eighteenth century. In about 1800 it was sold to the Claude family. Various Claudes owned the house through the 1970s, by which time they had turned it into an apartment house. The Claudes are as close as Annapolis ever came to having a first family; four Claudes in three generations served as mayor of Annapolis for a total of more than twenty years, starting in 1828. The building is still called the Claude House by some locals, but the Calvert House officially. Interestingly, the Calvert House does contain a small meeting room named after the Claude family; a piece of nineteenth-century history is tucked inside a piece of eighteenth-century history. All of this reflects Annapolis's focus on its eighteenth-century golden age.

Historic Annapolis operates three small museum buildings near the city dock: the Victualling Warehouse Maritime Museum (77 Main Street), the Tobacco Prise House (4 Pinkney Street), and the Barracks (43 Pinkney Street). All three are owned by the state of Maryland and managed by Historic Annapolis, with a budget for maintenance provided by the state. All three were acquired during the mid-1970s, to celebrate the American bicentennial, and are used to interpret the Revolutionary era in Annapolis. Three of Annapolis's major historic house museums—the Chase Lloyd, Hammond-Harwood, and Wm. Paca houses—are Georgian mansions built between 1763 and 1774. All of the institutionally produced presentations of Annapolis history, down to the costumes worn by Three Centuries tour guides, focus on the late eighteenth century.

If it seems that Annapolis's histories overemphasize the golden age, or that this discussion is becoming somewhat critical, then it is time to ask "What other parts of its past could Annapolis celebrate and put on display?" With this issue in mind, it is interesting to consider Annapolis's recent celebration of the 275th anniversary of its charter. Leaving aside the fact that at the Queen Anne's Ball, held to celebrate the anniversary, those who arrived in costume chose *late* eighteenth-century rather than *early* eighteenth-century dress; an element of the 1983 celebration was a remembrance of the 200th anniversary of the same event in 1908. It says a great deal that one of the few events from the period of genteel eclipse worth remembering was itself a historical celebration. The same argument holds for the 1976 reprinting of Riley's *"The Ancient City"* by the Annapolis and Anne Arundel County Bicentennial Committee. If these two commemorations reflect a difficulty in finding anything of value to celebrate from this time period, what then is there?

Annapolis in the nineteenth and early twentieth centuries was a small town. It had communities, such as the one made up of the families of black tradesmen and Chesapeake Bay watermen. Nineteenth-century Chesapeake Bay life could easily be a focus of historical attention. Given what we know about community structure in nineteenth-century Annapolis, both African-American and European-American, the nineteenth- and early twentieth-century period is particularly well suited for developing the concept of Annapolis: "placeness," an important topic that has been neglected in most historical presentations. Although there are several books on Annapolis in the nineteenth century (White and White 1957; Burdett 1974), they are essentially "anecdotal." What I am suggesting is that the nineteenth century could be a focus for studying Annapolis as a community, or a community of communities, and these studies could be particularly valuable now, when some Annapolis communities are actively disintegrating and others are in danger of fading from memory.

However, I think that Annapolis has sensed a danger in examining its local or community history too closely. Historians of Annapolis may be wary of finding that the local community, *as a community*, is not particularly unique, that it lacks a strong or usable identity, or that it lacks cohesion: that is, Annapolitans may fear finding that there isn't a "there" there, that there isn't a secure basis for defining localness. This, in turn, would provide precise quantification for the claim that Annapolis actually is not much more than the sum of its parts, a claim that strengthens the political position of the various institutions that make up Annapolis. These issues are discussed in more detail in chapter 7. It is sufficient for the moment to acknowledge that the golden age is a focus of historical attention in Annapolis.

Fragmentation

An overarching characteristic of much of Annapolis history is fragmentation. Architectural history is separate from archaeology, and both are separate from political history. Eighteenth-century history is separate from nineteenth-century history. African-American history is separate from the history of white Annapolitans. The various institutions in Annapolis have their own histories, rarely linked to those of other institutions. History, as it is usually presented in Annapolis, and as it has been for 100 years, is as fragmented as it could be.

This fragmentation is expressed in a number of ways. Most Historic Annapolis walking tours provide accurate historical information, but in all but the best tours it lacks a purpose or a point of view. Facts are attached to buildings, but seldom to each other or to the present. In Three Centuries Tours, which generally have a somewhat weaker commitment to scholarship and a somewhat stronger commitment to entertainment, the effect is largely the same. History books and guidebooks are usually divided into segments organized around discrete temporal episodes or prominent institutions. Many devote some pages to the city itself and some to the Naval Academy. The Warrens take this one step further, segregating their photo essays on the city and the Naval Academy into two different books. The underlying structure of Norris's title is relevant here, too. To Norris, Annapolis history has a colonial part and a separate naval part. However, with the exception of Ramirez's dissertation, no history of Annapolis to date puts all the pieces together and presents an interpretation of how Annapolis functions (or fails to function) as an integrated unit. The two most significant cleavages in the presentation of the history of Annapolis are the separation between African-Americans and European-Americans and the separation between the Historic District and the Naval Academy. Although each of these separations is worthy of examination, Archaeology in Annapolis did not move deeply into the archaeology of African-American sites until after I left the project, so a discussion of this issue is better left to others (Leone et al. n.d.).

The separation between the Historic District and the Naval Academy is expressed in two ways. First, some histories call the founding of the Naval Academy the dawning of a new day for Annapolis. They refer to this event as one that "restored [Annapolis's] national character" (Riley 1887: 5), as "a sudden change in the fortunes of the little town" (Norris 1925: 245), and as "an event . . . that was to have a profound and beneficent influence on the future of the town" (Stevens 1937: 176). Second, many guidebooks outline a tour of Annapolis that has a magical middle point, which marks the spot where one leaves the small, old, quaint, brick, slow city and enters the large, new, precise, stone, fast Naval Academy: "Our tour of dear, quaint, old Annapolis was completed and like Rip Van Winkle we had to rub our eyes before going down to our modern Naval Academy" (Thruston 1916). Says Randall (1911):

> It is a strange combination, or contrast, ladies and gentlemen, the most modern, expensive, and up-to-date technical educational plant in the world—with its palatial piles of buildings, its great battleships of steel, its destroyers—both submarine and aerial, its wireless telegraph, and everything that modern times and ingenuity has suggested to make conquest of the heavens above, the earth beneath, and the waters under the earth—all set amid a peaceful environment that carries the mind back to medieval times to the days of the simple life of our first settlers.

Slightly less hyperbolically, Dugan (1902) says on the first page of her *Outline History of Annapolis and the Naval Academy*: "The United States Naval Academy is placed somewhat like a modern gem in an antique setting, for the town of Annapolis is as old as we Americans count time, while the remodeled Naval Academy is intended to be the newest of the new. Those who visit the place, therefore, will do well to consider the town, or setting first, and go thence by easy and historic stages to the Naval School." Speaking of the view from the dome of the Maryland State House Dugan says, "The Naval Academy with its governmental care and Naval precision are close at hand while at one's very feet is the old town with its quaint, radiating streets, and its large old houses often hidden by the trees." Ramirez (1975: 397) calls the academy "a separate world behind its white wall." The city and the academy are presented in many histories and guides as being categorically different and thus unconnected.

Histories of Annapolis treat the academy as a separate entity, and histories of the academy (like Tilghman's [1984] history of St. John's College) tend to ignore the city altogether. While histories have been written about the academy, the academy provides little in the way of popular historical interpretation for the more than 1 million visitors arriving each year. The guided tour offered to visitors there makes little mention of the military careers for which midshipmen are trained and does not contain much history, either of the academy or of the academy's relationship with the city. The place is presented as a big, modern, but ahistorical university in a tour that tells how many pounds of mashed potatoes are consumed at dinner and the year in which Roger Staubach won his Heisman Trophy. Even at the academy's most historical spot, the crypt of John Paul Jones, below the chapel, history is overshadowed by discussions of the nonstop weddings that take place in the chapel just after graduation.

It seems as if, in the public context, the academy has simply decided to stress its modernity by not doing history. "The [academy's] disregard for Annapolis and ignorance of its contribution to American history has been almost continuous. The equal disregard for the historic qualities of the Academy and its site [by the academy] has deprived the Navy of evidence of its own growth" (Ramirez 1975:275). Why the academy has stopped doing history, or at least the kind of history that connects the city and the academy, one can only speculate. It may be that by doing history with John Paul Jones, the academy was competing with the city. The academy could have seen the reburial of John Paul Jones as a masterstroke, declared itself the winner, and retired from doing history. Or it may have stopped doing history after sensing that John Paul Jones was the best it could possibly do and that it could never beat Annapolis at history, or at least colonial history, which was defined as important by the widespread popularity of the colonial revival. A third possibility is that after John Paul Jones the academy simply decided that there was little value in developing a locally focused historical consciousness, leaving history in Annapolis to the rest of the city. It is also possible that the reburial of John Paul Jones had nothing to do with Annapolis but instead reflected the nationalistic pride of Teddy Roosevelt's new two-ocean navy. On a more pragmatic level, the academy's emphasis on modernity may be part of an effort to convince its visitors that their tax dollars are well spent by an institution that is relentlessly forward-looking.

The Naval Academy has, in certain physical ways, rejected eighteenth-century Annapolis history by pursuing "a development pattern that is oblivious to its setting" (Ramirez 1975: 275). Important evidence for this is the destruction of eighteenth-century houses and roadways before and during the early twentieth-century rebuilding of the academy. Not only did the academy reject Annapolis's history, it walled itself off from the rest of the city and was built massively, in gray granite, a look distinctly different from that of the generally small brick buildings of the Historic District. Stevens (1937: 269) suggests that the new academy was built in granite instead of brick because of the influence of a U.S. senator from New England who threatened to block appropriations for construction if any material other than granite was used. In any case, the new campus embodies both a rejection of history and a separation from the city. Ramirez (1975: 347), as noted earlier, refers to the academy as "a separate world behind its white wall." This presentation of the city and the academy as separate in the past and in the present is endorsed by both the city and the academy.

The eighteenth-century governor's house torn down to make way for the execution of Flagg's plan for the Naval Academy in the early twentieth century. (Photograph courtesy of M. E. Warren, Annapolis, Maryland)

This separation is particularly interesting in light of the many long-standing connections between the two. Annapolis lobbied for a naval school for twenty years before it got one and worried quite loudly when it feared that the academy would not return from Newport, Rhode Island, after the Civil War. Similar concerns were expressed just after the Spanish American War (Dugan 1902) and during the 1940s, when it looked as though the academy might be moved to California (Burdett 1974; Smith 1983). Housing for construction workers and other academy personnel filled out some residential neighborhoods in Annapolis and Eastport in the late nineteenth and early twentieth centuries. On nine occasions, the academy has expanded into Annapolis (Ramirez 1975), eroding the city's tax base with each expansion. Worry over academy expansion is strong enough today so that when the academy proposed buoying off a section of the Severn River to make a safe place for small sailboats, one Annapolitan wrote the *Capital*, slightly tongue-in-cheek, suggesting that the plan should be opposed because eventually the academy would claim that part of the river and fill it in to make more practice fields for athletics. It would not be the first time the academy has expanded into the Severn.

The town has been, and continues to be, dependent on the academy in a variety of ways. It depends on the discretionary spending of the academy, its students, faculty, and staff, and visitors to it: "The location of the Naval Academy at Annapolis," says Riley (1887: 268), "has been of large advantage to the business of the place. The social benefits have been well appreciated by its people, and the constant succession of interesting events occurring at the academy, has added to the enjoyment and culture of an already polished community." According to Norris (1925: 1), "The coming of the Naval Academy in the middle of the last century did not destroy Colonial Annapolis but merely enabled it to achieve sufficient material prosperity to maintain its gentility." In the view of Stevens (1937: 318), the academy brought "blessings to the community outside its gates":

> The rough, cobbled streets, for the most part gave way to pavements; garbage barrels, peeling paint, old board fences, and tangled dooryards disappeared in favor of an almost New England neatness. Even the alleys, where the darkies lived, no longer boasted the same fragrances from various obsolete remains of the vegetable and animal kingdoms. The great increase in Naval appropriations trickled through every street and lane like the waters irrigating a desert farm, and made the town bloom again as it had not done for over a century. It perked up with a new lease on life.

Annapolis, he continues, "is now enjoying a serene old age, secure in good days and bad, in the steady stream of Navy Department checks from a certain town nearby on the Potomac. . . . So, thanks to the presence of the Naval Academy, Annapolis is spared the humiliation of sinking into poverty on the one hand, or being vulgarized and exploited as an industrial town on the other. She is permitted to enjoy her memories in peace and plenty" (Stevens 1937: 327) These quotations demonstrate the basis for understanding the city and the academy as connected. But, appearing as they do, in books whose structure reinforces the idea of separateness between the city and the academy, their effect has been blunted.

Summary

This chapter has presented a history of history in Annapolis, demonstrating that Annapolitans are no strangers to historical thinking and that the city has long been the subject of historical discourse, if not study. Second, it has examined three characteristics of presentations of history in Annapolis: they assume that history is to be appreciated sensually or evocatively, they focus on the eighteenth century, and historians of Annapolis have thoroughly fragmented the city, allowing it to be put back together only in a limited way. In chapter 7 I discuss the ways in which these characteristics of Annapolis history have been put to use in the city.

7

Annapolis's Use of the Past

How do the versions and interpretations of Annapolis's past presented in chapter 6 constitute, or contribute to, the *use* of the past in Annapolis? This chapter presents a set of informed speculations that respond to that question.

It is important to remember at the outset the basic *assumption* of this study: that contemporary people use the past for social, political, economic, and even personal purposes (see Lowenthal 1985). This assumption will be demonstrated but not proven in any scientific sense. Thus, the main question of concern here is as follows: If Annapolis history is presented in the ways I outlined in chapter 6, what contemporary purposes could be served by these presentations?

The four issues examined in chapters 4–7 (Annapolis today, Annapolis history, the history of Annapolis history, and the uses of the past in Annapolis) are not, in reality, separate. I have separated them for analytical purposes, and while some facts seem to surface repeatedly, they do so in the service of different arguments. Any body of information becomes something different when used in a new argument.

Annapolis today uses its past in many ways. History has proved to be a good way to do business in Annapolis. Many bars, restaurants, and hotels in the Historic District have historical, or at least nostalgic, themes and decors. But this phenomenon is superficial and represents the least of

Annapolis's uses of the past. The real use of history, as I see it, is more dif-
fuse, more subtle, and much more powerful. The power of these uses flows
from their very subtlety, from their understated or unstated, rather than
blatant, character.

As I just mentioned, my principal strategy in this chapter is to suggest
some purposes that may be served by the characteristics of Annapolis his-
tory-telling I discussed in chapter 6. Specifically, I argue that the preservation movement strengthens its position by using the idea of inherent historical value, that the non–Naval Academy part of Annapolis is
empowered by a bias toward the eighteenth century, and that all factions
in Annapolis favor and appear, on the surface, to benefit from the fragmented telling usually given history in Annapolis. I also suggest that one
particular segment of Annapolis, the historic preservation community, has
attempted to create an identity for the city and make a place for itself by
curating the artifacts of Annapolis's past. Thus history is used by some to
overcome the difficulty many have found in establishing a claim to insider
status through productive activity. History has been used to create an identity for a place without placeness, by which I mean a place without a
strong basis for defining local identity.

Historic Quality as Inherent

As mentioned in chapter 6, most presentations of Annapolis history suggest that history is to be appreciated sensually, on the basis of proximity
to its artifacts. This attitude is evident in all the guides to Annapolis that
suggest that to walk through the city is to walk back in time, guides with
titles like Anderson's *Annapolis: A Walk through History* (1984).
According to this epistemology, all one needs to do is breathe in the
quaintness. A second epistemology, seemingly opposed, but conceptually
similar to the first, is the strong emphasis on accuracy that lies at the base
of Historic Annapolis's interpretation and preservation. These two
approaches, one seemingly uninformed, the other seemingly scholarly,
both see historical value as *inherent* in old buildings, streetscapes, and
town plans. So the question is: What interests could be served by the asser-
tion that historical value is inherent?

The argument that value is inherent in the things preserved can easily
divert attention *away* from all the contemporary social and political activities that make up modern preservation as practiced by Historic Annapolis
or by almost any other serious preservation organization, public or pri-

vate. It is one thing for a preservationist to say, "I'm doing X, Y, and Z to building A because I think the building needs it," and quite another to say, "building A deserves to have X, Y, and Z done to it." By making historical value inherent in old buildings, and not the product of contemporary social negotiation, the rhetoric of preservation defines preservation activities as necessary or as a moral obligation, rather than as a set of strategies worthy of debate. Thus, appeals to higher authority partly disguise the basis of preservation action in contemporary politics and economics. Sometimes the positive results of preservation activities are made explicit and are proudly claimed. For example, Historic Annapolis prevailed upon the State of Maryland to preserve as a small museum a building that had been, prior to its preservation, a pool hall and a hangout for a variety of unsavory characters (Wright 1977b: 156). Historic Annapolis also notes an increase in Annapolis property values (from $18 million in 1961 to $38 million in 1970) that has been brought about, in part, by the success of the preservation movement (Symonds 1977: 147). In both of these cases, Historic Annapolis acknowledges the benefits of preservation activities, but it does not say that it undertakes preservation in an attempt to achieve such results. Historic Annapolis, like other preservation organizations, chooses to be seen as a curator, answering to a higher authority, and through this stance of feigned passivity partly hides its active agency.

In this context, the ideology of historical accuracy, as espoused by Historic Annapolis, Colonial Williamsburg, and most preservationists, can be problematic. There are many aspects of eighteenth-century Annapolis that Historic Annapolis would never choose to replicate, among them the use of public streets as a receptacle for garbage and human waste, even though that would be "historically accurate." Even a "dirtied-up" outdoor history museum like Plimoth Plantation will go only so far in replicating seventeenth-century conditions (Zannieri 1980: 44). Whenever Historic Annapolis abandons historical accuracy, it is always careful to replace it with some other equally unassailable justification for its positions and actions. For example, in a recent appeal to the state legislature for funds to bury utility wires in the Historic District, Historic Annapolis publicly based its support for the project on the fire hazard posed by the existing overhead wires. In this case, Historic Annapolis portrayed itself as arguing not on its own behalf or for its own opinions, but as a custodian of the public welfare. Nobody would, or should, argue against sanitation or safe wiring, but it is important to understand that such categories are cultural creations just as much as "historical value" or preservation activities.

My point here is the length to which Historic Annapolis goes to obscure its own agency and activity in preservation by characterizing its activities as strictly in the service of unchallengeable ideals. It is important to note that accepting this point analytically does not entail a rejection of Historic Annapolis's actual motivations; they are often laudable. Yet, however one evaluates the results of Historic Annapolis's work, the organization's typical rhetorical posture flows, at least in part, from an ideology that places historical value in objects, not in the eyes and the minds of those who view those objects.

The Golden Age

The second theme in the presentation of Annapolis history is the idea that the city's colonial golden age merits far more attention than any other theme. This emphasis can be useful in at least three ways, especially to city-based interests.

Precedent

First, the history of the colonial golden age provides an ideal precedent or historical grounding for the city's present-day commercial boom. Today's boom times are based on taverns, sailing, and wealthy sophisticated passers-through, a picture of Annapolis that is similar in many ways to the most frequently painted picture of eighteenth-century Annapolis:

> Annapolis today is a mecca for out-of-town visitors. Some come in connection with the General Assembly or to visit state offices. Others come because it is a yachting center. Still others come to see the U.S. Naval Academy, St. John's College, the historic houses and gardens, or to canvass the numerous shops. As a result, there are many hotels and restaurants and bars in the city. The same, in large measure, was true in the eighteenth century. The General Assembly and the Provincial court drew many people to Maryland's "metropolis" either on business or the social activities that took place at the "publick times." And since Annapolis was a small town, even by eighteenth-century standards—with more than 1,500 or 2,000 inhabitants (a third of whom were black)—it had even then an unusually large number of inns, taverns, and ordinaries. (Middleton 1986: 11)

Norris (1925: 1) says that the Annapolis of his day "has retained something of the very atmosphere of the rollicking days before the Revolution. . . . [I]t has never changed its character and has preserved its old buildings, streets, alleys, and general air of cultivated, aristocratic complacency." This parallel between the eighteenth century and today can easily be used as a justification for the town's contemporary activities—a justification with some utility given the occasional outcries of residents against the Annapolis business community, which, in the eyes of local residents, has adversely affected the quality of residential life in Annapolis.

Precedence

A second value of a focus on the eighteenth century is that it may be used to deny history—and a privileged place in contemporary Annapolis—to certain elements of the local community. John Paul Jones aside, the Naval Academy cannot claim an eighteenth-century heritage. In any scheme that values the eighteenth century above all, the Naval Academy is a decided latecomer to Annapolis:

> It begins to dawn on the observer that the Naval Academy is, as compared with Anne Arundel's town, a mere child. To be sure it has passed its ninetieth birthday, but the city was the capital of Maryland one hundred and fifty years before the Academy was born. Thus, the famous school should be considered not even as the daughter of Annapolis, but rather as the granddaughter. "The Cradle of the Navy" is rocked by an affectionate grandmother who does her knitting the while and lives over the days of her girlhood when she was a famous toast among the colonial towns. (Stevens 1937: 327)

As Emery (1948: 1) points out, "Almost two centuries before the U.S. Naval Academy was even dreamed of, hearty pioneer settlers were holding 'pow-wows' with the native Susquehannock Indians. . . . A hundred years before the Academy was founded, Annapolis was one of our most cultured Colonial cities. . . . The city on the Severn was old, sage and refined long before the Revolutionary war—long before the birth of the American Navy itself."

Not only is the city older than the academy, it is able to claim a national importance on the basis of eighteenth-century events that occurred in Annapolis: Washington's resignation and the ratification of the Treaty of Paris. The Naval Academy may be a federal institution, but, the argument goes, Annapolis played a role in the birth of the nation seventy years before the academy was ever founded. In 1963 the residents of the city, led by Historic Annapolis, used both of these elements of Annapolis's historical vision of itself—its eighteenth-century heritage and its role in national affairs—to force the Naval Academy to abandon plans for the acquisition of, and expansion into, three residential blocks of Annapolis (Ramirez 1975: 326–30; Historic Annapolis 1963). The academy intended to demolish all the buildings on these blocks, but Historic Annapolis made a strong case for their historical significance. Among the buildings Historic Annapolis saved was the Peggy Stewart House, which was an important setting for the Annapolis Tea Party in 1763 and was also owned by Thomas Stone, a signer of the Declaration of Independence. In short, Annapolis's emphasis on its eighteenth-century history has utility as a method for denying the Naval Academy a history, or at least a history that matters in Annapolis.

An Imperative for Preservation

Third, Annapolis's focus on the eighteenth-century means that it pays less attention to the nineteenth- and twentieth-century aspects of its history. This lack of attention to post-Revolutionary times can be said to serve the local preservation community in an interesting way. By ignoring the nineteenth- and twentieth-century occupants of Annapolis historic houses, their contemporary curators foster the illusion that men like Edward Lloyd, Mathias Hammond, and William Paca simply turned the keys to their houses over to their present-day curators—underscoring the importance of preservation activities by making them seem to be the result of compacts between eighteenth-century worthies and contemporary Annapolitans. Such a turn of thought allows Mr. Paca to be a real presence in the Wm. Paca House, and many of Historic Annapolis's activities there appear as if carried out for him. A recent Christmas brochure welcomed visitors to "Mr. Paca's Christmas Celebration, 1985." This is the same sort of ideology that suggests historical value is inherent in old things.

In summary, by focusing on the eighteenth century, the city's history makers seem to be doing three things: (1) providing precedent for the city's commercial renaissance, (2) giving a part of the city's population some measure of power over (or protection from) the Naval Academy, and (3) strengthening the notion that preservation is a moral imperative by suggesting a false continuity between the eighteenth century and the present, which leads to the empowerment of those who practice preservation.

Fragmentation

The contemporary value of the fragmented telling usually given Annapolis history is more complex but no less significant. As described in chapter 6, Annapolis history is fragmented along cultural, temporal, geographic, disciplinary, and institutional lines. None of those breaks or lines of fracture is natural or given. Rather, each is a cultural product, either conscious and intentional or unconscious—but every bit as powerful. The cleavage I wish to consider in particular, in terms of its contemporary social utility, is the one between the city and the Naval Academy.

In chapters 4 and 5, I discussed the city's dependence on the academy and the academy's domination of the city. In chapter 6, I argued that the city and the academy both use history to present themselves as separate from each other, with the city's history anchored in the eighteenth century and the academy's, to the extent that it claims a history, in the nineteenth and twentieth—with the exception of the history surrounding John Paul Jones. Once again, the question is, given contemporary social relations, what purpose is served by this version of the past? In view of the significant connections between the city and the academy and the nature of those connections, the city and academy may be led to present themselves as separate for the following reasons.

The city, as already mentioned, has been dominated by the academy. By not telling this story, the city may be trying to avoid providing precedent for future domination. The city seems reluctant to give the academy ammunition with which to argue that since things have always been that way in the past, they should continue to be so. For its part, the academy seems reluctant to discuss history at all. When it does, it is strictly institutional history that stops at the main gate. By ignoring the historical connections between itself and the city in which it is located, the academy is able to avoid presenting itself as a dangerous neighbor. While the academy has the power to get almost anything it wants from Annapolis, depending on how much of its power it is willing to use, it pays considerable attention to being a good neighbor, on a superficial level. This appears to be an attempt to guarantee placid day-to-day relations between the city and the academy and thus to prevent local resentment from building up to the point where concerted local resistance would require a large-scale exercise of power. Such a display of power could only cost the academy a great deal of its Washington "capital" and make local living conditions for its employees based in Annapolis less pleasant. Except on a superficial and clearly ahistorical level, neither the city nor the academy is eager to tell the

140-year story of the city's submission to the academy. The city does not want to appear dominated; the academy does not want to appear dominating. Neither wants to give the other any more leverage than it already has. Even so, "the interdependence of the historic city and the Academy is essential if they are both to survive on the Annapolis peninsula" (Ramirez 1975: 276).

Transience, Visitation, Identity, and History

The utility of Annapolis's history becomes more evident when an aspect of Annapolis today is juxtaposed with a significant element in the city's portrayal of its history. This juxtaposition will serve as my principal example of the use of the past in Annapolis. The case I make is that some Annapolitans have turned to the curation of Annapolis's past and the creation of Annapolis history as a way of establishing local identity in a city where there are few other ways to do so.

As I have attempted to demonstrate, history in Annapolis is so fragmented that there is nowhere available, for any purpose, a comprehensive coherent view of how all the parts fit together. It would be easy to conclude that this fragmentation simply mirrors a complex struggle among several competing groups or institutions in Annapolis attempting to use history—or the lack of history—to gain an upper hand. No single group or institution is sure enough of where it will end up in a coherent history to actually produce one. This is especially true of the city-oriented white historical elite, which has been active in Annapolis for about a century. This group in particular has reason to fear that a comprehensive history of Annapolis would have no room for Annapolitans because such a history would be filled with midshipmen, legislators, Continental Congressmen, and other visitors. A study of visitation and the transient nature of many Annapolis historical figures and institutions provides a way of seeing the use of history in Annapolis as something more than simply a series of unconnected petty skirmishes.

The fighting with history that takes place in Annapolis is nothing short of a contemporary version of the age-old question, "Whose city is this?" As I have pointed out in previous chapters, Annapolis has a history of inviting individuals and institutions to the city and then becoming enmeshed in problematic power relations with those who respond to the invitation. The Naval Academy is an example of a guest who has grown dangerously powerful. My hunch is that civilian Annapolis finds the characterization of the Naval Academy as made up of outsiders a useful device for trying to limit the academy's claims to power. For the designation of certain groups as outsiders to be a successful strategy, however, there must be unambiguous ways of establishing and demonstrating a local "insider" identity.

In fact, identity problems are a recurring part of Annapolis history as well as a central thread in contemporary Annapolis politics. I have already mentioned the wide variety of fanciful nicknames Annapolitans have fashioned for their city. Further, Annapolis has made a number of attempts to regain aspects of its identity. For example, "the location of the Naval Academy here in 1845 restored its [Annapolis'] national character" (Riley 1887: 5), and the historic preservation movement helped Annapolis recover "a sense of place that is crucial to a well-ordered society" (Wright 1977b: 155). Put simply, the identity question has two parts: (1) What is Annapolis (or for whom does the city exist)? and (2) Just what makes a person an Annapolitan?

As I have already suggested, Annapolis seems to be a place without placeness. More precisely, most of its residents lack a direct relationship with the local productive environment. Few are directly tied to the natural environment by their labor. In contrast, Pittsburgh derives an identity from its natural location, which made it an ideal place to manufacture steel. Coal was available nearby and iron ore readily accessible. To be a Pittsburgher par excellence was, in the 1940s and 1950s, to be a beer-drinking, football-loving steelworker—or married to one. Chicago became hog-butcher to the world because it was ideally located to be a transhipment point. Milwaukee has beer, Dallas and Houston oil, and so on. Other urban identities work the same way. Boston and Philadelphia are known for their roles in the American Revolution. Los Angeles is tinsel town and New Orleans is jazz. All of these identities, of long historical standing, have, through the passage of time, taken on the status of naturally based identities. Although Annapolis is called Crab Town, its high rents have forced out all the watermen and their families, and Annapolis today does not have a direct productive relationship with the Chesapeake Bay. Far more Annapolitans buy crabs in restaurants than harvest them from the Bay. The city may have a developing identity as a yachting port, but only some yachters live in Annapolis; most pass through. Annapolis also lacks a coherent resident urban social identity. Annapolis lacks identity today just as its pleas for the relocation of institutions and industries signaled a lack of identity—and a willingness to assume one—in the past. Annapolis's history as a place filled with outsiders, and its understanding of itself as such, is well illustrated in a thin little book called *Yesteryear in Annapolis* (Burdett 1974).

Yesteryear in Annapolis reprints a series of historical vignettes published in the early 1970s in the Annapolis *Capital*. Although many are stories about nineteenth-century events, they all reinforce the city's bias toward eighteenth-century history since they are about people passing through Annapolis rather than about Annapolis or Annapolitans. Subjects of these stories include a Baltimore tour boat in Annapolis harbor, Union troops in the city, Spanish-American war prisoners, an incident with a Russian soldier, and a visit by P. T. Barnum—all visitors. The clear implication is that there was not much of historical importance in Annapolis itself. This is further justification for labeling Annapolis a place without placeness.

It is time now to consider the degree to which Annapolis, as a place without placeness, is like other American cities. On the surface, it is certainly similar to many small American cities whose livelihoods depend on a mix of educational institutions, administration, and tourism. If the comparison is restricted to tourism, Annapolis is hardly unique in its dependence on this particular form of transience.

In other respects, however, Annapolis is unique in terms of both its problems with transience and its use of history to solve these problems. Here it is helpful to recall MacCannell's (1976) idea about modern tourism: people visit other places to see solutions to the fragmentation and alienation in their own lives. They are seeking coherent worlds constituted by productive labor. One element of those supposedly coherent worlds that tourists visit is a clear productive connection between a group of people and the place they live. When this connection is in fact the case, history becomes the story of what makes insiders insiders and what keeps outsiders outsiders. In this way, history empowers insiders over outsiders.

But in Annapolis, which has historically lacked a strong identity based on production, history is the story of outsiders being wooed, answering the call, and becoming insiders. This is a dangerous story to put out for the consumption of visitors because rather than empowering the locals, it empowers visitors by highlighting Annapolis's dependence on them. As I will argue below, the historic preservation movement represents an attempt to establish a claim to localness in the absence of the usual foundations for such claims.

This lack of placeness is not simply my characterization of Annapolis. It was sensed, if not articulated, by Riley as early as the 1890s when, at the end of his Annapolis histories, he suggested that industries should relocate to Annapolis. With a traditional industry, Annapolis would have had the placeness the city lacks today and has lacked for nearly three centuries.

The city's principal identity problem is that it is simultaneously easy and difficult to become an Annapolitan. Until about twenty years ago, real estate in Annapolis was relatively inexpensive, and if the long-time residents did not beg for newcomers or welcome them with open arms, at least the real estate agents were willing to try to make Annapolis a suburb of Washington for faint-of-heart urban homesteaders. So, until recently it was easy to buy a house in Annapolis. But how to become an Annapolitan? One could not just get a job at the mill or in the meat-packing plant. And if one chose to become Annapolitan through yachting, one entered a lively community filled with all kinds of other transients, many similar, but few of them real Annapolitans. The ease of entry and the lack of a visible, occupationally coherent local community gave the impression that localness, a trait we usually think of as ascribed, could actually be achieved. Such is the lure of a fluid and malleable social environment. But how have people achieved or attempted to achieve localness?

One significant way of claiming localness is through a historic preservation movement. Because Annapolis was a small market town with no large-scale industrial development in the nineteenth century, by the twentieth century it had a remarkable legacy of colonial buildings. These buildings had been variously used and reused since the colonial golden age and thought of as anything from treasures to white elephants. However they were evaluated, many were allowed to stand.

Annapolis began to appreciate its architectural heritage fairly early, not long after the advent of the colonial revival in America. The pace of preservation quickened noticeably in Annapolis in the 1950s, and the great irony in the preservation movement in Annapolis is that many of the buildings treasured by preservationists, residents, and visitors alike are buildings built by transient eighteenth-century folk, people who were not natives and who could not be considered "true Annapolitans." Of the three builders of Annapolis's major historic house museums, William Paca owned his for fifteen years but lived in it only off and on, Mathias Hammond never lived in his, and Samuel Chase never even finished *building* his. Charles Carroll of Carrollton, who is as close as we can come to a true Annapolitan, moved to Baltimore long before his death in the 1830s. In short, much of Annapolis's splendid architectural heritage consists of buildings left behind by individuals and businesses that departed.

The particular irony of the "authorship" of Annapolis's rich architectural legacy is that the city's historic preservation movement is staffed, to a large extent, by relative newcomers to Annapolis, a phenomenon that probably is not unique to Annapolis. The wives of active and retired naval officers and the wives of corporate executives new to the community attempt to make themselves Annapolitans by taking care of the things left behind by previous short-term Annapolitans. In the same way that men or women who marry into ethnic groups tend to be more "ethnically correct" than their ethnic in-laws (Chock 1986), newcomers can take Annapolis history and architecture remarkably seriously. I have even heard it said by members of the preservation community that the long-time locals need a group like Historic Annapolis because the natives are not smart enough to know what treasures they have. It could, of course, be the case that native Annapolitans know exactly what they have but have no interest in—or reject—what the preservation movement tries to give them. In any case, the historic preservation movement in Annapolis is one vehicle some people have used to attach themselves to Annapolis, and to make themselves Annapolitans in the process. Ramirez (1975: 318, 320) says, "Delighted with Annapolis, many . . . newcomers began to see opportunities in Annapolis for attracting visitors through festivals and various special events [including historical activities]. . . . Within the oldest part of the city, its newest members are creating a new community activity." While it is difficult to find fault with the beauty or the historical accuracy of the restoration of the Wm. Paca House and Garden, many long-time Annapolitans have important personal memories associated with Carvel Hall Hotel. One of the prices paid for the restoration of the Wm. Paca Garden was the demolition of the scene of many local residents' wedding receptions.

Annapolis uses history in yet another way that is related to its past and present status as a host to large numbers of visitors. As a host, the city's challenge is to protect from the ravages of visitors those things that will help the city attract future visitors. As I discussed in chapter 4, this challenge is considerable. Among the things requiring protection are the city's small size, its historical character, and a general ambiance of sophistication created by expensive shops, up-scale saloons, and a well-heeled clientele. To preserve all this, Annapolis markets itself in certain ways (in yachting magazines but not motorcycle magazines), enforces laws against drinking (and urinating) in public, and publicly interprets certain parts of its history.

The book mentioned above, *Yesteryear in Annapolis*, is filled with stories of nineteenth-century visitations and may be read two ways. On one hand, it may be seen as just a collection of quaint stories; on the other hand, those stories may also be read as fables or parables about tourism, how to be a host city, how to behave as a visitor, and especially (as in the story of a riot between Annapolitans and Baltimoreans on a tourist cruise to Annapolis) what can and should happen to ill-mannered visitors. And while *Yesteryear in Annapolis* could almost serve as a guide for residents of a tourist town, the city's portrayals of George Washington and his approximately twenty visits to Annapolis appear to have great utility for teaching visitors how to behave in contemporary Annapolis.

George Washington visited Annapolis many times during his life, and those visits are celebrated as an important part of the city's history (Norris 1925: 191–225; Baldridge 1928; Stevens 1937; Anderson 1984; Riley 1887). Says Norris (1925: 191), "there are so many of these [visits], begun so early and continued so long, that it will be worth while to bring them together." Paragraphs and sometimes even chapters are devoted to Washington's visits, and Historic Annapolis has based a special tour for school children on them. Interestingly, portrayals of Washington in Annapolis tend to emphasize his social and domestic activities while in town. Norris (1925: 191) thinks these visits throw light on the personality of Washington, "especially because they illuminate a side of his character which has usually been overshadowed by outstanding and public traits as a general and statesman. . . . In Annapolis he appears at once as a great military figure, but at other times as the man of fashion, the friendly visitor, and the conscientious husband and step-father."

> By the year 1770, however, Washington had become a leading character in the Southern Colonies, and as a man of wealth and social standing became a fairly frequent visitor, for now Annapolis was distinctly the social center of the section that lay along the shores of the Chesapeake and the Potomac. Several visits are recorded in detail in the diaries that Washington, so methodical in all things, kept. They reveal the manner of the life he led and show his enjoyment of all the social activities of the period, the club, the races, the theatre, the balls . . . and the dinner table. (Norris 1925: 193)

This focus on Washington's socializing in Annapolis is not simply an artifact of old or out-of-date histories. Anderson's 1984 guidebook contains nine references to Washington in Annapolis, more than half of which are about the social aspects of his visits. In a well-attended public lecture on George Washington in Maryland presented in February 1987, a local history professor presented virtually the same information Norris used and focused almost exclusively on the horse races, balls, and dinner parties attended by Washington. At the same time, Washington's resignation of his commission in the Continental Army is by no means ignored. But rather than being treated as a political event, that act is "domesticated" in several paintings and engravings. Martha Washington is placed in the picture when, by all historical accounts, she was at Mount Vernon when her husband was in Annapolis. Thus in paintings, but not in reality, the future Father of his Country is portrayed with his wife, presumably the Mother of his Country. Other accounts of this event in Annapolis history play up the social aspects of even that Washington visit, some listing the toasts drunk (Riley 1887: 205), the ladies danced with, and so on.

Discussions of Washington's other visits focus on the dances, plays, and races he attended. Norris (1925: 194–99) even published parts of a diary that details Washington's wagering in Annapolis. Accounts are also given of consultations between Washington and the Reverend Jonathan Boucher, rector of St. Anne's Church and tutor of a small school attended by Washington's stepson, Jackie Custis (Norris 1925: 201–9; Anderson 1984: 131). There is even a story about a nightcap supposedly left by Martha Washington at the house of John Ridout, secretary to colonial Governor Horatio Sharpe, to indicate she intended to return (Stevens 1937: 108; Anderson 1984: 58).

There are many possible explanations for this pattern of emphasis. It may simply be an attempt to "humanize" the great man, or to lay claim to a special "behind-the-scenes" part of the Washington myth. Norris (1925: 200) has gone so far as to suggest that Washington gained a certain "polish" in Annapolis that helped prepare him for his role in the Revolution and the birth of the nation. All of these explanations for Annapolis's portrayal of Washington would help in marketing Annapolis as a special kind of historical place, giving them all some contemporary value. They may all be accurate at some level. Each would help do what any tourist town needs to do—attract visitors.

However, Annapolis' bigger problems revolve around controlling the behavior of visitors once they have been attracted, and making sure they end their visits and go home again. At least in terms of guiding visitor behavior, Washington is most useful. As portrayed in most historical accounts, Washington fits almost perfectly the profile of the "quality tourist" Annapolis has decided it wants to attract. The Washington who visited Annapolis was wealthy, sophisticated, and deferential to local authority. Washington is Annapolis's model tourist and serves, therefore, as a subtle model of behavior for contemporary visitors.

This notion finds some support in *Washington Bowed* by Theodore McKeldin (1957). McKeldin served as governor of Maryland during the

1950s and placed the name of Dwight Eisenhower into nomination at the 1952 Republican National Convention. McKeldin's interest in Washington may well have been a subtle attempt to draw parallels between Washington and Eisenhower as popular generals operating in the political realm. McKeldin's book, which evolved from an article he wrote for *American Heritage Magazine*, describes Washington's resignation. From McKeldin's point of view, this was the most important moment in American history and the greatest act in Washington's career. The crux of McKeldin's argument is that in carrying out this great act, Washington asked for instructions from the Continental Congress and then carried them out, to the letter. Washington is great, McKeldin contends, because he asked the Congress how they wanted him to resign and then did exactly as he was asked. The structure here is a visitor (Washington, who passed through town) demonstrating deference to local authority (the Continental Congress, based for about nine months in the city). Even in a heroic public act unlike anything any Annapolis tourist would ever do, Washington is portrayed to a national audience in a way that makes him a model for visitor behavior.

Note, too, the brochure called "Destination Annapolis," produced by the Tourism Council of Annapolis and Anne Arundel County. This brochure was directed toward corporate meeting planners and its first panel looks like this:

An-nap-o-lis

A great meeting destination since 1649.

Our first professional meeting planner, George Washington, who ousted Great Britain and started the good ol' USA, called his convention here a great success.

You may not want to start a new country, but take the advice of an original and your meeting may just go down in history.

And (it's true) George Washington *did* sleep here.

This brochure came out over a year after I formulated my Washington hypothesis and six months after "Archaeology in Annapolis" began presenting it to the public in archaeological site tours. It demonstrates local agreement that Washington-like visitors are desirable and it subtly presents a carefully selected group of potential visitors with a model for their deportment. "Do as Washington did," the brochure says, in the hope that its visitors will emulate all the sterling qualities that have come to be associated with Washington. If Washington is not a model for visitors, he at least provides a model for resident expectations of visitors and their behavior. As well, the brochure has served as a rebuttal to those who have found the idea of Washington as a model tourist overly fanciful or the figment of an academic imagination. The brochure makes explicit a potentiality very near the surface of Annapolis's typical historical picture of itself.

To recap, my hunch is that Annapolis's most complex use of the past involves the subtle portrayal of George Washington as a model tourist. Visitors who follow Washington's lead would constitute a happy solution to Annapolis's problem of how to maintain those aspects of the city that make it attractive to the kind of visitors who make tourism palatable and profitable to the residents of Annapolis.

Summary

The purpose of this chapter has been to suggest ways in which certain aspects of Annapolis history may be useful to contemporary Annapolis. Most of the uses of history in Annapolis today involve a central characteristic of both contemporary Annapolis and Annapolis in the past. That characteristic is the city's lack of identity, coupled with the transient nature of much of what is Annapolitan. Annapolis does not really know what the essence of the town is, or cannot agree on one, yet is host to more than a million visitors a year. As such, it needs to have an essence, something uniquely Annapolitan, to use in distinguishing locals from non locals. Attracting the right kind of visitor to Annapolis is vital because Annapolis's basic history is that the city *is* what it lets in. Unlike New York City, which attracts many immigrants but which folds them into a sort of multiethnic melting pot, Annapolis has little that could count as a central, self-generating essence. Annapolis does not do much to digest and synthetically incorporate its newcomers into a larger whole. It uses history to solve this problem in at least three ways. The city uses history to keep individuals, groups, and institutions in Annapolis separate—or to give the false impression of separateness. This is a move made by the white historical elite to protect its own social position from groups and institutions that would have too much power if fully enfranchised. In addition, while history is used to keep some visitors at bay, it is also used to attract yet more visitors and to keep them, too, at bay. This is all a sophisticated response to of the dilemma faced by any tourist town that hopes to attract the largest possible number of visitors and extract as much money as it can from them, at the least possible cost.

8

A Critically Informed Historical Archaeology

At this point my discussion turns to the question of how to do the archaeological part of a critical archaeology for Annapolis. In this chapter, I demonstrate a link between the ethnographic and historical data presented in the previous chapters and archaeological analysis. This demonstration serves as the basis for an archaeologically based discourse on Annapolis initiated by Archaeology in Public, which is the subject of the chapters that follow.

The central topic of this chapter is the invention, for Annapolis, of an archaeology of visitation and transience, themes that have characterized life in Annapolis for many years. The first part of this discussion considers various approaches to variability and meaning in the archaeological record along with several historical archaeological approaches to capitalism. It concludes by introducing a technique for measuring variability in the archaeological record. Archaeology in Annapolis has developed this technique (along with several others) with a view to using the city's archaeological record to explore the problematic solution Annapolis has found for its long-standing identity problem.

Both Annapolis's identity problems and its solutions for them are products of modern capitalism. That Annapolis has been able to survive and thrive without a strong productive base is a consequence of the specialization and segmentation that characterize the increasingly administered societies of late capitalism. Thus, the archaeology of transience and visitation I propose here may also be understood, more broadly, as an approach to the historical archaeology of capitalism.

A critical archaeology of transience and visitation in Annapolis serves two important purposes. First, it yields information on the early histories of these phenomena and a social world in which they were neither universal nor inevitable. Second, such an archaeology serves as the basis for a public discourse on the structures of everyday life often hidden by ideology. The topic of discourse I have proposed is the set of uniformly ambiguous claims to localness and authority held by most factions within the city. The Archaeology in Public interpretive program I discuss in chapters 9–11 does not advocate an alternative solution to this problem. Instead, it is based on the idea that an archaeologically based discourse that pierces the ideologies of nonlocalness and separateness can lead to a more productive coexistence in Annapolis. The result Archaeology in Annapolis hopes to bring about by using the analysis I discuss in this chapter is a better-informed interrelationship between the parts of Annapolis.

Archaeology and Contemporary Social Issues

Doing the archaeology of transience and visitation in Annapolis is not simply a matter of digging up the first tourist attraction in the city or the earliest buildings of the U.S. Naval Academy. Rather, it is a matter of using archaeological data to comment on the histories of the ways of thinking that have allowed visitation to be an activity, the category "tourist" to exist, and the distinction between outsiders and insiders to have meaning. Put another way, this critical archaeology is an attempt to explore the social, political, and economic foundations of Annapolis's ambiguous identity, as well as the reasons for the solutions various people have found for this central problem. It is not necessary to excavate the first tourist attraction to achieve this goal because, as I suggested earlier, Annapolis's ability to rely on outsiders is a product of capitalism. Thus, many different kinds of sites that represent early capitalism in Annapolis contain data relevant to the particular manifestations of capitalism I have identified as a problem in Annapolis.

Since a critical approach seeks ways of dealing with variability that will allow archaeological finds to comment explicitly on the origin or history of significant aspects of contemporary life, the first step here will be to determine how best to classify and measure variability in the archaeological record, a task that is, in fact, central to any archaeology, not just critical arachaeology. This vital step cannot be taken without careful attention to the construction of analytical categories and also to their implications.

Variability and Meaning in Historical Archaeology

It is widely accepted in archaeology that any archaeological find has many attributes, only some of which are considered germane to the purposes behind a particular classification system. Some variables are ignored whereas others are measured and become data. Any collection of objects may be classified many different ways according to classification schemes based on different attributes. To this extent, classification is considered an analytical task, or at least is carried out from a particular point of view (Potter 1982). Hill and Evans (1972: 251), Fontana (1973: 3), Dunnell (1971: 117), Clarke (1968: 13), Kaplin (1964: 51), Binford (1965: 206), and a host of others have pointed out that classification is directly influenced by the hypotheses tested with a particular body of data, but far fewer archaeologists have considered the potential impacts of their hypothesis testing on contemporary life.

The points I have just made, about the links between the measurement of variability and analytical purposes, is somewhat less accepted within historical archaeology. According to Noel-Hume (1973: 217), the terminology applied to British-made, eighteenth-century ceramic tableware by its makers is more correct than any other terminology. South (1977) has argued for his own etic classification schemes for historic period artifacts. What Noel-Hume does, largely by accident, is advocate a naming system far better suited to studying English pottery *makers* and the dispersion of their wares than the American—and other colonial—*users* of those wares. The ultimate utility of South's classification scheme, in the absence of any justification of the categories as meaningful in the lives of the people whose culture South purports to study, is the ability it gives other historical archaeologists to determine how like or unlike South's data their own are.

What neither Noel-Hume nor South seem to grasp is that although there may be wrong names for artifacts, there are no absolutely right ones. Rather, the appropriateness of the variables measured in artifacts and the correctness of the names applied to them can be judged only in relationship to the questions that any given archaeologist attempts to answer, using the artifacts as data. Consider the example of a blue, shell-edged pearlware plate. To answer some questions, it is enough to know that the plate is ceramic and not glass, metal, or bone. To answer other questions, say, chronological ones, its key quality may be its being pearlware and not creamware or whiteware. To answer yet other questions, it may be necessary to measure the regularity of the brush-strokes used to apply the cobalt to make the edging, or to measure the diameter of the plate. Any measurement of variables and any application of a name to an artifact is a *selection* based on the analytical use to which the artifact is put (see Potter 1982).

It does seem to be true that historical archaeologists are becoming increasingly skilled at creating measurements of the archaeological record that are linked to specific hypotheses. George Miller's work with ceramics (1980, 1984, 1991) and the studies reported by Suzanne Spencer-Wood (1987) are good examples. Again, for all these successes, there are far fewer examples of studies in historical archaeology that use variability in the archaeological record to comment on contemporary life.

Variability and Meaning in Critical Archaeology

One important step in constructing a *critical* archaeology is to determine what attributes of the archaeological record allow it to be used to explore the beginnings of an aspect of contemporary life masked by ideology. In some cases, preexisting measures of variability and classificatory schemes will be suitable, but in others, such as the ceramic analysis discussed below, a "known" variable, typically considered to carry relatively little information value, may emerge as quite significant. Whether the variables measured are new ones or old standbys, it is necessary to construct comprehensive and coherent arguments of relevance that demonstrate how the measurement of a particular variable contributes to understanding the history of some element of modern life.

Variability and Meaning and Archaeology in Annapolis

Since its inception, Archaeology in Annapolis has attempted to explore the roots of modern American capitalism. We have never claimed that capitalism was invented in Annapolis, only that its eighteenth-century remains were likely to be found in Annapolis. This likelihood is based on two factors: (1) Annapolis was home to some successful merchant capitalists and early industrial capitalists (who moved to Baltimore to do their business), and (2) Annapolis's eighteenth-century remains are extremely well preserved.

One of the most useful definitions of historical archaeology is that the principal object of study for the discipline should be European colonial expansion and the driving force behind it, European merchant capitalism (Schuyler 1970). Many historical archaeologists have followed this sound lead, including Handsman (1981b, 1982), Spencer-Wood (1987), Leone (1988), South (1988), Orser (1988), McGuire (1988), and Paynter (1988). Once Archaeology in Annapolis made a commitment to doing a historical archaeology of capitalism in Annapolis, it had the choice of two paths to follow, one trail blazed by South and the other by Deetz.

South's (1988) version of historical archaeology as the archaeology of capitalism is deeply rooted in the functionalism of Leslie White. There have been many critiques of a functionalist approach to archaeology, including those of Ian Hodder (1982, 1986), but relatively few within the literature of historical archaeology (see, however, Orser 1989). Here I focus specifically on South's version of historical archaeology. To South, following White, culture is a system for the capture and use of energy, but that definition offers little by which to distinguish between capitalist and noncapitalist systems; all are economic systems and all have the same basic goal. As with any functionalist analysis, the activities of any constituent part of the system can and must be understood in terms of its contribution to, or inhibition of, the smooth functioning of the system, and every part is understood as sharing the overall goals of the entire system. Stated another way, the implicitness of the goals of the system along with South's (*not* the system's) placement of those goals in nature makes human thought irrelevant. In South's view, all human activity is a chase for energy, regardless of whether this is acknowledged by individuals. What individuals or groups think is largely epiphenomenal.

In addition, although South agrees that historical archaeology should be about capitalism, his historical archaeology acknowledges but does not deal analytically with class, dominance, or resistance, which are central concepts in any study of capitalism (Paynter 1988). South's approach lacks the tools needed to understand conflicts between groups and classes. Similarly, ideology, where it enters South's analysis, is treated in the traditional functionalist fashion, as "vulgar ideology" and as a residual category like religion. In such formulations, ideology is just a synonym for ideas. In a typical reference to ideology, South (1988: 63) notes of copper stars from Santa Elena, "These stars probably acted in the ideological system much as the carved ebony amulets did—to ward off evil, bring good luck, and so on, when sewn onto clothing—because such stars with various points have religious symbolism." The argument of relevance for this claim is the statement that "crucifixes, rosary beads, and other religious symbols should reveal the Catholic nature of the town" (South 1988: 42). For South, the only artifacts of ideology are symbols that may be related directly to a specific explicit belief system.

South's mode of analysis may be inappropriate for the study of capitalism because it is so clearly a product of capitalism, or at least of the same kind of thinking that has produced and developed modern industrial capitalism. Stated another way, "functionalist theory is probably continuous with the Western European ideology emergent in the time periods studied by historical archaeologists" (Leone and Potter 1988: 5). Further, there is "the striking resemblance between functionalist theory and the phenomenon under study" and the way that this resemblance causes such an approach "difficulty in recognizing its own operation in the present" (Leone and Potter 1988: 5). South's functionalism is so similar to the main structural underpinnings of capitalism that it impedes rather than encourages the study of capitalism; many worthwhile objects of study are taken as axiomatic by the mode of study itself. Thus, although South says that historical archaeology is about capitalism, capitalism is made almost invisible by South's historical archaeology.

For example, South's idea that human life is, before all else, a pursuit of available energy naturalizes and takes for granted economic competition—a pursuit for profit—by participants in economic systems. Any activity that does not contribute to the pursuit of profit stands outside such a system, unanalyzed. As a result of these characteristics, South's program for historical archaeology is unable to measure the impact of the penetration of capitalism because the spread of capitalism is seen as natural and inevitable. South has devoted considerable energy to the creation of systems for classification, analysis, and comparison, but his categories are not tied to issues such as class, dominance, and resistance.

Whereas South explicitly states that historical archaeology should be the study of capitalism, Deetz says only "historical archaeology is the archaeology of the spread of European culture throughout the world since the fifteenth century and its impact on indigenous peoples" (Deetz 1977: 5). Nonetheless, Archaeology in Annapolis has found Deetz's work more useful than South's for constructing a historical archaeology of capitalism. I am not suggesting that the study of capitalism is on Deetz's agenda, only that his work has provided a valuable starting point for historical archaeologists interested in that agenda.

Deetz's principal contribution to historical archaeology to date has been his introduction of Levi-Strauss's structuralism, which has served as a counterweight to South's functionalism, and his introduction of the concept of the Georgian worldview based on his reading of Henry Glassie (1975). In Deetz's version of historical archaeology, the material record is the record of human thought. Within this conception, the Georgian worldview was a new way that people in colonial America began thinking in the eighteenth century, which signaled a shift from an earlier, postmedieval way of thinking. The Georgian worldview, as defined by Deetz (1977, 1983, 1988) and extended by others, is characterized by balance, order, symmetry, segmentation, standardization, specialization, and individualization. The earlier way of looking at and living in the world was less differentiated, less symmetrical, and so on. It is important to note that the Georgian worldview is not strictly conceptual; it is also a historical phenomenon. That is, not all symmetry everywhere is evidence of Georgian thinking. The Taj Mahal may be symmetrical, but it is not Georgian. The Georgian worldview is composed of the concepts listed above, as they emerged in Western Europe in the context of the Renaissance and the Enlightenment.

Deetz offers many examples of what this emergence looks like artifactually. The classic pre-Georgian house plan is the primarily vernacular hall and parlor design, an asymmetrical, two-room plan that features an off-center doorway and direct access to the main room of the house, the hall. The typical Georgian house plan has a symmetrical facade, a centered doorway, and a central passageway through the house, which in turn gives access to individual rooms within the house. The earlier house is asymmetrical and corporate with many of the household's daily activities taking place in the room called the hall; the later house is symmetrical and segmented, with particular activities assigned to particular rooms. Deetz's postulated shift to the Georgian worldview is also reflected in tableware, drinking vessels, and eating utensils. The pre-Georgian table was set with unmatched wooden and ceramic items from which diners ate communally, and with multihandled mugs that diners shared. When diners used utensils, they used knives and spoons but not forks. The Georgian table was laid with matching sets of ceramic or pewter tableware and glassware with each diner using his or her own plate, glass, and set of utensils. Furthermore, the Georgian era saw the rise of the fork, a utensil that made it possible to segment the process of serving and eating food into more and more steps, the sequence of which were governed by the increasingly complex rules of etiquette (Shackel 1993). These are some of the physical characteristics of the Georgian worldview; later on in this chapter, I consider what the shift to the Georgian worldview looked like archaeologically, and what archaeology can contribute to understanding this shift and its implications.

The structuralist aspect of Deetz's work is twofold. On the one hand, the claim that the material record is the record of ideas held in the minds of people is important for historical archaeological practice because it allows seemingly disparate classes of material culture to be brought together analytically. For example, the facade of the Jonas Green house, the front page of the *Maryland Gazette*, and the distribution of artifacts around the foundations of the Jonas Green printshop may be thought of as comparable because all three were the product of Jonas Green's mental manipulation of two-dimensional space. This, in turn, allows us to see Jonas Green in a world made coherent by his own patterns of thought rather than a world made coherent by the categories of an archaeological site report. (See Little 1987, 1988 for an analysis of the Jonas Green printshop site in Annapolis.) In this example, an analyst using a Georgian principle like symmetry or segmentation can see disparate and functionally unrelated objects as having something in common.

In addition, using the assumption of structural interconnections, one can examine disparate classes of material culture to discover previously unrecognized principles. This is well illustrated by Deetz himself (1988). He observed three seemingly unrelated shifts in early nineteenth-century material culture and examined them as ideas rather than as simple material phenomena. People stopped painting houses multiple natural colors and began painting them white. Gravestone carvers started working strictly in white marble rather than in variously colored stones. And, virtually simultaneously, more and more white ceramic items were produced, in place of multicolored wares. Deetz's move, and the one that demonstrates the value of his structuralist approach, is to suggest that the three shifts are linked and that the issue is not plates, gravestones, or houses and does not pertain to potting clay, mineralogy, or paint chemistry. Rather, the shift is about whiteness itself. Deetz takes whiteness to be an expression of a preference for artificiality over naturalness, and this opposition is, in turn, aligned with a series of similar, parallel oppositions including simple : complex, assymetrical : symmetrical, unsegmented : segmented, communal : individual, and organic : mechanical. The justification for Deetz's claim to be able to recover mind is that his work is not historico-psychology (an attempt to recover individual thoughts) but an effort to understand broad patterns of thought as represented by hundreds of houses, thousands of gravestones, and tens of thousands of ceramic sherds.

Deetz's work is an important step beyond South's in its recognition that human thought is not epiphenomenal. Thought is an important part of what shapes the material world. As for the nature of that thought, much of what Deetz deals with is at the unconscious level, but he allows that there is a clearly historical and cultural component to the worldviews he identifies. The shifts from one worldview to another may be understood as a series of binary oppositions, but the content of a particular worldview is not necessarily binary. Although Deetz does not use the term "ideology," those aspects of thought he considers a worldview are often the same phenomena labeled ideology by critical archaeologists, things like symmetry and standardization. Deetz has done a good job of describing these phenomena; it remains for others to deal with their operation in society.

These are the useful parts of Deetz's work, from the standpoint of a critical archaeology of capitalism. However, Deetz has been criticized for making a persuasive case for his own ability to understand seventeenth- and eighteenth-century New England without explaining his method. While Deetz (1988: 229–32) does suggest that local-level studies need to be done to refine his work, he provides no game-plan for how to do them. A second and related criticism is that although he presents abundant examples of the Georgian worldview, Deetz fails to answer certain key questions such as Why the Georgian worldview? What gave rise to it? How, precisely, did it emerge? and What did that emergence look like, at a fine-grained level of analysis? Both of these criticisms have been answered by Leone and his extensions of Deetz's ideas (Leone 1984a, 1984b, 1984c, 1986, 1988; Leone, Potter, and Shackel 1987; Leone and Shackel 1987, 1990).

As for "Why the Georgian worldview?" Leone does not make an argument of direct causality such as "The Georgian worldview was invented because. . . ." He does the next best thing. Essentially, he asks what the Georgian worldview was good for (Leone 1988). The response to his rhetorical question is that the ideas we call Georgian, such as symmetry, segmentation, and specialization, among others, were the very principles by which industrial labor was organized in America in the nineteenth century. Leone goes one step further than Deetz and calls the Georgian worldview the order of capitalism (Leone 1988). The Georgian worldview is an effective tool for the study of capitalism because the Georgian worldview is a *cultural* phenomenon. By following Deetz rather than South, it is possible to see capitalism as a historically conditioned human creation rather than as the inevitable by-product of cultural laws that operate as inexorably as the laws of physics. This use of the Georgian worldview makes capitalism visible rather than invisible and makes it a tractable object of study rather than something beyond analytical reach.

It is, Leone argues, no accident that some of the Annapolitans who in the late eighteenth century consumed most conspicuously the material expressions of the Georgian worldview moved to Baltimore and invested heavily in the industrial development of that city. Members of both the Catholic and Protestant Carroll families and the Dulany family, among others, invested in the Baltimore Iron Works in the eighteenth century. Charles Carroll of Carrollton, the longest-lived signer of the Declaration of Independence and at one time the richest man in America, was a founder of the nation's first railroad, the Baltimore and Ohio. More specifically, Leone suggests that the principles used to organize the elements in the facade of a Georgian house were virtually identical to principles used to rationally divide and subdivide land. This made land easier to buy and sell and land speculation an effective way of reaping a profit. Leone argues that the genius of some eighteenth-century people was their use of the ideas we call Georgian *and* their placement of these ideas in nature or in the supernatural realm where they were less challengeable and easier to use (Leone 1984b). All of these ways of asking what the Georgian worldview was good for constitute Leone's first extension of Deetz.

Furthermore, if Deetz is correct in saying that the principles he calls Georgian have continued to shape Anglo-American culture right up to the present day, then the Georgian worldview may be seen as a factor in both the segmentation that characterizes the treatment of African-Americans and the Naval Academy in Annapolis histories and the physical segmentation of the Annapolis peninsula into a civilian part and a naval part. In this way, Deetz's concept is well suited to the full range of issues addressed by Archaeology in Annapolis and by this book.

The second part of Leone's extension of Deetz is his characterization of material culture as having a recursive power, an ability to shape and teach behavior. Recursivity is the power of material culture to inspire the re-creation, in its users, of certain of its own characteristics. Recursivity is based on the idea that "material culture does not just exist. It is made by someone. It is produced to do something. Therefore, it does not passively *reflect* society—rather, it creates society through the actions of individuals" (Hodder 1986: 6). Discussing the recursivity of space, Tilley (1984: 122, 137) says that "space does not merely reflect social organization but once space has been bounded and shaped it is no longer a neutral datum; it exerts influence" and that "architecture, as with other types of material culture patterning, is both a product of organized action and a constraint on future action." What Leone understands as the recursive power of material culture can be expressed either explicitly or implicitly.

An explicit, large-scale example of material culture intended to teach people how to think and act is the town plan of Annapolis, laid out in 1695, with the State House and St. Anne's (Anglican) Church on the two highest points of land, and a series of streets radiating out from each. This setup was clearly intended to tell anybody who used the streets of Annapolis that the State House and the Church were the two most important institutions in the city and the colony. In this case, use of the street plan was intended to re-create in its users the messages about church and state encoded in the plan by Governor Nicholson.

In many cases, however, the recursive power of an item of material culture is more difficult to see, especially when a set of messages is delivered by a kind of object to which we do not normally ascribe the power to communicate. Consider, for example, a set of creamware plates, made in Staffordshire in the 1770s. Such a set of plates shaped lives in two ways.

In Staffordshire, creamware plates were mass produced through a process that radically segmented production, breaking it into a number of different tasks, each performed mechanically by a different group of workers (G. Miller 1980). (In terms of their impact on the twentieth century, Josiah Wedgwood's contributions to the organization of ceramic production and his innovations in marketing were far more significant than his experiments with the chemical composition of potting clays and glazes.) According to those initiating them, such production practices were more sensible, more economical, more efficient, and therefore better. What is left out, of course, is a disclosure of the point of view from which these practices are efficient and economical. From whatever economic, political, or other theoretical perspective we choose to judge the shift from craft-based to industrial production, there can be no question that the routinized, mechanical, wage labor required to produce thousands of sets of creamware plates played a large part in shaping the worldview of the workers who made them. A worker whose labor was measured by the clock had to measure his or her time off by the clock in order to be able to report to work on time. In these and other ways, participating in industrial production likely played a role in causing workers to re-create in their personal lives the order imposed on their work lives.

Sets of creamware plates taught not just their producers, but also their consumers, that the world works in certain ways. The shift from communally used ceramic items to sets of plates—one plate to one diner with each plate identical to every other plate—represented and helped to enact the idea that each person is separate from, but in some ways equal to and interchangeable with, every other person. At one level, the ceramic items on a table may be read as a model for the social relations of their users. Furthermore, those items of tableware were used by people. If we accept that different kinds of tableware were used differently, then perhaps the decrease in contact between diners called for by individual place settings encouraged plate users to see society as composed of separate individuals. Leone's argument is that such lessons, learned at home from a variety of mass-produced goods, served to instill a work discipline (Leone 1988: 240) and also to underpin the fiction that every worker is a free and independent individual selling his labor to a capitalist, on an equal footing. Those parts of the material world that were still handmade represented the degree to which capitalism had not penetrated all aspects of eighteenth-century life.

My premise is that encoded in a set of creamware plates used in Annapolis there was information about the kind of labor that produced them. If individuals learned the lessons in their plates, they may have become more amenable to having their labor managed according to the principles represented by those plates. This is not to suggest that Annapolitans were dominated by their plates or by the Staffordshire potters. Rather, when people bought creamware plates to be stylish, they got something besides style in the bargain. In this way, some of the basic concepts of the Industrial Revolution were exported to the colonies and demonstrated by its products. The order of the factory may well have been re-created in the lives of people who used the products of the factory. If we grant a recursive power to material culture, it is possible that as people were affected by their use of so-called Georgian material culture, they came to accept, more readily than they would have otherwise, the organization of their work and private lives in ways that were not in their individual interests. The ideas for which Georgian traits stand come from Deetz, but the statement of material culture's power to teach these ideas is Leone's extension of Deetz.

Leone's pivotal extension of Deetz is actually a follow-up to Deetz's own suggestion that considerable local-level research based on the idea of the Georgian worldview was essential for finishing the job he had begun. The need for local-level studies comes from the scale of Deetz's work. It is easy to get the impression from Deetz that the Georgian worldview was a monolithic entity that moved across the colonial American landscape incorporating all in its path. The danger in this reading is that it makes the Georgian worldview appear inevitable, which is probably not Deetz's understanding and is clearly not Leone's, and such a reading also puts the Georgian worldview and its cultural products beyond human agency.

If the Georgian worldview is or was a way of thinking, how did people come to think that way? When did they? And why? Did everyone think that way or was the Georgian worldview in some quarters resisted or even rejected? The basic structure of Leone's inquiry has been to focus on Annapolis in the eighteenth century and ask of it: Who started thinking this way before who else? What parts of life were affected before what others? Did merchants use these ideas before or after shipbuilders? What about lawyers? Did dining become subject to the Georgian worldview before architecture or after? And what about the organization of labor? These questions constitute an outline for a study of the penetration of the Georgian worldview (Leone 1988). This inquiry consists of three steps.

The first step, initiated by Leone (1984a, 1984c), and pursued by Shackel (1987, 1993; see also Leone and Shackel 1987, 1990), involves the use of the documentary record, principally probate inventories. Leone and Shackel have identified a range of material items related to segmentation, one of the characteristics of the Georgian worldview. Their list includes items that segment explicitly, such as clocks (time), musical instruments (sound), and surveying tools (land), and also items that are not explicitly used for segmenting but that, when used, do segment, items such as forks (which segment the process of eating) and sets of dishes (which segment the group of people eating a meal and the food that composes the meal). Leone and Shackel searched out the occurrence of these items in probate inventories, divided temporally and according to estate value, in an attempt to find out who in Annapolis, from a socioeconomic standpoint, used which kinds of segmenting items and when. Their preliminary research has shown that items that segment explicitly, such as clocks and surveying tools, (1) appeared in the inventories of the wealthy before they appeared in the inventories of the poor, (2) appeared in urban inventories before they appeared in rural inventories, and (3) appeared, in general, earlier than items that segment implicitly, such as plates and forks. And all three of these phenomena began during the 1720s and 1730s (Shackel 1993). It would be conventional to explain the appearance of segmenting items among wealthy urban individuals as a reflection of their wealth and education. Such an argument says that people owned segmenting items because they were rich. However, there is no good reason not to consider the opposite proposition, the idea that people got rich because they understood and could control the idea of segmentation. Perhaps people got rich because they owned and knew how to use segmenting items.

A second step in studying the penetration of the Georgian worldview, and a preliminary archaeological one, would be to investigate the material record for the presence or absence of Georgian traits. This kind of analysis involves selecting a particular problem typically addressed through material culture and then identifying a "pre-Georgian" and a Georgian solution. The challenge of shelter from the elements was met by some people, at some times, in some places, with a hall and parlor house and by others with a bilaterally symmetrical Georgian house with a central passage. Food was consumed from large, handmade, communally used trenchers or from mass-produced sets of individually used plates. In each case, the former item is the pre-Georgian and the latter the Georgian solution to a particular problem. To use these ideas analytically—that is, to gain a rough index of the degree of Georgianization that characterized any particular segment of the material world constituted by certain items—one need only examine an archaeological collection and quantify the relative frequencies of the pre-Georgian and Georgian artifacts. Such an analysis is not adequate for determining whether any individual has internalized the Georgian mind-set, but its results can be suggestive of further research questions.

A third way of doing the archaeology of the Georgian worldview on the local level is to measure the "Georgian-ness" of an assemblage of artifacts in a way that goes beyond presence and absence (Leone, Potter, and Shackel 1987; Shackel 1987; Little and Shackel 1989). This approach elevates to the status of data an aspect of variability previously unacknowledged as having much information value beyond simple identification. Specifically, we measure the rim sherds of plates to determine the size of the plate from which a particular sherd comes, listing for any given site the number of different-sized plates, by ware type, used by the occupants of that site. This listing makes it possible to characterize the degree of segmentation represented by a particular ceramic assemblage.

Before moving to that analysis, it is important to establish the links between contemporary Annapolis and variability in the archaeological record. These explicit links will replace my largely implicit argument for Deetz's cognitive approach, an argument based on the similarities between what Deetz calls the Georgian worldview and the capitalist economic order that began in colonial America in the eighteenth century and that clearly is still with us today.

The Archaeology of Transience and Visitation in Annapolis

As explained in preceding chapters, transience and visitations are the consequences of, and solutions to, Annapolis's ongoing problems with identity. If critical archaeology does not necessarily entail excavation of the first tourist attraction in the city, how then would one do the archaeology of transience and visitation? The first step consists of constructing arguments of relevance, arguments leading from tourists in Annapolis to broken plates in the ground or, more broadly, from transience and visitation to some measurable quality in the archaeological record of Annapolis. To construct such arguments it is necessary to examine the ideas that lie behind the transient nature of Annapolis. The second step is to undertake archaeological analyses of classes of material culture that express the ideas identified through the arguments of relevance.

Arguments of Relevance

Annapolis's transient nature has at least four components, which are essentially four different solutions to the city's lack of a productive base: (1) the city's status as a bedroom community for Washington, D.C., (2) state government, (3) tourism, and (4) the U.S. Naval Academy. Each component rests on certain cultural concepts.

The city's status as a bedroom community, for example, emanates from two ideas. First, people accept the commute from Annapolis to Washington each day because the separation of home and work is fully understood as a part of modern American life. This idea would more than likely have been incomprehensible to most seventeenth-century Marylanders. Second, although some of the gentrification of Annapolis has been accomplished by people buying houses to live in themselves, some has been accomplished by people buying one or more properties as investments and restoring them for rental. This activity stems from the idea that the qualities "house" and "home" do not always coincide. What a tenant views as a home, the owners see almost exclusively as an investment to be managed according to a whole set of rational principles that for the most part ignore the fact that the houses have human occupants. That is to say, life is segmented into a work part and a domestic or home part, and dwellings into a home part and an economic-value part. Far more important are the concepts that lie behind and structure state government, the Naval Academy, and tourism in Annapolis.

As noted in chapter 4, Annapolis's status as the capital of Maryland is responsible for a large daily influx of state workers who live outside the city. In addition, there are appointees who move into and out of town along with the governors they serve. And then there is the legislature. A centralized state government is based on ideas about efficiency and standardization. I do not claim that centralized government is a Georgian invention. However, there is a significant difference between the functional capital of fourteenth-century England, which was a mobile court that followed the monarch from castle to castle, and the permanent capital city of a modern nation or state, which contains a bureaucracy in residence regardless of the whereabouts of the head of state. The value of a centralized state government is that it provides a repository for precedents and statutes, as well as for interpretations and interpreters of them. This centralization of procedure in turn allows certain important economic and social practices to be standardized across the state. So, the idea behind having a permanent seat of government is that it allows for government to be standardized.

The principal concepts that lie behind the Naval Academy resemble those of any American institution of higher education. As mentioned earlier, the academy downplays its military aspect and stresses its similarities to other large universities. Thus, by ignoring the military part of the academy in this discussion, I am considering it on its own terms. The ideas behind institutionalized higher education have to do with the separation of learning from the application of knowledge. Through the eighteenth and part of the nineteenth centuries in America, most people learned to do the things that became their life's work by watching other people do the same things in either a parent-child or master-apprentice relationship. For example, William Paca studied at the Inns of Court in London but undertook a large part of his legal education by reading law with an already established Annapolis lawyer, Stephen Bordley (Stiverson and Jacobsen 1976: 13). Until learning to do things was separated conceptually from actually doing them, in the second half of the nineteenth century, the only professions that demanded formal education were those, like preaching, that people saw as inappropriate to learn on the job. Contemporary higher education is based on a separation of doing things from learning how to do them and often proclaims its value in terms of its removal from the larger "real" world. The academic community is a special place, where a higher level of morality applies, in which students may learn apart from the pressures of the world for which they are preparing themselves. The physical separation of home from school is considered valuable by all those parents who send their children off to college unconcerned with what they learn in the classroom and the grades they make as long as they get practice living away from home. So, a guiding principle behind the Naval Academy, like any modern American residential college or university is the separation of home from school and of school from the real world. In terms of its own history, the founding of the Naval Academy replaced a system in which naval officer candidates did all their training on ships. Both of these separations, between home and school, and between school and work, would be, as I have suggested above, completely alien to a seventeenth-century Marylander, who would not have had the conceptual categories to separate home from work and work from education.

Transience has yet another part, labeled tourism. Two concepts are relevant here. The first is that modern tourism is a search for authentic experience necessitated by alienation in the modern workplace, which disconnects people from the work they do and the things they help to produce (see MacCannell 1976). Tourism is clearly a product of a modern, capitalist economy, given that alienation is an almost inevitable by-product of capitalist notions that are conventionally called efficient and productive.

Second, the possibility of vacations, and hence tourism, may be seen as the result of the segmentation of time into work time and leisure time. In either case, vacations and tourism are products of a segmented way of thinking. The seventeenth-century Marylander would recognize neither the concept "nine to five" nor the idea of a weekend, let alone the idea of a "paid two-week vacation." At the risk of sounding evolutionary, the patterns of thought that gave rise, in the late nineteenth century, to vacations and tourism as we know them today may be traced back to the eighteenth century, through a series of transformations and extensions.

The separation of work time from leisure time was facilitated by the separation of work space from domestic space. The apogee of this separation was the removal of most work to facilities owned by people other than the workers, filled with tools also owned by people other than the workers. This step, however, was an extension of an earlier separation of work space from domestic space in the context of a single property. The classic example of this is a craftsperson's shop in which the craft worker and his or her family lived upstairs. This kind of arrangement characterized late eighteenth-century Annapolis and itself replaced a situation in which domestic and productive activities were not at all separated from each other temporally or spatially. This chain of transformations should not be seen as part of an evolutionary scheme: misuse of the biological metaphor to characterize cultural change introduces an element of inevitability that is incompatible with a critical perspective. However, this chain of transformations, presented as a description and not as an explanation, can serve as a connection between twentieth-century problems and their eighteenth-century roots.

The kind of tourism experienced in Annapolis today exists because people in the eighteenth century began to segment their lives and separate work time from leisure time. Thus, segmentation is one of the key ideas behind modern tourism.

To do the archaeology of transience and visitation in Annapolis is to do the archaeology of the concepts that have structured state government, the Naval Academy, and tourism, as cultural creations. As I have already argued, those concepts are standardization and segmentation. The value of Annapolis as an archaeological place is its potential to provide data on the introduction of these ideas in a particular context as ways people thought about and lived in the world. By searching for evidence of these ideas, it becomes possible to retrieve meaningful data from a range of sites far wider than the first tourist attraction or the first suburban house in Annapolis. The problem that remains is to find ways to structure archaeological analyses that can contribute to the archaeology of standardization and segmentation.

Archaeological Analysis

For several years, members of Archaeology in Annapolis have been creating artifact analyses based on the measurement of standardization and segmentation. The artifacts analyzed so far include buttons (Doherty and Knox 1986), marbles (Virta and Stabler 1986; Clark 1986), and ceramics. Each of these analyses is an attempt to go beyond simple assessments of the presence or absence of a particular artifact type. Each also involves characterizing a well-known artifact type or class of material culture in a way that has not been done before. The point of these analyses is to demonstrate a procedure for using a collection of artifacts to comment on the roots of a significant contemporary social, political, or economic issue. This exercise makes it possible to apply archaeological data to social problems.

All three analyses—of buttons, marbles, and ceramics—are structured similarly. However, neither the button work nor the marble work is as far along as the analysis of ceramic artifacts discussed in Leone, Potter, and Shackel (1987), Shackel (1986, 1987, 1993), Little and Shackel (1989), and Tubby (1986). That analytical program, discussed briefly here, is an attempt to do the archaeology of standardization and segmentation in Annapolis.

Throughout the late eighteenth and early nineteenth centuries, there was a rapid proliferation of sizes and shapes of ceramic items manufactured in England and available for sale in America and elsewhere. This proliferation was accompanied by an increase in the elaboration of table etiquette (Shackel 1993). The effect of a table fully stocked with creamware plates and serving pieces, and someone at the table knowledgeable enough to enforce the etiquette, was a two-fold segmentation. The food that made up the meal was increasingly segmented through the use of dinner plates *and* dessert plates, vegetable dishes *and* meat dishes, teapots *and* coffee pots *and* chocolate pots, and so on. Individuals at the table were separated from each other through the use of their own chairs (as opposed to benches), their own glasses (as opposed to communal mugs), their own plates (as opposed to trenchers), and so on. (To this list of tablewares Deetz adds individual chamberpots, which were also the becoming the rule at that time.) The problem, or limitation, however, comes in saying that coarse-bodied, slip-decorated earthenware plates signal an unsegmented, unstandardized worldview, whereas creamware plates always mean the opposite. Specifically, what of the person who used creamware in a distinctly non-Georgian way?

In part to address this issue, and as a measure of segmentation, Paul Shackel developed a formula for determining the amount of variety in the sizes of plates in any given ceramic assemblage. The basis of the formula is the assumption that a person who left an assemblage of nothing but 10-inch plates ate—and thought—differently from someone who left an assemblage containing plates of various sizes. The more varied assemblage would have made it much easier to signal the segmentation of meals into courses and, for that matter, to differentiate breakfast from dinner. However, saying that both people left large assemblages of creamware plates would mask such variation. The formula for variability makes it possible to break free from the assumption that underlies much archaeological analysis, namely, that most objects have their *full* meanings attached to them at the time they are made. The ability to measure how different people selected differently (or similarly) from the same range of available objects also provides an analytical basis for discovering the *rejection* of the Georgian worldview. An Annapolitan in 1787 with *all* 10-inch plates would have been different from most and would in all likelihood have known it.

The formula works in the following way. One collects all the plate-rim sherds from a layer or a site and divides them first by ware type, cream-ware, pearlware, and so on. Then one takes each sherd and compares it to a template to determine the size of the plate from which it came. The results of this measuring process would be placed on a chart like this:

Diameters in inches

	6	7	8	9	10	11	12

Ware types

Creamware	x				x	x	x
Pearlware		x				x	x

Each "x" represents the presence of at least one sherd of that type and size in the sample. These data are then inserted into the formula:

$$(TS/T) \times S = I,$$

where TS is the number of type-sizes, T is the number of ceramic types, S is the number of plate sizes represented in the sample, and I is the index of variety. This index can range from 1.0 (low variety) to infinity (high variety). Variety is, in turn, taken to be an index of segmented thinking. In the example above, $TS = 7$, $T = 2$, $S = 5$, and $I = 17.5$. The formula can be used to chart the increasing (or decreasing) acceptance of a segmenting worldview by occupants of a single site over time, or to compare the degree of use of such a worldview by occupants of different sites at the same time.

There are many ways to measure and characterize the archaeologically recovered fragments of eighteenth- and nineteenth-century plates. Not all, however, contribute to the study of segmentation. And the principal variable in this formula is something historical archaeologists have known to be a variable for many years, but for which most have had no use. Plenty of historical archaeologists have measured plate-rim sherds to determine the size and the name of the plates from which they came, but most such efforts have been strictly classificatory. Little *additional* meaning has ever been drawn from the fact that occupants of a given site used twice as many breakfast plates as dinner plates and no dessert plates at all. Such classificatory exercises have done little more than characterize the archaeological record in terms that would have been meaningful to Staffordshire potters without any explanation of how the potters' perspective is meaningful or advances archaeological analysis.

Summary

What makes an archaeological analysis critical is the explicit link it forges between variability observed and measured in the archaeological record and contemporary local social and political issues. In Annapolis, the central local issue is the lack of local identity, and the city's attempt to draw identity from transient individuals and institutions composed of transient individuals. One of the ideas behind much of the transience in Annapolis is segmentation. Thus, one potentially critical archaeology in Annapolis is the archaeology of segmentation. In addition to playing a role in Annapolis's transience, segmentation is an important part of capitalist production. The alienation of workers from the products of their labor, a central feature of capitalist production, is facilitated by the segmentation of production into a series of mechanical tasks carried out by a succession of workers.

More broadly, both the eighteenth-century archaeological record in Annapolis and much of the city's contemporary transience may be seen as consequences of capitalism, hardly a process unique to Annapolis. Further, many of the issues identified by the ethnographic component of a critical archaeology conducted almost anywhere in contemporary America will also be consequences of capitalism. This does not mean, however, that critical archaeology is reducible to a "one-size-fits-all" archaeological critique of the introduction and spread of capitalism. The local issues, the expressions of capitalism, in any given area will be different. These local differences will mandate different arguments of relevance linking the contemporary scene to a specific archaeological analysis. Such an archaeology grows out of ethnographic findings and its purpose, as discussed in the chapters to follow, is to provide a basis for demonstrating to contemporary members of society that the principles by which contemporary life is organized are not immutable.

9

Archaeology in Public

The next three chapters focus on the public interpretive program Archaeology in Public, developed as an exercise in archaeological practice that makes Archaeology in Annapolis a critical archaeology. Archaeology in Public represents the particular attempt of Archaeology in Annapolis to take on the task of putting its archaeological data to use. Of course, archaeologists can use their data in other ways to develop an archaeological practice, and I do not mean to suggest that a well-funded, full-scale interpretive program is the only way to apply critical theory to historical archaeology. Archaeology in Public is one attempt at archaeological practice, and it is important to bear in mind that the presentation of archaeological data to the public is not nearly as important as the application of archaeology to contemporary life. This chapter is about the techniques Archaeology in Public uses to inject the archaeological findings discussed in chapter 8 into the social context presented in chapters 4–7.

The first part of the chapter examines some of the problems in history museums for which Archaeology in Public was envisioned as an antidote, and the potential of outdoor history education to enlighten the public and serve as a basis for emancipatory social action. While Archaeology in Public does not have the same set of approaches and missions as places such as Colonial Williamsburg, I think it is likely that Colonial Williamsburg is an important part of what has taught Archaeology in

Public visitors how to learn history in an outdoor setting. From this discussion of outdoor history museums it is possible to abstract a comprehensive catalogue of what Archaeology in Public tries not to be.

Although this analysis of outdoor history education has been of specific use to Archaeology in Public in the development of its interpretive strategy, it is useful to *anyone* doing archaeology in any kind of setting that is remotely accessible to the public. Archaeologists are very good—perhaps *too* good—at recognizing the line (we draw) between cultural resource management (CRM) and "academic" archaeology. I suspect that members of the public are not nearly so precise, that instead they tend to see all archaeology as pretty much the same. Thus, if Archaeology in Public visitors use Colonial Williamsburg as a way of understanding their site visit in Annapolis, they probably use the same frame of reference to understand the contract archaeologist working on a sewer line survey back home.

The second half of the chapter is about what Archaeology in Public *is* and the ideas behind it. This public interpretive program represents the attempt of Archaeology in Annapolis to use the data it collects to provide Annapolitans and visitors with a clearer understanding of contemporary life in Annapolis. The goal of this discussion is to describe the tools Archaeology in Public uses to provide an emancipatory educational experience, one that puts archaeological knowledge into active, practical use.

Standard Approaches to History Education

The following discussion of the education available in history museums focuses on (1) the problems of outdoor history museums like Colonial Williamsburg, as identified by Mark Leone; (2) the problems of costumed interpretation; and (3) the kinds of learning that can take place in history museums.

Leone's Critique of Outdoor History Museums

Mark Leone has devoted considerable attention to outdoor history museums, notably to St. Mary's City (Leone 1980), Shakertown at Pleasant Hill (Leone 1981b), Sleepy Hollow Restorations (Leone 1983b), and Colonial Williamsburg (Leone 1981a). When Archaeology in Annapolis was initiated by the University of Maryland and Historic Annapolis in 1981, Leone saw an opportunity to experiment with and put into practice solutions to some of the problems he had identified in his ethnographic work at outdoor history museums.

Leone suggests that much of what is presented to visitors at Colonial Williamsburg, for example, is made up of "facts and data [that] are not tied to the present the way they may be" (Leone 1981a: 13). In the demonstration of a flintlock rifle, "the message is its meaninglessness; it had nothing to say because it did not use the social structural tie between past and present" (Leone 1981a: 12). When past and present are left untied, as they are so frequently in history museums, both scholar and visitor become trapped in the present and visitors are soon bored.

In his now famous analysis of the Raleigh's Tavern bakery, Leone describes a white, male adult baker and his young black male helper observed making a batch of gingerbread cookies. The baker spoke to the public and mixed the dough, a part of the task that required judgments to be made about the "feel" of the dough. The black helper was usually hidden from view, mute, and cut cookies out of the mixed dough, a mechanical task requiring manual dexterity but none of the subjective skills of the baker, who pronounced the dough ready for cutting:

> In this setting, the details of which we take safely to be true to another time, tourists see the following relationships acted out, relationships true also to his own time: master, helper; one who creates a whole product, one who fragments it through repetitive acts; one who orders, one who is ordered; one who can have several audiences and can change roles, one who is tied to one role and one audience. White and black are structurally related this way both historically and ethnographically in Virginia." (Leone 1981a: 9)

Leone's criticism of such presentations is that because of their ritual setting they become not so much statements of how things are and were, but rather statements of how things should be. The projection of contemporary race relations in Virginia back into the past—when they may in fact have been similar—has the effect of allowing the present to use itself as precedent. In this way, the present is made to appear as an inevitable outgrowth of the past. This is how presentations of the past can trap people in the present.

For both the public and the archaeological profession, the paradox of this entrapment is that "the past cannot be relived but knowledge of it is believed essential for our identity as a society" (Leone 1981a: 12). Of traditional solutions to this paradox Leone (1981a: 13) says, "For our culture and the archaeological profession, the problem is not as we all suppose, how did we get from past to present, the problem is what is communicated by going from present to past. That is where the news is." In their attempt to understand the progression from past to present, people put great faith in the value of accurate information about the past, but the accuracy of historical facts is no defense against the imposition of the present onto the past. Take the portrayal of Shaker life at Pleasant Hill, which is accurate up to the point that it imposes the present on the past "when it appropriates 'the meaningful realities of other people's lives by the secondary rationalizations of our own'" (Sahlins 1976: 73).

> This appropriation has two parts which make visiting Shakertown a dual process. The first event is the hiding of Shaker history. Shaker culture is fragmented, reduced to isolated terms like work, worship, celibacy, and some dates. The unintended hiding of their history is achieved, not avoided, by the premium put on accuracy and authenticity in the museum presentation. (Leone 1981b: 305)

The accuracy of the information in these categories tends to justify the appropriateness of the categories to Shaker life:

> The second part of the ideological process is the imposition of meaning from the [non-Shaker] present onto Shaker material. Efficiency, practicality, and wholesome materialism are the values we are allowed to come away feeling best capture the society we have seen. This is at best only partially true and is an inevitable imposition which can occur effectively only through the first half of the process, which is the masking of Shaker history by presenting it as organized into parts like our own society. (Leone 1981b: 305)

So, even *accurate* facts about the past provide no defense against entrapment in the present by interpretations of the past. What then, is the answer to this dilemma?

According to Leone (1981b: 309), "Naturalizing the present by imposing some part of it on the past is, as all historiographers know, inevitable and unavoidable." It is thus necessary "to allow the past to be the image of the present it must be" (1981a: 13). "There is nothing wrong with it; the difficulty comes when archaeologists working in settings involving public interpretation do not realize it and thereby are controlled by the process" (1981b: 309). The solution Leone calls for is a reversal of "our refusal to use self-reflection" (1981a: 12). If historical and archaeological interpretations cannot help imposing the present on the past, they can at least do so self-consciously, understanding the modern categories they use and the contemporary social implications of their interpretations:

> Once the process [of imposing the present on the past] is visible, then the composition of the ideotechnic artifact can be at our disposal, if we want it to be. And it is at this point that the museum collection offers a dual option paralleling the dual process that creates it. It can illustrate, in the cases I have mentioned [at Shakertown], the cultural processes in early capitalism and industrialism that formed the matrix of modern American society. Second, a museum can illustrate the misinterpretive or masking process, the ideological process wherein society appropriates the history and culture of others to ground its own in what seems to be the natural state of things. This second option creates consciousness of history and keeps the remnants of it housed in our museums from seeming useless. (Leone 1981b: 309)

Leone's second major concern with outdoor history museums is reflected in his observations about Colonial Williamsburg:

> Visitors to Colonial Williamsburg are frequently bored. This is a neutral observation and not meant to be critical. People at Williamsburg begin to wear a glazed look, children tire, husbands and wives squabble, older people begin to pat their clothes, and everybody starts to pick on the workers. They argue with guides, bully the waitresses, comment on high prices to salespeople, and doubt the reality of what they are being told. (Leone 1981a: 11–12).

As Leone points out, "when boredom accompanies archaeology, it is because the facts and the data are not tied to the present the way they may be" (Leone 1981a: 13).

Another reason for boredom among visitors to history museums is that the typical guide is disconnected from most of the data being presented. The interpreters in many of these settings have seldom had a hand in researching the information they are presenting in what is essentially a public performance. Such interpretations are based on recited facts and are given by someone who does not understand where the facts came from and, therefore, what they are. Such an interpretation is bound to be boring because the person giving it attempts to let the facts or the artifacts speak for themselves, which, as Leone (1981a: 12) reminds us, they cannot.

Leone points out yet another cause of boredom in his analysis of a Colonial Williamsburg flintlock demonstration by a single costumed worker who loads and fires a replica of an eighteenth-century flintlock and then answers questions about it. "The past," Leone observes, "cannot be represented in lifelike fashion with only one person in the demonstration representing another time. This means that there could not be any conversation between the past and the past" (Leone 1981a: 11). Without such conversation, it impossible to create and interpret the kind of connection between past and present necessary for historical interpretation that does not entrap its audience in a present that appears to be inevitable. Second, Leone notes that after the flintlock demonstration the interpreter and the audience engaged in little discussion that had to do with the past. He attributes this to the lack of social structure in the version of the past presented and to the lack of a structure for interaction between guide and visitor. The interpretation gives visitors nothing to do afterward and no model for setting up meaningful communication between interpreter and visitor. Most interpretations do not teach their audience how to question their teachers and in many instances discourage such a reaction. When interaction is foreclosed, boredom often follows. To extend Leone's analysis, it often seems to be the case that in museum settings where a model for communication is provided, the model is the archetypical American elementary school classroom, where knowledge and authority are closely associated in the person of the teacher. In these settings, an antipathy for authority often becomes conflated with an antipathy for knowledge, with the result that many students are bored by school and many museum visitors are bored by the interpretations they see.

Costumed Interpretation in Living History

As an extension of Leone's ethnographic observations of outdoor history museums, it is useful to consider the costumed interpretation employed in living history museums. Costumed interpretation needs to be discussed here because it represents the antithesis of the Archaeology in Public interpretive stance; Archaeology in Public was created in part to solve some of the educational problems exemplified in costumed interpretation. This mode of presentation has been widely discussed and debated within the museum world (Deetz 1971; Colwell 1972; Sidford 1974; Gerlach 1975; Alderson and Low 1976: 63; Alexander 1979: 200–201). Whatever scholars may think of it, costumed interpretation seems to be popular with museum visitors, which is another reason to examine it here. The following discussion outlines three significant shortcomings of costumed interpretation.

To begin with, role-playing or first-person interpretation, which is the subset of costumed interpretation that requires interpreters to disavow all knowledge of the twentieth-century, confuses visitors and hides epistemology. Zannieri (1980: 70) notes the frustration this technique has engendered in visitors to Plimoth Plantation, where more than 50 percent fail to understand how the technique works. More significantly, this mode of interpretation offers a visitor no means of finding out how an interpreter learned what he or she knows. Ask a costumed tobacco planter at a place like St. Mary's City how he learned to build his tobacco barn and the best he can tell you is that he copied a neighbor's, used a design from England, or learned from his father. The visitor can learn how a seventeenth-century tobacco planter learned but not how a twentieth-century actor did. At the very least, such a technique mystifies the process of discovering and creating historical knowledge. It privileges and reinforces the position of the expert, making the visitor completely dependent on such experts for historical information and interpretation. Costumed interpretation, in character, does nothing to teach people how to learn about history because it masks epistemology. There are occasions when costumed interpretation can teach people how to learn, but these occasions occur when the interpreter explicitly steps out of character, making himself or herself a contemporary of the audience and bracketing his or her own performance by making it into an artifact.

A second issue has to do with what is actually taught and learned through costumed interpretation of either the first-person variety or the third-person, craft-demonstration variety. Visitors are often overheard praising a costumed performance for its "realism." The question is, on what basis can *any* contemporary person judge the realism of a portrayal of an earlier century? The emphasis that such performances of history place on research, detail, and accuracy encourages visitors to attempt judgments that are essentially nonsensical. "As the past no longer exists," says Lowenthal (1985: 215), "no account can ever be checked against it, but only against other accounts of the past; we judge its veracity by its correspondence with other reports, not with the events themselves." Thus the concept of historical accuracy has little meaning in this case. When one calls a performance of living history accurate or realistic, one is really saying that the performance agreed with his or her preconceived ideas about some part of the past. The more highly approved a performance is, the better it matches—and reinforces—what the visitor came to the performance already knowing. The more it does that, the less it teaches. The process by which some kinds of historical interpretation reinforce preconceptions is similar to that noted by Lowenthal (1985: 301), wherein an authentic object, like the Mona Lisa, is judged on the basis of its fidelity to well-known copies, which, by virtue of being better known, have greater reality than the original for most people. Experience with the real thing does not validate the copy; the copy validates the original! This impediment to teaching is part of the larger problem of how to judge a costumed interpretation. Without access to epistemology, one is left with few alternatives other than treating such performances as theater and evaluating them strictly on the basis of their entertainment value.

Beyond hiding epistemology and reinforcing preconceptions, costumed interpretation has an additional flaw. By placing costumed guides into a restored building or set of buildings, it becomes much more difficult for visitors to keep track of what is old and what is not. The "reality," or at least the tangibility, of the architecture and the costumes tends to suggest that everything else, physical and nonphysical, is "accurate" too: "Like restorers, re-enactors start with the known elements and fill in the gaps with the typical, the probable, or the invented" (Lowenthal 1985: 295). Thus, much of what is presented in such contexts is either underresearched, based on assumptions, or deliberately inaccurate. The most typical form of deliberate inaccuracy is well illustrated by a story I once heard about Colonial Williamsburg. A faculty member at the College of William and Mary told me that Colonial Williamsburg once bought several oxen and spent an entire year experimenting with mixtures of beans and grain in an attempt to develop a diet that would help the oxen to produce manure that was easy to remove from the streets. The fact is, "Eighteenth-century odors in Williamsburg would be such a shock to twentieth-century noses that every other impression might be blotted out" (Lowenthal in Burcaw 1983: 162). Obviously, this is not meant to be an indictment of a hygienic environment for visitors, but the ox dung story, like all the other critiques of inappropriately sanitized outdoor history museums (Alexander 1979: 94; Zanneiri 1980: 34–44; and Lowenthal 1985: 300, to cite just a few), points up one of the many ways in which expressions of contemporary values are placed in outdoor history museums.

The danger comes when these impositions of the present go undetected because of the power of suggestion exerted by the costumes and restorations and the willing suspension of disbelief they induce. The process by which this takes place has been called "faction": it is the blending of fact and fiction practiced by authors like Michener, which "includes so much known to be true . . . shown with so much patient expertise, that the rest of it is swallowed in . . . easy credulity" (Brogan in Lowenthal 1985: 230).

A powerful or engaging medium may thus inspire confidence in the accuracy of the message it conveys and suggest a contemporary ability to know the absolutely unknowable (see Lowenthal 1985: 367).

For example, it is easy to wonder if a costumed interpreter speaks the way an eighteenth-century person would have spoken, and even to think that such an interpreter does indeed sound like an eighteenth-century person. Upon reflection, however, most would agree that the sounds of an eighteenth-century language are in no way directly recoverable through the techniques of *any* historical discipline. To restate: a real danger in this kind of interpretation is that visitors will be induced by the historical accuracy underpinning certain aspects of the interpretation and vividness of the medium to think that absolutely everything they see, hear, smell, taste, and feel is historically accurate. The problem is not that visitors are stupid or gullible, but rather, that this mode of interpretation encourages people to misplace the line between what parts of the past can and cannot be known and leads them to misunderstand the historical disciplines that provide information about the past.

Modes of Learning in History Museums

Three distinctly different modes of teaching and learning take place in history museums (see Potter and Leone 1986: 98). These modes of presentation are based on appeals to the emotions, to sense experience, and to the intellectual imagination.

Much of the historical interpretation presented in the United States appeals to the emotions, as can be seen in displays and exhibits intended to inspire patriotic feelings. I am not objecting to patriotism, only suggesting that when one files past the Liberty Bell, the Declaration of Independence, or a moon rock, after standing in line forty-five minutes to do so, one does not *learn* anything from the experience. This iconographic use of items from the past, in a celebratory way, touches people's emotions by reminding them of what they already know and believe. What more can one learn about American history, that one does not already know, from looking at the Liberty Bell? "For most people, relics render the past more important but not better known" (Lowenthal 1985: 249). Relics "light up the past" and are visited precisely because people know what they are and what they mean before they ever visit them. Exhibits of the type described here unquestionably provide emotional satisfaction by reinforcing the beliefs of the millions who visit them each year, but they do not teach anything new.

Some presentations of historical material appeal to the senses of visitors. Such presentations can be found in a wide range of outdoor history museums, as well as all kinds of hands-on history exhibitions. They offer the visitor an opportunity to experience what the past looked like, felt like, smelled like, and so on. This mode of presentation has been widely embraced by the museum community as an effective teaching tool (Alexander 1979: 92). It seems also to have been embraced by the visiting public. Some presentations of this kind even suggest that they allow the visitor to go back in time because the experience they provide is so enveloping. Unlike appeals to the emotions, which use objects from the past as mnemonic devices to remind people of their values, beliefs, and feelings, education of this second sort does encourage the acquisition of fresh knowledge. This mode of education adds to the knowledge people have already acquired in various conceptual categories, but does so without questioning or altering the categories themselves. That is, a visitor to Colonial Williamsburg can think, "I know what a typical twentieth-century house looks like; I wonder what a typical eighteenth-century house looked like?" and arrive at an answer. Colonial Williamsburg does not, however, encourage its visitors to examine categories like "house" and "looking" to determine whether *they* were constituted in the same way in the eighteenth century as they are today.

Furthermore, sense experience is actually an inappropriate way to learn about the past, for "all past events are more remote from our senses than the stars of the remotest galaxies, whose own light at least still reaches the telescope" (Kubler 1962: 79). The past cannot be verified "through observation," "can never be known like the present," or be "directly confronted" (Lowenthal 1985: 87, 91, 258). The past is *not* visible, smellable, tastable—and not even the most meticulous restoration can make it so.

The visitor's frame of reference compounds the problem. How, for example, does one interpret the small, dark houses lived in by seventeenth- and eighteenth-century common folk? It is easy to be awed by the hard conditions under which those people lived, but the only real standards we have for making such a judgment are our own. It is exceptionally difficult to apply eighteenth-century standards to an eighteenth-century house when our knowledge of it comes from our contemporary activity of walking through it. We think of it as "cramped" when we bang *our* heads on it (implicitly comparing it to our own higher-ceilinged homes). We often pass such judgments without knowing what eighteenth-century folk thought or would have thought. They could easily have learned to duck their heads and been able to ignore what we call an inconvenience. Or they may have known of no other houses where ducking was *not* required, which would mean that they did not have a "cramped/spacious" category to cover the situation. Both possibilities are likely. Thus, although historical presentations based on sense experience are good at filling categories of knowledge, they rarely use the knowledge they provide to challenge the categories it fills. Part of the problem is the logical fallacy in seeing the houses at Plimoth, Sturbridge, and Colonial Williamsburg, say, as steps along an evolutionary path toward a modern three-bedroom, split-level ranch house, which is certainly not the way they would have been viewed by their eighteenth-century occupants (see Lowenthal 1985: 34).

Second, upon seeing the well-kept, cozy little houses in places like Colonial Williamsburg, many visitors think of suburbia (Boorstin in Lowenthal 1985: 145), and these attractive houses certainly give the impression of being pleasant to live in. However, in thinking of Colonial Williamsburg as residentially desirable and life in that period as comfortable and quaint, we tend to see ourselves in an eighteenth-century house along with our twentieth-century conveniences and assumptions. Of course the eighteenth century appears delightful when eighteenth-century daily life is invisibly underpinned by central heating, air conditioning, and running water. Obviously, sense experience is no way to understand the absolute otherness of a past from which we are completely and irrevocably separated.

If anything, these first two kinds of historical education actually trap visitors more tightly in the present. Appeals to the emotions are based on what people already know and do not teach them anything at all, especially about the past. Appeals to the senses cannot teach about the past because logically the past is inaccessible to the senses. Instead, visitors are led to focus on their own emotions and frames of reference, while being told that they are focusing on the past. What one sees most clearly is one's own self and culture.

A third mode of historical presentation in museums appeals to the intellectual imagination of the visitor. Hexter (in Lowenthal 1985: 236) suggests that "the most illuminating works of history are those governed by the most imaginative and capacious regulative fictions." According to Leone (1981a: 13), "the past, like foreign cultures for ethnography, is entered through the imagination—the agreed upon source of all hypotheses." Imagination in this sense is not the free play of undisciplined fantasy, but rather the creative element inherent in constructing any version of the past, even the most academic. The goal of interpretive appeals to the intellectual imagination is to teach people what they did not know they did not know. This is in contrast to the kind of history education based on sense experience, which can add to knowledge but which does not challenge the categories of knowledge or the assumptions that structure it. This third kind of education encourages visitors to question things they normally take for granted.

For example, "After the Revolution," the Smithsonian Institution's permanent exhibition on late eighteenth- and early nineteenth-century America, presents a series of statistics showing that around 1800 far more women were pregnant at the time of their marriage than today (Smith 1985: 20). If one simply learns the fact without examining the category, his or her conclusion would be that morals were looser or that people were more sinful 200 years ago than they are today. However, if one goes a step further, to examine the social and cultural construction of marriage at that time, the ideas people held about it, and the social context in which these marriages took place, a different picture emerges. From that picture one can learn that "marriage," easily considered an immutably defined institution, actually changes and means different things to people in different societies and times. This is the kind of thing that many people do not know they do not know.

The same argument may be applied to the other bits of quantified demographics and other kinds of data presented in "After the Revolution," including, among other things, statistics on the seemingly prodigious consumption of alcohol by Americans in the late eighteenth and early nineteenth centuries. Any presentation of historical information that also helps create an appropriate frame of reference is education of this third type. Such education is based on the intellectual imagination because it focuses on the made-up quality of the past, the fact that people in the present create the past, both its content *and* its categories. In sharing this insight, the idea is to demonstrate that the past need not be created exclusively by experts and specialists and that each person creates his or her own version of the past on the basis of an active and critical engagement with historical facts and interpretations. This is the kind of education Munley (1987: 118) refers to when she says, "The museum fulfills its educational mission only to the extent that its exhibits affect people's lives."

Interestingly, it seems that the more strenuously we strive for historical accuracy, the more completely we cut ourselves off from the past (Leone 1981b: 305). As Lowenthal points out, "Those who assert their objectivity also tend to minimize the difficulties that prevent its realization" (1985: 236), with the result that "every advance in our knowledge of the past paradoxically makes it more remote, less knowable" (1985: 258).

Happily, the solution to this paradox is obvious: we will gain our greatest access to the past not by striving for it but by acknowledging that we create it.

Archaeology in Public Interpretation

The foregoing sections have described what Archaeology in Public was created to counteract. We may now turn our attention to the substance of this program.

Theoretical Issues

Presentations of history that trap people in the present can be counteracted, first, by paying close attention to the implications of seemingly innocuous aspects of depictions of the past. This attention should be directed toward both the form and content of historical presentations.

On the matter of form, Leone (1981b: 306) notes that by placing artifacts of Shaker industry "in bedrooms and [the] little buildings where [they] are now stored. . . . Present displays often make the work [Shaker industry] look like hobbies." Shaker life is misrepresented and trivialized by the way that *authentic* relics of it are displayed. The 1986 interpretive program at the Main Street site in Annapolis provides an example of the kind of content problem that can arise. Paul Pearson, a local hotelier, owned a property that he allowed us to excavate and interpret as the Main Street site. The focus of our investigation and interpretation was an eighteenth-century owner of the property, Thomas Hyde. Coincidentally, at that time, Pearson owned *another* of Hyde's eighteenth-century properties just up the street from the archaeological site. This coincidence clearly qualifies as an interesting tidbit, but it was not included in any Archaeology in Public programming out of concern that by pointing out one similarity between eighteenth- and twentieth-century owners of the property, we would encourage some visitors to see other similarities for which there is no basis in fact. The danger is the ease with which Hyde and Pearson could become transformations of one another and finally identical. The process by which this occurs is similar to that by which gaps in outdoor history museum interpretations are filled by visitors with the corresponding aspects of contemporary life. Gaps in our knowledge of Pearson could be filled with Hyde and gaps in our knowledge of Hyde could be filled with Pearson. Although there may be little harm in seeing Hyde as a jazz-lover or polo player (both of which Pearson demonstrably is), danger does lie in filling in missing pieces of Hyde's business life with pieces of Pearson's because such a process makes Pearson (or Hyde as Pearson) the precedent for his own contemporary business activities in Annapolis. This process of linking Pearson and Hyde would impede our ability to see differences between the two men and also would contribute to making Pearson's activities today—as beneficial as they generally are—appear natural and inevitable, as a part of the march of history and not open to contemporary examination, question, or challenge.

This kind of attention to detail is an important part of a public interpretive program using a critical perspective. It helps prevent the dissemination of unintended messages, and it helps control the use of interpretations of the past for purposes other than those for which the interpretations were intended.

Returning to the question of what Archaeology in Public is, the program was conceived and designed to do two things: (1) help reenfranchise people with control over their own consumption of history and (2) illuminate the origins of certain aspects of contemporary life usually taken for granted, but which, when given histories, become easier to question, challenge, and change.

In addition to its primary goal—which is to provide sophisticated history education for adults—the program has a variety of secondary goals, some of which may be primary goals for other archaeological projects. Archaeology in Public has provided good public relations for the University of Maryland and Historic Annapolis, as well as for Archaeology in Annapolis itself. The work it does has been construed as public service. The ethnographic component of Archaeology in Public allows the archaeology to be integrated smoothly into the community. An original justification of the ethnography was the idea that in a community with a 100-year historical tradition, it was important for the archaeologists, as creators of yet another line of historical evidence, to know what the town already thought about its past, as a way of understanding how new archaeological knowledge would be fitted in, accepted, or rejected. It was considered important to be able to predict or at least understand the impact of new knowledge. This sort of "local knowledge" is well within the grasp of all those CRM operations that have developed expertise in particular locales, and although such knowledge can simplify archaeological logistics, it may also be useful in the formulation of research questions.

Archaeology in Public has attempted to reenfranchise people by demystifying archaeology, a mission that can be undertaken by *any* archaeological project. First, we explain archaeological logic, step by step, trying not to tell visitors our conclusions without explaining how we reach them. Second, we try to discuss the social context of the archaeological project in as much detail as is practical. We include information on who funds the work, where the excavators come from, and what will happen to the site after the archaeologists are finished with it. When practical, this second step would seem especially appropriate for CRM projects. The purpose of both of these steps is to place archaeologists and site visitors on the same footing as members of modern American society. At a slightly more technical level, considerable attention is paid to the language used by Archaeology in Public in addressing the public, to make sure that it is neither jargon-laden nor incomprehensible, but, at the same time, adequate to express the sophistication of the ideas being discussed. By taking this position, and linking it to critical theory, Archaeology in Public rejects Alexander's (1979: 198) contention that "the guides should have at their command human interest materials that emphasize colorful personalities, lively happenings, and underlying concepts." Such approaches patronize visitors by placing entertainment ahead of education. Archaeology in Public aims to be understandable but not condescending to its visitors and strives not to "talk down" to them. The intention is to present archaeology as a contemporary social activity that creates a version of the past. Rather than hiding agency and point of view in that process, Archaeology in Public attempts to be as explicit as possible about the social context in which it operates and the influence that context exerts on the version of the past produced by Archaeology in Annapolis.

This approach aims to go beyond the idea that history is facts about the past connected to the present only because they are inherently interesting. Archaeology in Public tells contemporary Americans things about the past and the creation and use of the past that are important because of the ways such ideas are used to organize contemporary American life. Archaeology in Public deals with the past as an active force in modern life. The active quality of the past needs to be understood, not because those who do not understand the past are doomed to repeat it, but because people who do not understand how the past is constructed and used are certainly at risk of having history used to trap them in contemporary relations of social inequality by arguments that use the past to ground, naturalize, and legitimize the present: "Every act of recognition alters survivals from the past" and "to see why and how we ourselves change the past helps free us from myths that constrained previous perceptions" (Lowenthal 1985: 63).

Interpretive Tools

This philosophy informs all three components of Archaeology in Public: (1) *Archaeological Annapolis: A Guide to Seeing and Understanding Three Centuries of Change* (Leone and Potter 1984), a twenty-four-page guidebook to one section of the Annapolis Historic District; (2) *Annapolis: Reflections From the Age of Reason*, a twelve-projector, computer-synchronized audiovisual production, fully produced but not yet mounted, intended for showing in the Historic District; and (3) a twelve- to fifteen-minute tour of a working archaeological site. This multimedia approach to public programming was designed by Leone and me with considerable conceptual assistance from Philip Arnoult, director of the Theatre Project in Baltimore. Arnoult has served as the media consultant to Archaeology in Public since its inception. Both the guidebook and the audiovisual were professionally designed and produced to the specifications of Archaeology in Public and in close consultation with Leone and me. *Archaeological Annapolis* was designed by Kell & Chadick, Inc., of Silver Spring, Maryland, in cooperation with the publications office of the University of Maryland, and *Annapolis: Reflections from the Age of Reason* was designed by Telesis, Inc., of Baltimore. Each piece of Archaeology in Public can stand alone, but its impact is far greater as a multimedia experience, for the individual elements, while independent and not redundant, interlock with, reinforce, and extend the meaning of each of the other elements. One objective in selecting media has been to present each part of the Archaeology in Public message in the most suitable medium available. The first two elements, the guidebook, and the audiovisual, are discussed in this chapter; the tours, which represent the most fully elaborated expression of Archaeology in Public, are discussed separately, in chapter 10.

Archaeological Annapolis is a twenty-four-page, 7-by-10-inch, soft-covered, staple-bound, three-color, illustrated guidebook published in 1984. Its first press run of 2,000 copies was exhausted after thirteen months of distribution. Nearly half of the copies were distributed as complementary; the rest were sold for $1.50 in Historic Annapolis museums, in local bookstores, by mail order, at an open archaeological site, and through the Historic Inns of Annapolis. It seems to have been purchased by both residents and tourists and received two favorable reviews in the local press. A second printing in 1989 produced 5,000 copies.

The book contains two maps. One directs visitors to the part of the Annapolis Historic District covered by the guidebook. while the other depicts the area covered by the book and suggests a path to be followed by its readers. The main part of the book consists of eight two-page sections containing a set of historical photographs of a particular spot on the left-hand page (from the collection of noted Annapolis photographer M. E. Warren) and a 500-word essay about the spot on the right-hand page. The principal purpose of *Archaeological Annapolis* is not to teach archaeological findings—there are, in fact, few test pits or artifacts in the book—but, rather, to teach one part of the critical point of view adopted by Archaeology in Annapolis. Each essay focuses on a particular spot and explains how different generations of Annapolitans have chosen to understand it and its history.

A typical example is the discussion of the Wm. Paca House and the sharp contrast between its two main historical identities. In 1907 the Paca House was "renovated," added onto substantially, and renamed the Carvel Hall Hotel. At that time, Richard Carvel, a fictional character, must have been a more attractive historical figure than William Paca, son of liberty, signer of the Declaration of Independence, and three-term governor of Maryland. During the mid-1960s, Historic Annapolis purchased the building, demolished the hotel addition, and began the meticulous restoration of the Paca House proper. In place of the connection to the fictional Richard Carvel, Paca was reemphasized and scientific accuracy replaced romance as the way to a better understanding of the eighteenth-century past at 186 Prince George Street, Annapolis. As the conclusion of the Paca House essay states:

> The Wm. Paca House, as does any historic place, shows aspects of the past, but at the same time cannot help but show how the present understands the past. At one time the "history" of the house centered more on artistically portraying fictionalized people in a real colonial house. But our own age has chosen to interpret the history of this house and its era through displaying genuine period objects and through applying scientific accuracy. (Leone and Potter 1984: 19)

This was intended to demonstrate that historical identities are not intrinsic but continually negotiated. The proprietors of Carvel Hall were not ignorant of Paca; they *chose* Carvel over Paca. And today's focus on Paca is *not* inevitable or necessary; Historic Annapolis could easily focus on any number of eighteenth- and nineteenth-century owners or occupants—including Carvel's creator, Winston Churchill, who lived in the Paca House briefly just before the turn of the century.

The guidebook also contains sections on Francis St. and the State House; vistas; the harbor; Cornhill, Fleet, and Pinkney streets; the

Governor Calvert House; the State House, Government House, and Rowe Boulevard; and the Chase-Lloyd, Hammond-Harwood, and Wm. Paca houses, as a group. The point of the book is to demonstrate that the view of the past taken in any era is in large part a product of the unique challenges, conditions, and needs of that time, that the past is created, used, and subject to varying interpretations, and is not immutable fact. The book is undoubtedly more valuable for the way of thinking it teaches than the specific details it contains.

The guidebook format is particularly well-suited to this part of the Archaeology in Public message because it lends itself to leisurely use and contemplation in the presence of the buildings and streetscapes it interprets. This quality makes *Archaeological Annapolis* different from inventory-style guidebooks, which are useful primarily as a place to check off visits to significant sites and monuments. Furthermore, the potentially challenging point of view in the guidebook can be restudied at home or wherever else the user desires. The guidebook is critical because its peeling back of layers of historical interpretation, uses of the past, and uses of buildings challenges the idea that history is a set of objectively collected facts about the past. It does this by reestablishing agency in the creation of history.

Annapolis: Reflections from the Age of Reason, discussed in detail in Potter and Leone (1992), functions somewhat differently from the guidebook. The twenty-minute show consists of about 600 slides, shown by twelve computer-synchronized projectors on a wide screen, with a taped narrative backed by a soundtrack composed of six musical selections, some eighteenth-century, some modern. Originally produced as an audiovisual, *Annapolis: Reflections from the Age of Reason* was reformatted as a videotape in 1990.

In comparison with the guidebook, the audiovisual is less about how to see and more about what one can learn by examining eighteenth-century material culture. The audiovisual takes a wide range of eighteenth-century material culture—some archaeological, some architectural, some from the decorative arts, some from the fine arts—and demonstrates how such material is, among other things, an expression of the traits Deetz has amalgamated into his conception of the Georgian worldview: balance, symmetry, and segmentation. Then it goes a step further, using Charles Willson Peale's famous painting of his own natural history museum. The painting contains Peale's conception of the natural order. It shows a wall of display cases containing lower orders of animals near the bottom, higher orders of animals nearer the top, and portraits of Revolutionary War heroes just below the ceiling. The audiovisual suggests that people in the eighteenth century studied the natural world in order to build a more orderly human society based on natural principles, forgetting or concealing the fact that regularities and laws were not discovered in nature but placed there by the observer. The audiovisual concludes by noting that the ideas we call Georgian applied not just to aesthetics or early science, but to a wide range of economic activities. The orderly survey and subdivision of land made speculation easier and more profitable. Improvements in navigational techniques made transatlantic voyages more predictable and trade more profitable. Organizing the industrial workplace according to the principles of mass production and wage labor made it easier for capitalists to profit from the labor of workers.

A multiprojector audiovisual is a particularly effective medium with which to cover such topics because multiple projectors, focused on different parts of the screen, create multiple, simultaneous, parallel images, illustrating graphically the ideas of segmentation and standardization discussed by the script. In this way, the spoken and visual aspects of the audiovisual presentation reinforce one another. The audiovisual is critical because the usually unexamined ideas that lie behind the material culture featured in it are not simply "logic," "common sense," or "efficiency"; are still operating today; and make it easier for some individuals to exploit and profit from the labor of others.

A drawback of both the guidebook and the audiovisual, however, is that in being a stylish work of graphic or visual art in its own right that matches the upscale kinds of products that sell well in Annapolis, each is slightly at odds with the critical perspective. On the one hand, the polish and the seamlessness of each piece serves to divert attention away from its creators. At the same time, any medium affects the message that it conveys. It is easy for the reader or the viewer to make the leap from an artistic presentation of some class of material culture to the interpretation of the material culture itself as art, even though that is the antithesis of the stance of Archaeology in Public. This is the same point Leone makes when he says that Shaker tools displayed in bedrooms make Shaker industries appear to have been hobbies.

To make the point a bit more broadly, if Archaeology in Annapolis was to produce a longer print piece, in the format of a coffee-table book, it would be difficult to keep that book from being transformed into a coffee-table book by its readers. To the extent that people do not expect to be challenged by such books, a critically informed work turned into a coffee-table book has in some sense failed because it has been coopted by the dominant ideology.

Summary

Archaeology in Annapolis has important implications for CRM archaeology and for other projects that are not "long-term," "citywide," or funded specifically to provide public interpretation. As noted earlier, few people are likely to distinguish between the National Science Foundation, the National Endowment for the Humanities, or a state's department of transportation as the primary sponsor of an archaeological project. All archaeologists are faced with a public that is, generally speaking, interested in both the techniques and the findings of any archaeological project that is publicly accessible.

This broad public interest in archaeology needs to be explained by archaeologists to all of our various partners, sponsors, and clients. Simply suggesting that contract archaeologists insist on a line-item for public education in every archaeological contract is too facile a solution, but, in fact, more and more CRM companies are developing sound strategies and programs for public outreach and education. This trend should be continued and intensified.

As more CRM archaeologists move into archaeological education, they will face all kinds of decisions about media, personnel, and costs. It would be foolish for me to attempt to anticipate every possible scenario and to prescribe an appropriate public program. However, some elements of Archaeology in Public are better candidates for export than others. In particular, we have found print to be an especially flexible and useful medium. In addition to *Archaeological Annapolis*, the project has produced dozens of interpretive signs for on-site use, and a variety of fliers and brochures for use by visitors both on-site and elsewhere.

A book like *Archaeological Annapolis* requires a certain depth of local knowledge that may be developed in a variety of ways—including long-term attention from well-established CRM firms. At least two sets of contractors working for the Delaware Department of Transportation have produced fine, informative print pieces for the public (Klein and Friedlander 1983; Gardner and Walker 1990). As I suggested in chapter 1, it is wrong to think that critical archaeology falls exclusively, or even primarily, within the domain of academic archaeology. Precisely because they are *not* insulated from the "real world" or ensconced in an ivory tower, contract archaeologists are well situated to make important contributions to the development of critical archaeology, and vice versa.

Perhaps the most useful educational medium for relatively mobile CRM programs is the brochure. These do not have to be elaborate; a well-written, well-designed, photocopied brochure of four or eight pages can communicate a considerable amount of sophisticated information. There is no technical or logistical reason why even a fairly small, fast-moving survey team armed with a good brochure could not undertake a critical archaeology. In mounting a critical archaeology, the expense of the medium matters far less than the quality of the message. An elaborately presented archaeological interpretation that does not challenge its audience to think about contemporary life is *not* archaeological practice in the critical sense; a simply presented interpretation that *does* use archaeology to comment on contemporary life *is* archaeological practice.

10

Site Tours

The number of archaeologists with the resources and the inclination to replicate Archaeology in Public is undoubtedly fairly small. As a result, it seems more appropriate to concentrate here on the philosophy that underpins Archaeology in Public and the content of tours given at two Archaeology in Annapolis sites (the Victualling Warehouse and Main Street) rather than on a great deal of "how to" material. In any case, simply emulating the technical aspects of Archaeology in Public will not produce a critical archaeology. What *can* produce a critical archaeology, and what I hope *will* be emulated is the pattern of thought that seeks to discover just how knowledge of the past can be and is linked to contemporary life by contemporary creators and users of that knowledge.

My point here is that we have done a great deal in Annapolis that may be attempted elsewhere, with substantially less funding and in less ideal circumstances. An archaeological project with *no* public program can be a critical archaeology as long as it is carried out with an audience in mind. Most archaeologists do not give site tours, but *all* archaeologists can be prepared to deliver critically informed responses to the questions that people inevitably ask archaeologists. In the same vein, most archaeologists do not select their sites (at least not any more), but even with a site that has been "preselected" by the alignment of a new highway, there is no reason why a contract archaeologist cannot think about who would be likely to visit the site, how visitors would get there, what they would already know, and what they would want to learn. And there is no reason why an archaeologist working on a preselected site or set of sites cannot devise an interpretation that constitutes an archaeological practice, an application of archaeology to contemporary social life. In short, and at the risk of sounding like a Zen archaeologist, most archaeologists working in most situations can *think* a critical archaeology. Furthermore, once a use is identified for any piece of archaeology, it becomes that much harder for someone else with a different agenda to misuse that work. This is precisely the point of archaeological practice; the explicit use of archaeological knowledge is a safeguard against misuse.

Acknowledgment

Much of the technical polish achieved by Archaeology in Public is straightforward and relatively easily acquired. Well-designed tours and attractive print pieces are the products of sound advice adequately followed. Early in the history of Archaeology in Public, however, the project benefited from an important piece of advice that was rather more philosophical than technical.

Midway through the first summer of Archaeology in Public, Philip Arnoult of the Theatre Project in Baltimore became the project's media consultant. He developed a basic tour outline, which we have used for almost every Archaeology in Public tour; he established a guide-training program; and he designed the site "decorations" used to attract visitors to and through a half-dozen sites. More important than any of these contributions, however, was his concept of acknowledgment. Arnoult does not design archaeological theater pieces, or even tours. Rather, he designs *meetings*. Before any archaeological or historical information is conveyed in an Archaeology in Public site tour, each archaeologist/guide clearly acknowledges and establishes a unique social relationship: the archaeologist/guide is a specific member of contemporary American society talking to a specific group of visitors about the process and the products of one particular archaeological attempt at understanding the past. This specification of the contemporary social context provides Archaeology in Public visitors with a kind of grounding that is unavailable from interpretive settings in which the interpreter plays a role or attempts to be as inconspicuous as possible.

The concept of acknowledgment is expressed in a variety of ways. An

Helen Sydavar delivering a tour at the Shiplap House site.

Archaeology in Public guide explains the cleanup procedures for a notice-ably muddy site after an all-night rainstorm. An Archaeology in Public guide acknowledges the rumbling of buses and trucks passing by during a site tour, and he or she does not try to talk over the loud ones. A new Archaeology in Public guide acknowledges that he or she is new and still learning the ropes. Each of these is a small detail, but when added up and forged into a performance technique, these acknowledgments let visitors know that their tour is a unique meeting. This reinforces the critical idea that interpretations of the past are highly dependent on the circumstances of their creation. All of this is opposed to a memorized, one-size-fits-all tour, given identically day in and day out. Such a tour, which treats its text as revealed truth, suggests that there is a single, correct interpretation of the past, the very point of view critical theory was invented to counteract.

Acknowledgment seems especially germane to the process of creating critical interpretations for CRM projects. Sometimes in Annapolis we had to work hard to find the proper contemporary social context on which to hang a particular archaeological interpretation, but in CRM, by definition, an element of contemporary life is *always* colliding with something that remains from the past. The superimposition of past and present land use can be a very productive focus for archaeological interpretation. The juxtaposition of past and present that is inevitable in CRM forms the basis for my earlier suggestion that CRM archaeology could well be the setting for future advances in critical archaeology.

Two Examples

By the time I left Archaeology in Public in 1987, a total of eight archaeological sites had been opened to the public, and nine tours had been written. One site had three different tours for three different seasons, and one site with light visitor traffic, Reynolds Tavern, was opened with just placards. Sites that have been opened to the public are the Victualling Warehouse (1982, 1983, 1984), Reynolds Tavern (1983), Governor Calvert House (1984), Newman Street (1984), the State House Inn (1985), Shiplap House (1985), Main Street (1986), and the Charles Carroll of Carrollton House and Garden (1987). The remainder of this chapter is devoted to the tours for the Victualling Warehouse and Main Street. As I have suggested several times, the most important lesson that may be drawn from these tours is their attempt to link past and present. This pattern of thought, rather than some sort of interpretive technique, is the hallmark of a critical archaeology.

The Victualling Warehouse

The Victualling Warehouse is a two-and-one-half-story, three-bay brick building erected in the very early nineteenth century. It stands on the foundations of a presumably identical building, constructed in the 1750s and destroyed by fire in the 1790s. Today the first floor of the Victualling Warehouse is occupied by a Historic Annapolis museum devoted to maritime activities between 1750 and 1780. The second floor houses a laboratory for Archaeology in Annapolis.

The archaeological site is in the backyard of the extant building and consists of the foundation of a second warehouse also built in the 1750s, destroyed in the 1790s, but not rebuilt. The site was excavated in the hope that it would provide evidence of eighteenth-century commercial activities in the city dock area, to go along with Annapolis's elaborate understanding of eighteenth-century colonial social life centered in the city's great Georgian mansions. The Victualling Warehouse is located at the base of Main Street, at the city dock, in the center of Annapolis's tourist district. The site was opened to the public in 1982, 1983, and 1984.

In 1982 the site was open in August and again, with the same tour, in October, for the U.S. Sailboat Show. The tour was given during the early stages of excavation at the site, and there was relatively little to report in the way of results. As a consequence, the tour was principally about archaeological method. It explained how the archaeologists knew what they knew:

> These foundations probably represent the remains of a second warehouse, built in the 1750s, at the same time as the building on whose foundations the present Victualling Warehouse stands. How do we know that?
>
> The 1750s deed to the property refers to two buildings, one with exactly the dimensions of the standing building and another adjacent to it 42 feet long by 16 feet wide. We cannot determine the length of the building that stood on these foundations because they have been torn up by subsequent construction activities on the site but it *is* 16 feet from the foundation I am standing on to the parallel line of foundation over by where you are standing. We think that the match between the deed and this measurement means that these foundations are the remains of the second 1750s warehouse. . . .
>
> We think that the building that stood on these foundations was probably two or two and a half stories tall. We think that because standing buildings in Annapolis, built around the same time, with foundations the same width as these foundations, are usually two or two and a half stories tall.

The intention of these two short explanations was simply to demonstrate archaeological reasoning. It is the practice of Archaeology in Public not to present information without explaining *how* that information is known. For example, when ceramic dating is needed for an interpretation, it is introduced with references to English manufacturing records and price-fixing agreements, and the use of ceramics to date buildings is always accompanied by an explanation of builders' trenches. And so on. The idea is to demystify archaeology by presenting as much of the epistemology as possible in a straightforward way.

Further, the 1982 Victualling Warehouse tour stressed the "thought-up" quality of historical interpretation by discussing a feature of the site for which there was no explanation:

> Well, I've told you about some of the things on the site we do under-stand. There is in addition one fairly large thing we don't understand. The brick thing you can see back over my shoulder remains a mystery to us. When we first uncovered it, lots of people from around town told us it was the roof of a tunnel. One thing we have learned is that Annapolis is full of tunnel stories, referring to the use of tunnels for the underground railroad or for smuggling. So, we decided to test that idea. Just two days ago we took off some of the bricks on top and dug down below them. What we found—and I actually did some of that digging myself—was perfectly clean sand with no artifacts in it at all. The lack of artifacts suggests that the sand was natural sub-soil, undisturbed by previous human activity. This means that our brick feature, rather than being the top of something, like a tunnel, was probably the bottom of something. But of what, we don't yet know.

In addition to demonstrating the logic of archaeological thinking, such a tour attempts to break down the basis for popular dependence on histori-cal specialists in an attempt to lay the groundwork for Carl Becker's ide-alized world in which everyman is his own historian (Becker 1935).

In 1983, the Victualling Warehouse site was opened again, from early July through mid-August and for the October boat shows. Between the summer of 1982 and the summer of 1983, an interim report had been written (Crosby 1982), and with a few tentative conclusions in hand, we decided to present some of the findings of the 1982 season in the 1983 tour (Leone 1983a).

The principal archaeological finding had to do with the layers of debris remaining after the building's fire and demolition. There were two distinct layers of rubble: a lower burned layer and an upper unburned layer. In addition, the ceramics from the two layers differed chronologically by ten to twenty years, with the older ceramics in the burned layer and the newer ceramics in the unburned layer. This was taken to indicate that at least a decade had passed between the 1790 fire and the final demolition of the building. This information was used in the tour in the following way:

> Now that I've told you a little bit about who I am and how we dig, let me tell you about what we've found here at this site.
>
> Step over this way with me, if you will. Take a look at the sidewall of this square. Note the three different layers of soil. That bottom layer

is the natural subsoil. It has no artifacts in it showing that it had never been disturbed by people until we dug into it a couple of weeks ago.

Now look at the layer right on top of the subsoil. See how dark it is? That darkness is from charcoal produced by the fire that burned the building in 1790. How do we know the fire was in 1790? Not just from digging holes in the ground. The charcoal made us think that there had been a fire here and the burned up ceramics—bits of plates and dishes— were of varieties made in England during the 1780s. We know that because the folks in England who made ceramics in the 1700s and 1800s kept detailed manufacturing records. What we do is match our sherds to information from the manufacturing records to determine when the ones we dig up were made. As I said, the ceramics from the burned layer dated from the 1780s, mostly. So, using that information we carefully read the *Maryland Gazette*, Annapolis's eighteenth-century newspaper, and discovered that on the 20th of January, 1790, a fire broke out at a bakeshop on the corner and burned out the whole block.

What's interesting here is the layer of rubble on top of the burned rubble. This rubble is not burned and has unburned ceramics in it 10–15 years newer than those in the burned layer. That leads us to think that the warehouse burned in 1790 but did not burn all the way to the ground. We think it stood as a burned-out shell, collecting neighborhood trash for 10 or 15 years before it was finally pushed in. That's an important thing to learn in light of what Annapolis is like today.

I can't imagine a burned-out building standing empty for 10 years in the Annapolis dock area of the 1980s, but in the 1790s that's just what happened. Annapolis in the 1790s was a very different place from Annapolis today. Around 1800 Annapolis's economy started becoming much more local. During the second half of the 1700s Annapolis was the "Queen of the Chesapeake," the social, political, and economic center of the area. But by 1800 Baltimore was on the rise and Annapolis began to decline in importance. In 1790, when this building burned, it was not worth anyone's while to rebuild it, which is a graphic commentary on the city's economic slowdown. This slowdown lasted for about 150 years; the bustling city you see today, filled with shops, bars, and restaurants is the product of a commercial renaissance which began in the 1950s.

The interesting thing about this commercial re-birth is the effect it has on work like ours here. What we're doing by digging this site is commercial history. Thirty years ago Annapolis would have had no use for commercial history, and virtually none was written. The city wasn't doing much business and therefore, commercial history would have been the story of failure. But, when the city's re-birth as a commercial place took hold, commercial history was no longer the story of failure, but was instead the story of success. And as a commercial place once again, Annapolis could make use of eighteenth-century commercial history as a precedent, as historical grounding for contemporary commercial activities.

And just as the kind of history done in Annapolis today is different from what was done 30 years ago, so too will historians 30 years from now probably focus on different aspects of the past than historians do today. The histories written 30 years from now will serve the needs of the society that produces them, just as contemporary versions of history serve the needs of today.

My broader point is that Annapolis is not unique; history is always a product of the circumstances under which it is written. We bring this up so that the next time you see a presentation of history, rather than swallowing it whole; you can question it to find out the ways in which it is a product of the contemporary circumstances of its creation. We hope this helps you view interpretations of the past with new, more critical eyes. The goal of this tour is to arm you with questions to ask the next time you visit a historical interpretation and tools for taking it apart for yourself, so you gain a better understanding of its connections to the circumstances of *its* creation.

With that, I'd like to thank you very much for your attention. If you have any questions about anything I've said, or something I've not said, I'd be pleased to answer them.

Archaeology in Public tours are nothing if not explicit in articulating what they are intended to teach. The broadly stated intention of the 1983 Victualling Warehouse tour was to use specific Annapolis data to show the ways in which the present creates the past for its own purposes.

This example, as well as those that follow, point up one important value of the critical perspective with regard to some other antipositivist or antiobjectivist positions. The danger in a relativist position informed by radical epistemological skepticism is that after throwing away a positivist search for a scientific-style explanation, proof, and facts about the past, such a stance can leave one with little to say other than any past is as good as any other, and not much basis for understanding the creation of any one version beyond individual idiosyncrasy. But, by asserting that versions of the past are created to protect or expand the power of those in positions of social authority, a critical perspective offers the possibility of explanation.

Yet a third tour was created for the Victualling Warehouse site. At the end of the 1984 summer season, after putting on tours at the Newman Street site for a relatively small audience, we opened the Victualling Warehouse site for one week, during which time the final touches were put on the excavation of the site. Concurrently, a tour was offered, different from either of the Victualling Warehouse tours given during previous seasons.

This tour acknowledged that work was being completed at the site, and it looked to the future. The tour suggested that the Victualling Warehouse property would eventually become a museum exhibit space of some sort. It then laid out a series of possibilities for museum exhibits that could go there, from partial reconstruction of the buildings with an eighteenth-century or a modern interior, to a conjectural reconstruction using tubular steel to outline the house (as at Franklin Court, in Philadelphia), to the placement of a sheet of plexiglass over the area, preserving it as an archaeological site. The tour explained that each possibility contains a judgment as to which elements of the past are more important than others. Exterior reconstruction with a modern interior says that architecture and exterior appearance are important. Presentation of the area as an archaeological site says that the techniques used to learn about the past are as important as the results achieved through those techniques. And so on.

The tour went on to say that while the tubular steel framing technique was attractive because of the explicit way it forced visitors to use their imaginations to understand the past, *any* historical reconstruction effort depends on both the imagination of its builder, to fabricate parts of the structure for which there is no direct evidence, and on the imagination of the visitor, who must at the very least mentally animate such a reconstruction to use it to understand life in the past. Any version of the past, the tour asserted, is a product of the intellectual imagination.

The tour concluded by saying that although all of the options presented were under consideration, none had been selected as the way of exhibiting information from the site. The tour told visitors that if they came back in ten years, they would likely see a museum presenting itself as the picture of life in the past in that spot, but reminded them that whatever version of the past the exhibit presented, the shape of the exhibit would be the product of a decision *yet to be made*. Contemporary discussion and debate will play a *major* role in determining the way the past will be made to look at the Victualling Warehouse site museum, and the contemporary interests to which that version of the past will be helpful. Although the *result* of the discussion will be the exhibit, the exhibit most likely will not contain the full discussion that gave rise to it, thereby obscuring the negotiated nature of presentations of the past and implying that the exhibit presents a true version of the past rather than being one version selected from many. The conclusion of the tour suggested that this museum exhibit would in no way be unusual, but rather that *any* presentation of the past is a version selected from many and that any exhibit is as much a reflection of the discussions that surrounded its creation as it is a reflection of the past it attempts to report on.

Like the 1983 tour, the 1984 update tour was explicitly critical. It simply took the earlier argument about the relationship between written histories and current social needs and extended that logic to museum exhibits. The objective of the tour was to teach people something that museums often tend to hide, namely that their exhibits are created and have authors. The deeper point is that by concealing authorship and point of view, museums cultivate the appearance of objectivity in order to make themselves authoritative. This is important for us to understand because when museum exhibits change, or even when the basic theories behind them change, rather than being called changes in point of view, most of these changes are explained in terms of new and improved, more accurate, modern scholarship and the new products passed off as unconnected to interests.

All three of the Victualling Warehouse tours make general points based on a critical perspective. Even the 1983 tour, which discussed the value that commercial Annapolis places on commercial history, was directed primarily toward making the general point that the topics taken up by historians depend on the social and political needs of the social contexts in which they operate. The reason for this level of generality is that my ethnographic research was not far enough along, even by 1984, to provide a specific contemporary political issue whose roots could be examined archaeologically. By the spring of 1985, when we gave a tour at the State House Inn site (Potter and Leone 1986), we were beginning to incorporate my ethnographic research, and by 1986, we were able to present a tour that was fully informed by critical theory.

Main Street

An explicitly ethnographically based tour was offered at the Main Street site during the summer of 1986 (Leone, Potter, and Shackel 1987). This

Creative signage at the Main Street site.

site was a parking lot next to a movie theater torn down during the summer of 1987. The entire property, theater site and parking lot, was subsequently redeveloped into a shopping and office complex, and archaeological access to the property was a product of its redevelopment. (In fact, roughly half the Archaeology in Public sites have been excavated and interpreted shortly in advance of construction—mirroring quite nicely the world of cultural resource management archaeology.) Deed research, nineteenth-century insurance maps, and old photographs all suggested that the parking lot had contained, from the mid-1760s through the 1930s, the two-and-one-half-story, five-bay, brick house of Thomas Hyde, a successful Annapolis entrepreneur.

A preliminary archaeological survey in the winter of 1985–86 showed that in addition to Hyde's house, the property contained the remains of several eighteenth- and nineteenth-century outbuildings indicated by the documents, and also, the remains of a foundation of an entirely unexpected early eighteenth-century building. Summer excavations focused on Hyde's house and the early eighteenth-century foundation in an attempt to examine variation in the use of items reflective of the Georgian worldview. The Main Street site is two-thirds of the way up Main Street in a neighborhood of shops and restaurants well traveled by both local residents and tourists.

The Main Street tour went as follows:

> Now that I've told you about who we are and how we dig, I'd like to tell you about why we're digging here.
>
> As I mentioned a few minutes ago, one important class of archaeological finds is ceramics. Most ceramic tableware used in this country through the mid-1800s was made in England, and since we know when these items were made, we can use fragments of them to help us date archaeological sites.
>
> Ceramics, however, are useful for far more than dating. There was a revolution in the manufacture and marketing of English ceramics led by Josiah Wedgwood in the middle of the 1700s. Wedgwood and others developed materials and techniques that allowed the mass manufacture of relatively inexpensive tablewares—in matched sets. Before the middle of the 1700s ceramic items usually didn't come in sets and were generally used communally, several people eating from one vessel and sharing another for drinking. The Wedgwood revolution changed all that. Wedgwood introduced plates that allowed each diner to have his or her own plate, separate from but identical to those of each other diner. He also created sets of dishes which included many different sizes and shapes of vessels for different courses. A proper set of dishes had soup plates *and* breakfast plates *and* dessert plates *and* butter plates, in addition to regular dinner plates.
>
> We feel that the use of a fully elaborated set of dishes, then as now, was not simply a matter of manners, unconnected to the rest of life. The elaboration of sizes and shapes of dishes is a process of both segmentation and standardization. Separate plates separate the diners at a table from each other, along with the use of proper manners—using the right fork and so on. Manners and dishes provided clear rules and divisions which showed individuals how to relate to each other. The meal became segmented in Annapolis by around 1750.
>
> Meanwhile, the process of mass production was beginning to standardize dishes and many other kinds of manufactured goods. The plates whose sherds we are digging up here served to regularize the eating behavior of those who used them and at the same time, their own regularity was the product of both a regulated manufacturing process and a regulated life for the workers who made them. Everything was getting more standardized, including much of human behavior. Stan-

Patricia Secreto explaining stratigraphy at the Main Street site.

dardization and segmentation are worth our attention because while they were new ideas in the middle of the 1700s, they are still with us today and are taken for granted as given, as ways we assume the world has always operated. This is how we think about the ceramics we dig up.

These ideas about segmentation don't just have to do with dishes. Just as individual plates and specialized serving dishes separated food and diners, houses came to have more and more rooms with different activities being performed apart from each other in separate rooms. Before 1700 many work-related and domestic activities took place in the same room of the house. By 1750 people were building houses with separate rooms for eating, sleeping, cooking, and working. And the richer folks, like those in the Paca and Brice houses, carried this even further with music, card, and ballrooms. Dishes and eating were segmented. Houses and domestic life were segmented. So too were lives segmented into a work life, a social life, and a family life. In the early 1700s work and domestic activities usually all went on in the same place. By 1800 in Annapolis people divided work from home life by working in shops, taverns, and offices in separate buildings from their homes. Houses like the one we are digging up were used only for domestic activities by 1800. By the time large-scale manufacturing

Another perspective on the Main Street tour.

began in Baltimore in 1850, work was located farther from home and the distance became greater and greater.

We think that people learned how to divide their lives and accept the divisions and the rules for division by learning them at home at the table and at all the other tasks which were also becoming separate.

So far I've talked about several different separations beginning to enter American life in the 1700s, separations between diners at the table, the separation of different activities into different rooms in the house, and the separation of home and work. I would like to turn to one final separation, that between work time and leisure time. The distinction between work time and leisure time creates the possibility of something that many of you may be involved with right now, a vacation. Bear in mind for the next few minutes, if you would, that this particular cultural invention, the idea of a vacation, only entered American life about 100 years ago, about 100 years *after* Thomas Hyde built his house on this site.

Vacations and tourism are a major industry and a big issue in Annapolis, as in many other small historic towns. Each year over

1,000,000 people visit Annapolis, a city of only about 32,000, so it is easy to understand the city's interest in paying close attention to tourism; the city works hard to protect the things that attract visitors. As I said, the need to control a large influx of visitors is not at all unique. What is unique is one part of Annapolis's solution to this potential problem.

In some very subtle ways, Annapolis attempts to use George Washington to guide visitor behavior. For as long as the town has considered itself historical, local guidebooks and histories have included many references to George Washington and his 20 or so visits to the city. In many of these accounts there is a strong emphasis on the social and domestic aspects of his visits, his trips to the racetrack, the balls he attended, the plays he saw, and the friends and family members he visited. The picture of Washington that emerges is very similar to the profile of the kind of visitor Annapolis has very publicly said that it wants to attract, the "quality tourist." As defined during a local election campaign and since then in the local newspapers, a "quality tourist" is one who spends some money in town without causing trouble or leaving a mess behind. The effect of stories about Washington that make him like the kind of visitor that Annapolis tries to attract today is that Washington ends up as a model tourist or as a model for tourist behavior. What makes this subtle, or even unconscious portrayal of Washington as a model tourist so interesting is that tourism and vacations were not even invented until 80 years or more after Washington died. George Washington could never have been a tourist because tourism, as we practice it today, did not exist during his lifetime.

In the last 12 minutes I've tried to do two things. By discussing the origins of some-taken-for-granted aspects of contemporary life, separations, and segmentation, I have tried to show that our way of life is not inevitable; it is open to question and challenge. The second thing that I've tried to do, through the George Washington example, is to show ways in which history is often made and presented for contemporary purposes. This tour will have been a big success if, the next time you see a presentation of history, a museum, a tour, a television show, or whatever, you ask yourself what that version of history is trying to get you to do. In the meantime, I'll be happy to answer any questions you have about things I have talked about or other things I haven't mentioned. (Leone, Potter, and Shackel 1987: 289–91)

At the time it was presented, the Main Street tour was, if one can measure such things, the most critically informed tour that Archaeology in Public had yet presented. Its message has two critical aspects, one general and one specific. The general part of the message is an extension from what was said in the 1985 tour at the State House Inn (discussed in more detail in Potter and Leone 1986). In discussing the Annapolis street plan, the State House Inn tour concluded that "things we normally understand as utilitarian often contain messages." The Main Street tour suggested that versions of history contain submerged messages. On the specific side, the issue of relations between Annapolitans and visitors discussed in the Main Street tour directly affected virtually every person who took a tour of that site. Every tour taker was either a resident of or a visitor to Annapolis. The tour they all heard discussed the roots of the categories that structure the relationship between visitors and residents in Annapolis. The intent of the tour was to demonstrate that rather than given, the relationship is changeable, therefore challengeable.

Summary

This chapter has presented the site tour portion of a multimedia program of public interpretation based on archaeology and critical theory. Several other sources (Leone 1983a; Potter and Leone 1987, 1992) are better guides to the actual implementation of public programs. The purpose here has been to focus on those aspects of Archaeology in Public tours that make them critical, rather than "show-and-tell" performances on an archaeological site. The achievement of this goal is attempted in two ways. First, every Archaeology in Public tour begins with a discussion of archaeological technique and method. The purpose is to present insights into archaeological thinking in an attempt to demystify the process of archaeology. In addition, each tour contains a specific statement about the contemporary use of versions of the past, demonstrated with data from Annapolis. Second, tours like the one at Main Street are critical because they attempt to do more than merely present a standard historical archaeological tour that would be equally appropriate on any other historic site. At each Archaeology in Public site, the archaeological questions and interpretations presented grew, to some extent, out of an ethnographic analysis of the contemporary social context of Annapolis.

This does not, however, mean that every element of every Archaeology in Public interpretation is unique to Annapolis. Deetz's concept of the Georgian worldview as extended by Leone into a model for the study of capitalism has been very useful to Archaeology in Public. It would likely prove just as useful for many others using a critical approach for historical archaeology in a wide variety of places. This is simply a reflection of the fact that capitalism, in one form or another, has been the dominant economic system for most of the time in most of the areas studied by historical archaeologists. What will change, however, from locale to locale, is the contemporary expression of a capitalist economy. Variable as well, from place to place, is the specific set of social and economic issues that should be examined through archaeology. In Annapolis, a major contemporary issue, the relationship between residents and visitors, is clearly a product of an economic system that separates home from the workplace and that separates work time and leisure time. In other places, dealing with visitors may not be important, but another significant issue is likely to arise from and be structured by the local expression of capitalism. In any such context, historical archaeological analysis drawing on Deetz and Leone's extension of Deetz will probably prove helpful.

A final question to consider is whether the interpretations presented in this chapter are "real" archaeology. What they obviously are not is simple descriptions of things dug up out of the ground. Each major tour presented here does flow from an archaeological discovery, the burned and unburned layers of rubble at the Victualling Warehouse and pre-Georgian and Georgian ceramics at Main Street. Each tour moved fairly quickly from a discussion of things to a discussion of ideas. In each case, however, the leap was a part of the process of searching for meanings and frames of reference for understanding the archaeological record. A ten- to fifteen-year span between a fire in a building and its ultimate demolition obviously means different things at different times, in different places. In Annapolis in the early nineteenth century, it may have been standard operating procedure in a town in which there was relatively little commerce. In Annapolis today, the same phenomenon would be highly unusual and would point to some large, specific, and difficult issue like an insurance problem or competing claims to ownership. From the data collected in an attempt to understand the archaeological record came data shedding light on the contemporary social context of the project. The point is that all of the tours discussed here began with archaeological findings, and the discussions that flowed from the strictly archaeological portions were products of the search for meaning to attach to the finds, both meanings in the past and meanings for the present.

That it is proper for archaeologists to take up some of the seemingly nonarchaeological issues mentioned in these tours is substantiated by the fact that archaeologists are also members of societies, and most societies are capable of finding all kinds of political uses for all kinds of scientific and historical data. Archaeological data are no exception. Public presentations of the type offered by Archaeology in Public are simply a way for the producers of knowledge to acknowledge its contemporary social value and to take some of the responsibility for attaching meaning to it, as a way of guarding against its use by others for purposes entirely at odds with the intentions of the creators of that knowledge. Such a presentation, carried out critically, does not make an unchallengeable expert out of the investigator; rather, it makes the knowledge produced *more* available to the public at large, and members of the public are less likely to have such knowledge, particularly interpretations of the past, used against them.

11

Evaluating the Experiment

In chapter 1, I proposed that this book be read as a report on an experiment in critical archaeology. So far I have discussed the three components of a critical archaeological project: ethnographic findings, archaeological research, and archaeological practice. Although I have generally eschewed the language of scientific experimentation, the question remains as to how to judge results and determine whether Archaeology in Annapolis and Archaeology in Public are successful experiments. In this chapter, I discuss four approaches to evaluating the success of Archaeology in Public. These discussions focus on: (1) the logistical feasibility of opening archaeological sites to the public, (2) informal indicators of public acceptance of Archaeology in Public, (3) formal visitor evaluation conducted on site after tours, and (4) measures of success suggested by critical theory. In evaluating Archaeology in Public, I concentrate primarily on the site tour aspect of the project because that is the part of Archaeology in Public that is best developed and has been formally evaluated in the greatest detail.

Feasibility

An evaluation of Archaeology in Public begins by asking whether opening archaeological sites to the public, in a structured and rigorous way, is a feasible and reasonable way to do archaeology. After helping to provide an educational opportunity for more than 36,000 people at eight open sites for six seasons, I have come to the conclusion that Archaeology in Public demonstrates the feasibility of open sites, with certain qualifications. A detailed analysis of more than 1,000 visitor evaluation forms indicates that 97 percent of Archaeology in Public site visitors have found their tours "clear;" less than 2 percent have claimed not to have gained a better understanding of how interpretations of the past are produced; and more than 85 percent would walk three blocks to take another similar tour (Potter 1989: 373–80).

A full-scale program of critically informed site tours, professionally presented, can be conducted in the context of an on-going, research-oriented excavation. Such an endeavor depends, however, on a solid commitment of time, money, expertise, and other resources. As a rough rule of thumb, putting on a competent, full-scale interpretive program at an urban historical archaeological site increases the cost of a typical excavation by at least 25 percent. Archaeology in Public does not advocate the excavation of archaeological sites solely for purposes of interpretation, nor does it suggest that the needs of a public program should be put before the requirements of proper archaeology. However, to be effective and educational, public programs cannot be a secondary priority, either. To take one example, guide training takes time and will sometimes pull crew members out of their squares and off the site. At the same time, without adequate training, most archaeological workers—and student archaeologists in particular—will not be equipped to present a site tour that is legitimately educational. So, there is no question that the excavation of an open site goes more slowly than the excavation of a site that is not open.

Therefore, once an informed decision is made to open a site, there needs to be a firm commitment to an interpretive program. A useful goal is to attempt to do the interpretation as proficiently as the archaeology. A dig foreman is unlikely to tolerate mislabeled artifact bags, poorly drawn profiles, or out-of-focus photographs; by the same token, poorly delivered tours should not be accepted. Structurally speaking, one way to protect the integrity of both the archaeological and the interpretive components of a project is to keep their funding and administration separate. Coordination is essential, but it is very easy for one side or the other to be short-changed if both sides are supported from a common purse and if both are run, on a day-to-day basis, by the same person. In the experience of Archaeology in Annapolis, when a single individual is in charge of both excavation and interpretation, neither is done as well as it could be.

Further, presenting a high-quality public program involves two key moves. First, crew members should not be obligated to give tours. A guide who fears speaking in public and who does not want to give tours will communicate those fears to the audience. Without time-consuming and prohibitively expensive training, such a guide will never be comfortable enough to give good tours. Second, the participation of a media expert is essential. There are simply too many variables involved in effective public communication to leave the creation of a public program solely in the hands of people who have not been trained in the use of the media. The media should not dominate the message, and archaeologists should remain in full control of scholarly content. It is important to remember, however, that ineffective use of the media can kill a public interpretive program before it ever starts. Hiring a media consultant, to aid in signing a site and training guides, is the same thing an archaeologist does when consulting with a faunal expert or hiring an experienced remote sensing technician rather than undertaking, poorly, such tasks on his or her own.

Even with the costs involved, public interpretation benefits archaeology. Site archaeologists know that their analyses will be incorporated into tours, and they often end up listening to guides presenting elements of those analyses twenty-five or thirty times a day. This keeps the archaeologists on their toes, pushing them to think through their interpretations more frequently and more comprehensively. I would go so far as to argue that all archaeologists—and all archaeology—would benefit from imagining a public audience for archaeological results, even when there is *no* possibility of mounting a public interpretive program. We can all develop specific, appropriate attempts at archaeological practice by thinking of our work, *at all times*, as a performance. Further, there is the distinct possibility that hundreds of fresh perspectives on vexing archaeological features can help lead to valuable identifications, interpretations, and understandings for the archaeologist. This possibility is clearly enhanced by interpreters who attempt to reenfranchise visitors with control over the past by illuminating rather than mystifying archaeological techniques and method.

More specific prescriptions for mounting public programs may be found in Potter and Leone (1987). The short answer to the question of feasibility is that competent and sophisticated site tours can be presented and will be worthwhile as long as there is a clear commitment of time and money to mounting a public program as professional as the archaeology it reports on.

The foregoing assessment of feasibility is based on our experience in Annapolis, which is, in some ways, unique. Less frequent public access (weekly rather than daily site openings), greater reliance on printed materials, off-site static exhibits, and off-site public talks are all techniques that may be used to create a successful program of archaeological practice. The only nonnegotiable requirement in using any of these media to create a critical archaeology is acknowledgment; a critical interpretation in any form must place itself in relation to its authors, its audience, and the contemporary social world that surrounds them both. Beyond this single requirement, I recommend professional guidance in the use of various media. Slick publications or perfectly delivered tours are not a guarantee of a critically successful program of archaeological practice. However, even the most sophisticated message in the world will have little or no impact if it is poorly delivered. With a good, strong message in place, the next step is *not* to telephone me and ask for the name of the Archaeology in Public sign painter or brochure printer; the next step is to get good, local professional advice in matching an appropriate (large- *or* small-scale) media package to the particular circumstances of a specific project in a specific place. As with archaeological analyses, one size does not fit all when it comes to public programs.

Archaeology in Public and Historic Annapolis

Feasibility is only half the argument for attempting a program like Archaeology in Public someplace else. If such a program *can* be done, given the costs of doing so, the next question is, what kind of results does such a program produce or generate?

Archaeology in Annapolis has generated a good bit of local interest, as demonstrated by newspaper coverage, funding from the City Council, invitations to teach at nearby Anne Arundel Community College, and so on. This sort of response, which constitutes a positive, but informal evaluation of Archaeology in Public, is relatively commonplace and has been generated by many other archaeological projects. The one local response to our work worth focusing on here in some detail is that of Historic Annapolis, which is best understood in terms of the three principal benefits Historic Annapolis draws from its cosponsorship of the project.

First, Historic Annapolis often ends up wearing the black hat in local politics. The organization is not afraid to take unpopular positions. For example, Historic Annapolis opposed the construction of a parking garage for the Anne Arundel General Hospital in the 1970s and a decade later stood strongly against the erection of a private residence near the

One result of Archaeology in Public.

Wm. Paca Garden, which is operated by Historic Annapolis. For taking stands like these, Historic Annapolis is sometimes attacked in the local press by both editorial writers and editorial cartoonists. At the same time, Archaeology in Annapolis is one Historic Annapolis program that is almost universally appreciated in the city and that generates considerable positive publicity for the organization.

A second benefit is that Archaeology in Annapolis gives the organization the character of a research institution. It is important for Historic Annapolis to be able to cite its research activities because it uses its superior knowledge, as validated by research, as the public basis for its claims for local authority. As the argument goes, Historic Annapolis knows a great deal about Annapolis history and architecture and therefore deserves a loud voice in local development and other issues. Archaeology in Annapolis is one means by which Historic Annapolis knows what it knows. Historic Annapolis gains the opportunity to use Archaeology in Annapolis in this way by granting a considerable amount of academic freedom to members of the archaeological project to use both archaeological data and material from the Historic Annapolis data bank to come to their own scholarly conclusions. All Historic Annapolis requires is a modest disclaimer, and with this disclaimer Archaeology in Annapolis members have published interpretations that easily could be construed as critical of the organization.

Yet another benefit is property-specific. On rare occasions, Historic Annapolis has asked members of Archaeology in Annapolis to testify at public hearings on the archaeological value of properties scheduled for development, as a way of blocking or slowing down construction. Much to its credit, Historic Annapolis makes such requests infrequently, understanding the risks it would run if it politicized the archaeological project.

None of these uses of Archaeology in Annapolis by Historic Annapolis is necessarily a goal of Archaeology in Annapolis. However, the value Historic Annapolis finds in the project is a function of Historic Annapolis's recognition of the esteem in which Archaeology in Annapolis, or archaeology in general, is held by Annapolitans. In that light, Historic Annapolis's use of Archaeology in Annapolis represents, to some extent, the impact of Archaeology in Annapolis in the local community.

Few archaeologists work with sponsors like Historic Annapolis; there cannot be more than two dozen local preservation organizations with the resources and the interest to take on an archaeological project in the way Historic Annapolis has. However, many archaeologists work under contract to clients, and one anonymous reviewer of my original manuscript wondered, in a marginal note, just how clients might react to a public program like the ones we have put on in Annapolis. Of course, some of the clients who require archaeological services want as little publicity as possible and would refuse to support any kind of public program. Other clients recognize the public relations value of publicly interpreted archaeology. As for being willing to put up with archaeological interpretations that are critical (in the non-Frankfurt school sense), most archaeological clients, unlike Historic Annapolis, are not in the business of making history; they make bridges, sewage treatment plants, and new highways. This eliminates for most archaeologist-client relationships one of the most fertile grounds for conflict between Archaeology in Annapolis and Historic Annapolis. In any event, the archaeologist-client relationship does not automatically foreclose the possibility of critically informed archaeological interpretation. The necessary first step is the kind of negotiation that preceded the establishment of Archaeology in Annapolis.

Formal Visitor Evaluation

The next important question to consider is what, precisely, audience members learn from Archaeology in Public interpretations. Since 1982, Archaeology in Public has employed a one-page questionnaire, completed by self-selected visitors at the conclusion of their tours, to monitor the impact of site tours. The initial format was based on a model provided by a major source of support for Archaeology in Public, the Maryland Humanities Council. Their form was designed to evaluate the quality of presentation in the programs it sponsored. Archaeology in Annapolis revised that form with a view to collecting data in four areas: (1) visitor interest in archaeological presentations in media beyond the site tour, (2) visitor demographics, (3) visitor assessments of the quality of the presentation, and (4) the capacity of the tours—both individually and as a medium—to contribute to the kind of enlightenment or illumination that is the goal of any critical theory. Of the four kinds of data we have collected, those that relate to "critical value" are of primary concern here.

A clear audience profile emerges from the demographic data. The typical Archaeology in Public visitor lives more than 40 miles from Annapolis (47.5 percent do), will be spending a day or less in the city (58.8 percent do), and visits the site with his or her family (60 percent do). However, approximately 12.5 percent of the people who fill out evaluation forms are Annapolitans, and given the predilection of locals *not* to be treated as tourists, the figure of 12.5 percent in all likelihood underestimates the proportion of local residents in the audience of Archaeology in Public site tours. Beyond that, it is common for people who live or work near a site to visit regularly to check on the progress at the site. Few of these regulars are represented in the data from visitors evaluation forms. So, although many visitors to Annapolis take Archaeology in Public tours, the program reaches a significant number of Annapolitans as well.

With regard to tour quality, the extremely positive responses mentioned above suggest that most visitors have liked what they have heard in Archaeology in Public tours. They seem to think that the tours are well presented, and that their site visit has been educational. This means that Archaeology in Public has mastered its medium and thereby created the *possibility* of education. In terms of the experimental nature of Archaeology in Public, these data offer quantified substantiation for the claim I made earlier, that it is possible, without great hardship, to present high-quality tours while conducting archaeological excavations with appropriate scientific respect for the archaeological record. While these responses confirm the technical quality of the presentation of Archaeology in Public site tours, and the feeling of visitors that they have learned something, such results do not demonstrate *what* visitors have learned.

This is an important issue because most visitors come to an open site with some opinion of archaeology, perhaps from *National Geographic*, perhaps from *Raiders of the Lost Ark*. Given that most visitors do arrive with knowledge of and opinions about archaeology, and a whole host of other issues central to the message of any given tour, it is important to learn from visitors specifically what they have learned from a tour, and whether what they have learned is what Archaeology in Public has intended to teach. Because visitors arrive with all kinds of ideas—they are *not* blank slates—it is important to be aware of the possibility of visitors fitting Archaeology in Public interpretations into their previous knowledge through some kind of transformational process. Needless to say, if and when such transformations take place, and despite a visitor's approval of the educational value of their tour, that tour serves only to support and replicate a visitor's previous understandings; when this takes place, the message of the tour is coopted and education in a critical sense may not occur.

In order to move beyond questions that simply measure the preconceptions of visitors and their predisposition to like anything archaeological, Archaeology in Public began, at the Shiplap House site in 1985, asking one or more questions requiring a short answer, in addition to questions that could be answered with a check mark or a circle. Such questions were intended to allow Archaeology in Public to ascertain the success of the tour as an educational tool. These short-answer questions were designed specifically to find out if visitors learned things from the tour that they did not know beforehand, or things that they did not expect to learn. Questions of this nature on the Main Street site evaluation form in 1986 pertained directly to the argument of the tour. It was thought that even if they were not effective for evaluation, they would at least help visitors grasp the tour's main points by having them repeat for the questionnaire what they had just been told.

Shiplap Short Answers

The Shiplap House site tour was largely about the Georgian worldview and the use of archaeology at that particular site. This information was expected to improve visitors' understanding of the penetration of that way of thinking into Annapolis. Georgian ideas were contrasted to their antecedents in the realm of ceramic tableware and architecture. Shiplap House was presented as an excellent place to examine archaeologically the penetration of Georgian thinking because, first, it was built early enough (c. 1713) to be occupied from the time that Georgian ideas were introduced to Annapolis through the time by which they had become well-accepted and even "old hat," and, second, because it had a number of eighteenth-century occupants with a wide range of occupations. The tour concluded with the suggestion that the ideas called the Georgian worldview are important to us today because they serve to organize much of contemporary social and economic life, while being treated as givens or taken-for-granteds, rather than as social and cultural creations with beginnings, histories, and uses. The tour attempted to use archaeological evidence to demonstrate that because human interests played a role in the establishment of certain aspects of our contemporary lives, those parts of life are not inevitable. The way things are today is not the only way things could have turned out.

In an attempt to determine whether the tour had any impact, in a critical sense, the evaluation form posed the following question:

What did you learn about Archaeology that you did not know before you visited the site?

Three blank lines were left for visitor responses.

Of the 318 visitors at Shiplap who filled out evaluation forms, 239, or 75.2 percent, answered this question, most with a phrase or a sentence, some with more. Willingness to respond to such a question certainly validates the effort to collect visitor data in such a manner and also suggests a commitment on the part of visitors to the educational value of the site tour. Of those who answered the question, only 7 (2.9 percent) said that they had not learned anything from the tour, most citing previous archaeological experiences. Of those who did learn something new, some gained understandings that could be labeled "critical," whereas others did not.

The principal kind of noncritical knowledge gained from the site tour was a greater understanding of the techniques of archaeological excavation. Of the 239 respondents, 104 (43.5 percent) learned about field techniques. Their responses were of two kinds: some cited a specific archaeo-logical technique, like the grid or stratigraphy, and some simply mentioned the meticulousness of the work. These answers are taken to represent non-critical knowledge, for although the specific facts may be new to visitors, field techniques constitute a category about which most visitors likely expected to learn from the tour. New facts filled a preexisting conceptual category, without affecting the construction of the category itself.

Far more interesting, from a critical perspective, are responses that sug-gest a visitor learned something that he or she did not necessarily expect to learn. Such learning concerns things that the visitor did not know that he or she did not know and consists of knowledge that challenges that individual's categories of knowledge. Visitor responses to the Shiplap tour that seem to indicate this kind of learning fall into three broad categories.

The first group of responses show visitors learning something *new* about archaeology, rather than simply collecting the facts they expected to learn. Typical of such responses are those that register surprise concerning (1) archaeology being conducted in an urban setting and applied to the recent past, (2) the amount of lab work required after excavation, and (3) the fact that even the smallest and "commonest" artifacts can carry impor-tant information. Each of these "surprises" represents the replacement of one idea about archaeology with another, in the mind of a visitor. Such new insights are similar to critical insights because they challenge previous knowledge and categories, rather than simply adding new information to unexamined categories. Among the most pointed responses of this type are the following:

Q: What did you learn about archaeology that you did not know before you visited the site?

A: • The questions they ask to find answers to.
   • That questions serve as motivation for their digging.
   • How archaeologists operate from theory to reality.

Learning that archaeologists dig to answer questions, rather than digging to find things, implies the understanding that archaeological data, like any scientific or historical data, are collected from a particular point of view, which is one of the most important and most accessible insights of critical theory. Responses like those cited above seem to show an under-standing of the role played by any question in shaping answers to it. Such responses were written by 16 visitors, or 6.7 percent of those responding to the question.

The second broad class of responses that may signal the dawning of a critical awareness are those showing visitors seeming to leave a site thinking that archaeology is about more than excavation, digging, and artifacts. Someone who claims to have learned about "the connection of archaeology to behavior" may well have learned to challenge the traditional popular perception that archaeology is about objects. This response, like those in the previous category, challenge previously held knowledge about archaeology itself and go the next step, by suggesting that a visitor has reconsidered the boundaries and relations between archaeology and other disciplines. Thus, two kinds of taken-for-granted knowledge are called into question. The following are examples of such responses:

Q: What did you learn about archaeology that you did not know before you visited the site?

A: • Connection of archaeology to behavior—very interesting.
   • How the digging is done. The relationship between archaeology and culture history.
   • Learned about the Georgian order—how to use archaeology to study the imposition of new patterns of living on the people.
   • Georgian period as a time of reorganizing family living structure.
   • Structure of the house indicates the philosophy of the day.

Of the 239 responses to this question, 83 (34.7 percent) were of this type. The 83 responses can be divided into two subsets, those that say that archaeology can tell us about the Georgian worldview without directly defining it (n = 29) and those that are more specific about the idea that archaeology can be used to answer questions not popularly perceived as archaeological (n = 54). Either type of response may offer some reason to hope that visitors, using their newly acquired abilities to see beyond the cultural myths about the nature of archaeology, could possibly be better able to pierce other instances of cultural mystification or ideology. This is by no means a certainty, only a hope.

Responses of the third kind are those in which visitors demonstrate a willingness to understand archaeology as relevant to today. At one level such a response is like those previously discussed: it suggests an ability to challenge the idea that archaeologists dig up old things unconnected to today by anything other than their curio value. However, in the context of the tour of the Shiplap House site, which was about the origins of some typically unexamined aspects of contemporary life, acknowledgment of archaeology's relevance to today may indicate a willingness to challenge the inevitability of some of the foundations of contemporary life. Examples of this kind of response include the following:

Q: What did you learn about archaeology that you did not know before you visited the site?

A: • Principles of the Georgian Period relating to the start of the industrial revolution.
   • Some of the reasons for digging in the site and how you tie it to today.
   • More about today's living (symmetry, workplace habits, etc.) and how it is based on early 1700s. Very interesting.
   • I learned that it teaches us—in the present day—about how some of our living habits evolved. So a study of the past really teaches us about our present.
   • Correlation of society 200 years ago with today. Industrial Revolution, mass production beginnings.

Of the 239 respondents, 25 (10.5 percent) gave answers of this kind.

Two conclusions may be drawn from these responses. First, some visitors clearly think that archaeology is relevant to today, that it contributes to our understanding of the roots of contemporary life. The critical position is that seeing contemporary taken-for-granteds as having histories makes them more open to question and challenge. However, the relevance of archaeology—or of any historical discipline—can be viewed in two ways: in the critical way, in which the present writes the past; or in a more conventional way with the present portrayed as an inevitable and natural outgrowth of the past, which is valuable as tool for teaching us how to prepare for the future. For some visitors, the Shiplap tour apparently supported this second position. Interpretations like this are likely to continue as long as biological evolution is our primary cultural metaphor for long-term change of any sort, including social change. The idea of "continuity of evolution into our own day"—expressed by a visitor as a lesson of the Shiplap tour—makes change inevitable and its direction beyond the control of human agency. It is the purpose of any historical critical theory to oppose such formulations because they teach individuals to be passive victims of history rather than agents for change. So, the preceding responses, and others like them, demonstrate both the possibility of imparting critical perspectives to visitors and also some of the impediments to their embracing this point of view.

Beyond responses in these three broad classes, several combined elements of the second and third into an understanding of archaeology as being about more than objects and as having the power to illuminate contemporary life. Such responses include the following:

Q: What did you learn about Archaeology that you did not know before you visited the site?

A: • Process of archaeological digging. How artifacts dug up show past story of how people lived and how it relates to today. (Nice touch!)
   • It was interesting that archaeology was explaining sociological questions—the idea of Georgian culture evolving to the present—finding when it started.
   • The connections between archaeological data and the way people thought and lived and the connection to modern life.

Although these responses do not suggest that the people who wrote them are ready to change the world, they do suggest that the rank-and-file American museum-goer may be prepared to think critically, or at least experiment with critical perspectives.

In all, visitor responses to the Shiplap tour suggest a mixed success. At least 95 respondents (39.7 percent) answered the short-answer question in a way that indicated, if not a fully formed critical perspective, at least the basis for thinking critically, which is, to be sure, a different thing. Such visitors clearly have done some intellectual work rather than just collecting archaeological facts to paste into some mental stamp album, and this unquestionably counts as a success. Those visitors for whom the tour "failed" are those whose preconceptions were reinforced. This process of reinforcement will be discussed in greater detail later in this chapter.

Main Street Short Answers

The evaluation form for the Main Street site tour in 1986 included the short-answer question we asked at Shiplap, which received fairly similar responses, along with two new questions:

1. What connection do you see between this site and everyday life today?
2. What did you learn about how Annapolis presents George Washington?

The first of these new questions was answered by 78.5 percent of the 219 people who filled out evaluation forms at the Main Street site, and it received a variety of responses. There was no particular "right" answer to this question, but the best that could be hoped for, from a critical perspective, was a statement that the site contains archaeological evidence of the beginnings of some taken-for-granted element of contemporary daily life. Tours given by some guides said this explicitly; all contained the elements from which a perceptive visitor could draw such a conclusion. In their responses, some visitors simply affirmed that the tour showed that there was a connection between the site and everyday life today, but did not specify the connection. Others repeated a part of the tour, typically the part about shifts to items of material culture indicating a Georgian worldview. Some visitors mentioned that the present shapes or manipulates the past. And a few (7 of 172, or 4.1 percent) did mention specifically that the site offered evidence of the roots of some contemporary taken-for-granteds. This is, or is the basis for, a critical perspective.

However, a plurality of visitors who responded to the question, 64 (or 37.2 percent), gave responses such as the following:

Q: What connection do you see between this site and everyday life today?

A: • We need to know about the past to understand our present and future.
   • Better understanding of how things evolved (vacations, etc.).
   • Life goes on.
   • History repeats itself.
   • The continuity between history and life today.
   • Everything. Whatever exists today is built from or on the past.

These, and a host of other similar responses show visitors using an understanding of history entirely antithetical to that used by Archaeology in Public as a way of understanding the tour presented to them by Archaeology in Public. "Life goes on" or "history repeats itself" are responses that show visitors understanding history as composed of objective facts and the present as a consequence of the past largely beyond the reach of contemporary action—despite the use by Archaeology in Public of a theory based on the relativity of versions of the past and the efficacy of contemporary action to change things. People who say the things listed above use history to trap themselves in their present lives, and the traps are so powerful that they are able to make Archaeology in Public site tours a part of the trap. This is probably a commentary on the inability of a fifteen-minute archaeological site tour to "undo" a lifetime of previous learning.

Beyond the set of responses demonstrating visitor preconceptions, there is a fascinating bit of contradiction in responses to this question. Some visitors found that the tour taught them how similar the present is to the past. Others found just the opposite. And several visitors found that the tour highlighted both the similarities *and* the differences between then and now. While this is a good example of the three blind people describing an elephant, it is something more; in either of the two extremes there is the danger of mystification.

Those who learn from the tour about the similarities between past and present risk losing the ability to see the real otherness of the eighteenth century, particularly the different conditions of daily life and the different cultural "givens." Without a clear perspective on those givens, the degree of change between then and now is underestimated, which makes it all the easier to naturalize. Take for example something as innocent-sounding as calling a privy an "eighteenth-century bathroom." This easy equation replaces an absolute difference in kind with a relative difference in degree, which effectively disguises the fact that during the second half of the nineteenth century waste treatment and sanitation in most urban areas was transformed from a private concern to a public one. But once changes like these are minimized and naturalized, it becomes difficult to locate the agents of change and the interests served by it.

Thus it would seem that the alternative understanding, that the eighteenth century was very different from today, is intellectually "safer" in terms of providing a viewpoint that makes individuals less vulnerable to having history used against them. This is probably the case *except* for respondents who discussed the difference between then and now and phrased this understanding as a celebration of progress, not hiding but glorifying the agents of change. The difference of the past is used to validate modern life, as if to say, "look how far we have come." Although such a perspective does not naturalize change, it takes as a foregone conclusion that *any* change that helped bring about our contemporary way of life has been a change for the better (on this point, see Smith 1985: x–xi).

Thus, both perspectives gained from the tour have the potential to be used in support of the organization of contemporary American society and life. Critical theory, or at least critical archaeology, does not automatically seek to bring down the establishment, but it does reject research and interpretation that support the status quo by placing it and its antecedents beyond examination, question, and challenge. The conclusion here, as above, is to use responses to this question to discover the structures of popular historical thinking that typically absorb and transform the interpretations presented by Archaeology in Public. When discovered, frames of reference like "history is cyclical" or "things really don't change that much" can be discussed explicitly in subsequent tours.

The second short-answer question—What did you learn about how Annapolis presents George Washington?—is fairly complex. It asks visitors to repeat the tour's foil, the idea the tour attempts to counteract. A response that shows that a visitor has grasped the point of the tour is not a simple, declarative sentence, "George Washington was the father of his country," but rather, a conditional statement, "Annapolis presents George Washington as the father of his country." The ideal response goes one step further, to say *why* Annapolis presents George Washington as the father of his country. Despite, or perhaps because of, the complexity of the question, and the kind of response it called for, it elicited a much narrower range of responses than the previous question, for which there was no clearly articulated, direct response available in the tour. Of the 174 respondents to this question, 119 (68.4 percent) indicated that they had absorbed some part of the tour's argument that contemporary portrayals of George Washington, emphasizing certain aspects of his visits to Annapolis, are used to attract "quality tourists" and to control their behavior in Annapolis by subtly making Washington appear to have been something he could not possibly have been, a tourist in the modern sense of the term. Some visitors, but very few (2.9 percent) got the idea reversed, learning from the tour that George Washington *was* a tourist in Annapolis. Some (7.5 percent) claimed to have learned nothing about how Annapolis presents George Washington. And others (12.6 percent) learned things entirely beyond the intention of the tour, principally that Annapolis presents George Washington either as a heroic figure or more as a "real person" than is usually the case.

Among the respondents who indicated that they understood the tour, there is a relatively large range of ways in which their understanding is articulated. Some respondents suggested that they had learned the idea that history can be used long before they ever visited the site:

Q: What did you learn about how Annapolis presents George
   Washington?

A: • It's always fascinating to see the ways that events or history can be
     manipulated in different ways.
   • For its own benefit, as we often use history.

- Like everything else, truth is presented selectively.
- Typical manner in which writers and historians place emphasis on what their perceptions were to start with & then write to substantiate them.
- I wasn't surprised about what I heard. This is the way I would have guessed it was.

Other visitors gave fragmentary responses suggesting only that Annapolis presents a biased, slanted, or inaccurate version of the past:

Q: What did you learn about how Annapolis presents George Washington?

A: • Vacations at a time when the theory of vacation was nonexistent.
  - Somewhat biased.
  - He was portrayed as a figure not from his own time, but from the time of the portrayal.
  - He's presented as a "tourist" but vacations weren't really in existence until about 100 years ago.
  - He was a tourist 100 years before tourism was invented.
  - As a tourist which is inaccurate.
  - As a tourist which didn't exist.

Yet others suggested that Annapolis has presented its past in a self-serving way:

Q: What did you learn about how Annapolis presents George Washington?

A: • George was a "vacationer" before it existed: if he came here, so should a lot of people.
  - From their perspective/advantage.
  - He was used as a tourist draw—obviously George slept here.
  - Annapolis presents George Washington as a tourist. They do this because of the economical aspects. Money is all they are concerned with.
  - False, what they want you to know.
  - Biased by self interest.
  - Presented him as a tourist, perhaps as a role model for today's tourists.
  - I found it interesting to discover how he is "used" to promote tourism today.

Some responses are so complete that they sound almost like paraphrases of the tour:

Q: What did you learn about how Annapolis presents George
    Washington?

A: • I learned that although vacations are a modern invention (c. 1760s
     or after) Annapolis presents Washington as a "visitor" role model.
   • He is presented in a way, it seems, to enhance tourism. He is presented as a tourist when in reality he probably was not.
   • Annapolis is a city of tourism and they paint a picture of "George
     Washington the tourist on vacation" when back then vacations as
     we know them probably didn't even exist.
   • It's as a role model for tourists (not truly consistent with history).

Whether these responses indicate that actual learning has occurred, it is at least the case that a visitor who has heard the argument, called it back to mind, and written it out has internalized the point of the tour deeply enough so that he or she may reflect on it later, off site.

Another interesting group of responses call Annapolis's use of George Washington good advertising or shrewd public relations:

Q: What did you learn about how Annapolis presents George
    Washington?

A: • They had great P.R. men!
   • Good P.R.
   • They use him in an advertising sort of way.
   • Historians were proud of GW visiting their city and when tourism
     began here a P.R. person "directed" history to emphasize the
     leisure activities over the business activities of his visits.

There are two ways to respond to such responses. One could argue that by seeing the use of George Washington *only* as a marketing tool, visitors risk trivializing the larger issue of the political use of the past. On the other hand, it is useful to recall the concept of assimilation, the impulse to transform new information to make it fit into preexisting mental categories, the process that allows some visitors to see Archaeology in Public as a version of Colonial Williamsburg, despite the content of Archaeology in Public tours. This process is partly cognitive but not exclusively; it is probably also an example of the power of capitalism, as an ideology, to coopt opposition. In the case of Annapolis, visitors attempted to place Annapolis's representation and use of George Washington into the spot in their minds where examples of representation (or misrepresentation) for specific purposes reside. That place seems to be alongside cases of overaggressive public relations and false advertising of the sort often exposed on television's *60 Minutes*. This information suggests the circumstances under which typical members of the American public have encountered ideas like those academically termed "critical theory." These popular forms of discourse can then become important points of reference for constructing and presenting critical interpretations. Good examples, accessible to members of the public, can be used both as analogies serving as starting points ("The way Annapolis uses George Washington is similar to the way that. . .") and also as foils ". . . and while Juan Valdez is probably only useful for selling coffee, the use of George Washington in Annapolis has far deeper implications. . ."). The point is that by making reference to popularly held ideas that resemble critical theories, it may be easier to create a critical consciousness and bring about real illumination.

The 1986 Main Street tour was the first about which there was any measurable disagreement. Two examples:

Q: What did you learn about how Annapolis presents George Washington?

A: • They slant the old boy's activities to their own benefit. But who's to say that he didn't vacate? A man of wealth with others to take care of his responsibilities? Surely the concept of holiday is not so new.
   • He shopped & went to the races & taverns. He was not classified as a tourist. The guide said tourism started about 100 years ago. I think she was about 4,000 years off.

There were not many visitors who disagreed, and disagreements usually focused on relatively small points. While the generation of conflict for the sake of conflict is not the goal of Archaeology in Public, we do take it as a measure of success that at Main Street, we created an educational context in which visitors could interact with our interpretation and disagree with it. A visitor who disagrees is not a passive consumer of historical facts, and encouraging active and thoughtful consumption of historical information *is* a goal of Archaeology in Public (for more on this phenomenon, see Potter and Leone 1992: 494).

Questionnaire Summary

The broad conclusion that may be drawn from a close analysis of the short-answer responses to both the Shiplap and Main Street tours is that

Archaeology in Public is a mixed success in imparting critical insights into the organization of contemporary social and economic life. Some visitors have gotten the point. Others have missed it. Yet others have claimed to understand the point, phrasing their claim in the language of an entirely antithetical point of view. This last group may be composed of people who bring such strong preconceptions to a tour that what they hear from guides can only become evidence in support of those previous understandings. This is the transformational process alluded to throughout this chapter. As noted above, this process has both a cognitive part and an ideological part. The ideological part of the process, called absorption, is what Barnett and Silverman refer to when they say that "opposing views do not challenge the ideology at its root, but are accommodations with it" (1979: 72) and that "often one remains internal to the ideology through the very form of appearing to break free" (1979: 77).

The strength of people's previous understandings and their predisposition to like anything archaeological, while potentially useful to Archaeology in Annapolis in the local political arena, are impediments to critical education and may well account for a curious phenomenon, the fact that strenuous objections to the messages of Archaeology in Public are almost unknown. Although Archaeology in Public does not casually publicize its use of Marxism, its interpretations have become, in small increments, increasingly radical. Yet, there have been virtually no challenges. This lack of serious challenge could be simply a product of context; visitors may consider it inappropriate to loudly confront a friendly young interpreter presenting a short, free tour. Historic Annapolis may have decided that such a performance does not have the capacity to alter dramatically anybody's thinking or even begin to shape behavior. This surmise may be the basis for the organization's relative lack of censorship of a program that at least some Historic Annapolis officials know to have a radical message and the goal of affecting its audience. More unaccountable, given the profile of the average Historic Annapolis volunteer interpreter as the spouse of a career military officer or a corporate executive, is the lack of challenge to the Archaeology in Annapolis point of view when presented in considerable detail and with considerable vigor at Historic Annapolis interpreter training sessions and in courses at Anne Arundel Community College offered by members of the Archaeology in Annapolis staff and attended by Historic Annapolis interpreters. My best guess is that when the ideas behind Archaeology in Public are presented as ideas, but without easily attacked labels like "Marxism" and so on, many Annapolitans with a commitment to historical interpretation find them worth thinking about.

The lack of serious challenge to Archaeology in Public guides may indicate that Archaeology in Public tours have not made themselves clear, that the ideas are old news, or that the ideas, as presented, are just too easily assimilated into or captured by preexisting conceptual categories and do not adequately challenge the categories themselves. For the tours to be truly effective, and truly critical, they must challenge the structure of visitor knowledge as well as add to its content. The way to inspire such rethinking might be simply to be even more explicit about the ideas against which a critical approach is arrayed. Since we have found the concept of evolution to be a stumbling block, perhaps cultural evolution and the ideas it may be used to support should be a central topic of a future tour. But ultimately, it indicates no failure on the part of the site tours to suggest that critical enlightenment is too complex and faces obstacles too large to be inspired by a fifteen-minute archaeological site tour. Such enlightenment is more appropriate to expect at the conclusion of a visitor's two-hour experience with the full, multimedia Archaeology in Public we hope to mount.

Long-Range Outcomes of Archaeology in Public

Skirted throughout this chapter is an articulation of precisely what would constitute the best possible response to a site tour, from a critical perspective. It is worth recalling, at this point, that in the classic formulations of critical theory by the Frankfurt school, enlightenment is intended to serve as the basis for corrective action to rectify social inequality. The two most fully realized critical theories—political Marxism and psychoanalysis—both have action steps. In Marxism, enlightenment leads to revolution; and in psychoanalysis, understanding the early childhood basis for adult neurotic behavior allows the patient to deal with the past, dismiss it, and be rid of neurotic behavior (Leone n.d.). Archaeology in Public clearly attempts to achieve enlightenment, specifically enlightenment as to the origins of certain aspects of contemporary social and economic life. The evidence cited above suggests some success in encouraging some people to move some aspects of the structure of daily life from the category of given or natural to the realm of the culturally created and challengeable. But what is the action step, the behavior Archaeology in Public wants to inspire, and the consequent behavioral evidence for success in educating the public? What does Archaeology in Public want to get people to do?

The principal behavioral response or action step Archaeology in Public attempts to elicit from visitors is *active* questioning, mainly about the pre-sentation of the past and aspects of daily life not normally considered open to question. Our hope has been to help our visitors become more critical consumers of historical information. For each of the tours mentioned in chapter 10, there is a question or a type of question Archaeology in Public wanted to teach visitors to ask of other historic sites. At the Victualling Warehouse in 1982: "How do you know that?" At Victualling in 1983: "How do present circumstances shape this presentation of the past?" At the same site in 1984: "What were some of the alternative ideas discarded in designing this exhibit?" And "Why?" At the State House Inn in 1985: "What subtle lessons are encoded in this aspect of everyday life?" Finally, at Main Street in 1986: "What is this version of history trying to get me to do?" Any of these is a simple enough question, but none is regularly inspired by most presentations of the past in the United States. The inten-tion of "Archaeology in Public," derived from critical theory, is that by asking such questions visitors can take more control over their consump-tion of historical knowledge, making them less likely to have history used against them. Archaeology in Public stops short of prescribing a particular understanding of the past that is better than any others, given its commit-ment to liberation and its desire to avoid replacing one rigid orthodoxy with another. The difficulty with the goal of teaching visitors a new mode of questioning, from the perspective of evaluation, is that the truest indi-cations of a successful tour will be virtually invisible. They will come next week when a visitor goes home and reads the new *National Geographic*, or next semester in a history class, or next summer on a trip to Colonial Williamsburg. How best to gauge the *critical* success of Archaeology in Public programs is a question as yet without a complete answer.

Any Archaeology in Public tour has the dual intent of inspiring people to question presentations of history and trying to help them learn how to do so. All have explicitly acknowledged their place in the history-making process of Annapolis. Beyond that, among the tours discussed in detail in chapter 10, the Main Street tour was particularly deeply rooted in findings from the ethnographic component of Archaeology in Annapolis. That tour, more clearly than any other Archaeology in Public offering, follows the critical prescription for putting on display social and political relation-ships hidden by local history. Of a tour like this, further questions of inten-tion and impact must be asked. What was the purpose of telling Annapolitans and visitors about the sometimes tense relationship between visitors and residents, as was done at Main Street?

The situation surrounding the Main Street tour is nicely illustrated by a major concern we had during the training sessions, namely, making sure that the tour, as delivered, was not insulting to its audience. The tour, largely about tourism in Annapolis, was given to an audience that was *at least* 80 percent tourists. (This is an excellent illustration of the idea that any critical theory is in part about itself.)

Was the tour, which discussed Annapolis's need to control visitor behavior, actually trying to tell visitors to stay away? Did it expose Annapolis's use of George Washington in an attempt to help visitors do exactly as they pleased while in town? No, on both counts. However, the tour did intend to remind visitors that whatever else Annapolis is—yachting center, mecca of Georgian architecture, upscale shopping enclave—it is also *home* to 32,000 people. This may seem a small point, but with no language barrier, no currency exchange difficulties, and relatively easy access, it is easy for visitors to think that they are in some version or extension of their own homes and should therefore have the run of the place. In short, it is easy for visitors to forget that they are visitors. By reminding them, gently, of that status, it may be that a tour based on the roots of tourism helps visitors better understand some of the steps Annapolis takes to protect itself.

On the other hand, what did the tour have to say to Annapolitans? Did it intend to suggest that Annapolis is and has been deceitful and wrong in its use of George Washington to attempt to control visitor behavior? Again, the answer is no. The tour suggested that *any* presentation of history is a selection, slanted to the social needs surrounding its creation, and that the use of George Washington was simply a particularly creative use of history to help solve a very real problem. If there is any lesson for the city of Annapolis in being reminded of its dependence on visitors and their money, it is simply that any attempt to solve problems between residents and visitors that forgets the city's dependence on visitors risks an arrogance that could, to use a cliché, kill the goose that laid the golden egg.

The local political goal of the Main Street tour was not revolutionary. It did not seek to inspire the end of tourism in Annapolis nor did it seek to strengthen one side, residents or tourists, against the other. Rather, it simply attempted to remind each side of its dependence on the other in the hope that by acknowledging the nature of the relationship, along with the fact that the distinction between residents and tourists is not a natural division, but a constantly renegotiated cultural creation, both sides could coexist more happily and more productively. One might argue that in comparison with some issues taken up by various critical theories, the archaeology of tourism is a trivial pursuit. In some contexts, the archaeology of tourism might be insignificant, but in a city that has depended on visitors of one sort or another for literally hundreds of years, the archaeology of tourism is not unimportant.

Summary

This chapter has examined the attempts of Archaeology in Annapolis and Archaeology in Public to gauge the impact and measure the success of an archaeological project informed by critical theory. This discussion has centered on evaluating the public programs aspect of Archaeology in Annapolis, trusting that peer evaluation of the strictly archaeological component of Archaeology in Annapolis will be forthcoming as other members of the project staff, more directly involved in the archaeology itself, begin to publish on it.

To rephrase the results of both informal and formal evaluation, it is clear that short site tours, delivered by student-archaeologists, are an effective medium for communicating with the public and can be presented without an undue disruption of primary archaeological activities on a site. From this standpoint, Archaeology in Public has been a fully successful experiment. However, knowing that we can speak to people effectively is not the same as knowing *what* we are able to teach. Results of visitor evaluations call into question the degree to which Archaeology in Public site tours reproduce and reinforce old knowledge rather than creating new understandings. Finally, given the goals of any critical theory, which include altered behavior based on new understandings of the nature of knowledge and the conditions of life, serious questions remain as to whether the critical success of a public interpretive program is measurable, in that the new behavior Archaeology in Public attempts to inspire occurs off site and is, in any case, largely introspective. In all, the question of evaluating a program like Archaeology in Public is not unlike the problem faced by the Sisyphus of Albert Camus. Even if its ultimate effects appear unmeasurable, the attitude of self-reflection represented by evaluation is essential to any critical theory and in the case of Archaeology in Annapolis, it seems fair to claim some measure of success.

12

Conclusions

In chapter 1, I described both this book and Archaeology in Annapolis as experiments in the application of critical theory to historical archaeology. The results of the Archaeology in Annapolis experiment are the subject of this chapter. I also discuss the applicability of a critical approach to other archaeological contexts.

Results of the Experiment

The results of the experiment can be assessed in terms of the application of critical theory to archaeology and the application of critical archaeology to Annapolis.

Critical Theory and Archaeology

Critical theory, when applied to archaeology, has two expressions, one logistical and the other social. Logistically, critical theory can be seen as an attempt to create an archaeological practice, parallel to the concept of practice in many other disciplines. For Archaeology in Annapolis, archaeological practice has consisted of the presentation of archaeological techniques, methods, and conclusions to the interested public. As I noted in chapter 11, a full-scale program of archaeological interpretation can add 25 percent to the cost of an excavation. Fund-raising to meet these costs often requires that archaeologists explore unfamiliar sources of funding like humanities councils, arts councils, and groups that sponsor historical celebrations. In addition, an on-site interpretive program requires careful coordination between a project's interpretive aspect and its research aspect to ensure that neither is compromised.

These challenges are daunting but not insurmountable. Archaeology in Public demonstrates that from a strictly logistical standpoint, it is feasible to create a performance-based archaeological practice informed by critical theory. Beyond the logistical possibilities, the use of critical theory has provided a significant practical benefit for Archaeology in Annapolis. Archaeological vandalism and looting are considerable problems in the middle Atlantic region and in the nation at large, but not in Annapolis. The openness of our work and the respect we try to show our visitors, both underpinned by a critical approach, have, without doubt, contributed to the lack of archaeological vandalism in Annapolis. Critical theory is certainly not the only tool for counteracting vandalism, but it has helped in Annapolis.

More important are the social questions that surround the application of critical theory to archaeology. As formulated by members of the Frankfurt school, critical theory is about discovering, exposing, and overcoming domination and the hegemony of powerful interests. Unlike most of Marxist archaeology, which is content to find the social relations described by Marx in the archaeological record (Spriggs 1984), critical archaeology is concerned with ideology, dominance, and resistance in the present and the ways in which these are tied to knowledge of the past. This raises two questions. Can archaeology deliver a radical message to members of contemporary American society? And if archaeology does deliver a radical message, can it retain the support of the various mainstream agencies that currently underwrite archaeology in this country? Archaeology in Annapolis can provide only a limited response to these two related questions.

The radical content of Archaeology in Annapolis is at best moderate. This moderate radicalism has been noted by scholarly commentators on Archaeology in Annapolis (Blakey 1987; Durrans 1987; Paynter 1987). Their most pointed criticism, and an appropriate one, is that Archaeology in Annapolis interpretations lack a class analysis. An analysis of eighteenth-century class relations does exist in Paul Shackel's new book (1993) and his 1987 dissertation, but this work has not yet been incorporated into the interpretive program and whether it is ever used or not, Shackel's work does not constitute a commentary on *contemporary* class relations.

There are two obstacles to using archaeology to present a radical message. First, visitors seem to have strong preconceptions of archaeology as apolitical (and by default, conservative) or as sophisticated middle-class entertainment. This confirms Adorno's doubts that something as bourgeois as archaeology could be used for emancipatory education. Whatever their preconceptions, most people just do not expect archaeology to provide any kind of commentary on contemporary life, let alone a mildly radical one. And when visitors are unprepared for a radical message, it is easy for them to transform something intended as radical into something else, namely evidence for a much more conservative position. This is Barnett and Silverman's point about the absorptive power of capitalism, the power of capitalist ideology to coopt critiques. Recall all the visitors I discussed in chapter 11 who turned one Archaeology in Annapolis tour into an evolution-based celebration of modern life when the tour was intended to throw those very aspects of modern life into question. So, on the one hand, visitor expectations can limit the radical effect of archaeological interpretations.

At the same time, a sensitivity to context can easily cause those of us who create archaeological interpretations to be wary of presenting a radical message. In the interest of protecting our working relationships, Archaeology in Annapolis has at times been reluctant to present interpretations that our local sponsors could find embarrassing or objectionable. We have done so in order to maintain access to sites, facilities, and funding that are necessary to the very existence of Archaeology in Annapolis.

On balance, Archaeology in Annapolis has yet to demonstrate the use of archaeology as a means of presenting a radical social critique; we and our visitors have in some ways conspired in the creation and consumption of a public program that is somewhat timid, if judged by the standards of critical theory. It is, however, too early to abandon the attempt to create a more critical archaeological interpretation for Annapolis. And beyond that, it is important to remember that there are successful archaeologies elsewhere (Handsman 1981b, 1982; Schmidt 1977) that contain a critical perspective. What Archaeology in Annapolis demonstrates better than anything else is the difficulty encountered by members of a contemporary capitalist society attempting to create and present a critique of that society to other members of it.

Any attempt to create an archaeology radical enough to deserve the label "critical" raises the question of what would happen if and when this attempt is successful. As the previous paragraph indicates, we have not reached this point in Annapolis, so my response here can only be hypothetical.

My best guess is that a radical archaeology, closely tied to a local context and interpreted widely and effectively, would be difficult to sustain. It is no accident that people expect archaeology to be conservative. All the critiques of archaeology (and anthropology) as extensions of colonialism in the third world (D. Miller 1980) apply at home, too. Much of American archaeology is sponsored, in one way or another, by the same conservative agents and institutions targeted for intensive criticism by critical theories. Thus, I do not think it is realistic to expect that traditional sources of archaeological support would underwrite a fully critical archaeology. (Although it should not be forgotten that a considerable portion of American archaeology is conducted under and protected by the principle of academic freedom, I suspect that the strength of academic freedom for archaeology is inversely proportional to the degree to which archaeology is seen to have a practical aspect connected to contemporary social and political life.) As Durrans (1987) understands, the creation of a solidly critical archaeology would almost inevitably put archaeologists in the position of biting the institutional hands that feed them. Durrans suggests that the possibility of a critical archaeology may require significant alterations in the institutional context of archaeology, alterations in the ways archaeology is supported by and integrated into society at large. Durrans may well be right, but to this point Archaeology in Annapolis has produced no interpretations threatening enough to undermine the project's mainstream bases of support.

To restate the results of the first part of the Archaeology in Annapolis experiment, the project has yet to adopt and enact a fully critical perspective. Logistically, it is possible to build an interpretive program to serve as the basis for archaeological practice. However, Archaeology in Annapolis has proceeded cautiously in the creation and presentation of a radical message. This is a different kind of negative result, however, than a hostile or destructive reaction to a fully radical message. Given that, the failure of Archaeology in Annapolis as radical critique should not be used as a justification for abandoning the application of critical theory to historical archaeology. Archaeology may ultimately prove to be an inhospitable disciplinary location for serious critical analyses, but Archaeology in Annapolis is not the necessary proof of this, especially after the critical successes cited above. In view of this situation, the experiment should perhaps be identified as an application of a less-than-critical archaeology to the Annapolis context.

Critical Archaeology and Annapolis

In this section I discuss the effects of Archaeology in Annapolis interpretations on visitors as well as local reactions to Archaeology in Annapolis. As indicated in Chapter 11, the most positive visitor reactions to Archaeology in Annapolis are to the technical quality of the tours we give, but this strength of the project is not attributable to the use of critical theory.

Directly attributable to our critical approach, however, is our attempt to respect visitors rather than pander to them. Both formal and informal evaluations suggest that the visiting public, at least the public that visits Annapolis, appreciates our efforts to link archaeology to social issues not normally associated with the study of the past. Archaeology in Annapolis tours are always given a fair hearing, even if they are not what visitors expect archaeology to be. Paired with this piece of success, however, is the discovery noted earlier, that some of our visitors have such strong preconceptions that they transform our interpretations into something that they are not. So in this context, the implementation of a mildly critical archaeology is a mixed success, suggesting two things: (1) that some members of the visiting public are prepared to consider historical interpretations that are more adventuresome than those found in most American museum settings and (2) that some members of the visiting public will bring considerable internal unconscious resistance to such interpretations. Put the other way around, archaeology has some capacity as a medium for a critical social analysis but this capacity is clearly limited.

Given the commitment to praxis that is central to critical theory, it is apparent that the greatest successes and failures of a critically informed educational program lie beyond the reach of traditional modes of museum evaluation because they will take place off site. As formulated by members of the Frankfurt school, critical theories are intended to teach people new ways to think and to inspire them to act on those new patterns of thought. Almost any action that visitors take in response to an Archaeology in Annapolis tour, even the relatively limited action of becoming more aggressive museum visitors, is inaccessible to us. Accessible, but only through painstaking research, are data that can shed light on the degree to which Archaeology in Annapolis is successful in addressing the problem I set out in chapter 1, helping Annapolitans come to a more productive understanding of the place of transience in the city's history and its contemporary life.

If held to the strict standard of inspiring enlightened and emancipatory political action, almost any critical archaeology is likely to fall short—or at least resist evaluation. In this respect, it is inappropriate to consider Archaeology in Annapolis a failure. But if Archaeology in Annapolis cannot claim to have decisively influenced the political behavior of its visitors, it can claim to have expanded the range of topics considered appropriate for archaeological discourse. At this stage in the development of critical archaeology, this should be enough to justify the continuation of the experiment.

Tour visitors are not the only people with opinions about Archaeology in Annapolis, and this multiplicity of points of view puts the project in an interesting position. As I noted above, some scholarly commentators on the project have found Archaeology in Annapolis to be insufficiently radical. At the same time, some members of the local historic preservation community find the project's interpretations too radical. Their concern with Archaeology in Annapolis is an excellent illustration of Geertz's observation that increasingly the subjects of anthropological research are also an audience for the products of that research (Geertz 1988). Historic Annapolis is enmeshed in a wide range of local political situations and has a considerable interest in making sure that Archaeology in Annapolis is not a political liability. In attempting to protect its interests, Historic Annapolis may be hypersensitive, taking our attempts to examine the underpinnings of modern life as an outright condemnation of American society and its capitalist economy. Nonetheless, to allay the fears of an indispensable sponsor, Archaeology in Annapolis makes available to Historic Annapolis for prior review all interpretive materials and some scholarly products.

On the basis of these negotiations, I think it is fair to suggest that if Archaeology in Annapolis were to undertake a serious program of radicalization, Historic Annapolis would find the project too radical before Paynter, Durrens, and Blakey found it radical enough. To be fair, Historic Annapolis is a good bit more open-minded than many sponsors might be, which leads me to pose three questions that surround the establishment of any radical archaeological practice. First, is "mainstream" sponsorship—in any of its forms—desirable at all, under any circumstances? If not, two choices are possible. Are we content to operate on the margins, as "guerilla archaeologists" (Handsman 1987) resisting the sort of institutionalization that would make the ideas inside critical archaeology into a new ortho-doxy? Or, do we work "to advance awareness of the past by changing the institutional framework that reflects the particular social classification of knowledge and its associated activities characteristic of late capitalism, while at the same time recognizing that critical archaeologists cannot oper-ate on ideas alone but need to be employed within that framework in order to protect their arguments" (Durrans 1987: 294). "This problem," accord-ing to Durrans (1987: 294), "cannot be solved within traditional forms of scholarship" and will require "more effective and conscious collective organization."

To return to the broader issue, just what is the applicability and value of critical archaeology for Annapolis? The city does seem to attract a vis-iting public that is in many ways up to the challenges imposed by a pro-gram of critically informed public interpretation. At the same time, some local interests sense a threat in this mode of interpretation. This simply means that archaeological interpretation in Annapolis has not existed in a context of unlimited possibilities. However, within the parameters that Archaeology in Annapolis has chosen to accept, we have found sufficient latitude to undertake a program of archaeological interpretation we find educational enough to justify the costs of mounting it.

There is also the question of whether Archaeology in Annapolis has done anything to solve the problem I laid out in chapter 1, concerning the unreflective solution Annapolis has used to overcome the city's lack of a productive identity with which Annapolitans can identify. In chapter 1, I suggested that an acknowledgment that Annapolis is composed largely of transients could make it easier for the various factions in Annapolis to get along with one another. I have no evidence that Archaeology in Annapolis has had any impact in this area. Archaeology in Annapolis does help soften Historic Annapolis's public image, but in doing so, the project prob-ably strengthens the ideology behind Historic Annapolis's claims to local-ness rather than challenging it. The failure of Archaeology in Annapolis to affect life in Annapolis is probably attributable to a failure of technique rather than a flaw in the message. Public archaeological interpretation pre-sented through site tours may not be the best way to build an archaeolog-ical practice, if the goal of such a practice is to inspire social action.

In summary, my assessment of Archaeology in Annapolis as an experi-ment in the application of critical theory to historical archaeology can be divided into two parts. Some site visitors have without doubt seen Archaeology in Annapolis interpretations as an instance of archaeology that is relevant to modern life, but at the same time I have no way of knowing whether or not they have acted on this understanding. Archaeology in Annapolis by itself is clearly not sufficient to "prove" the value of critical theory to archaeology, but its results are positive enough to justify continuing the experiment in Annapolis and elsewhere.

Critical Archaeologies Elsewhere

Despite the substantial resistance to critical thinking among some American archaeologists, critical archaeologies are being developed in other places besides Annapolis. Archaeology in Annapolis has already served as a model for other interpretive programs in Maryland and beyond. But even with a commitment to using a critical approach, there seem to be significant obstacles to creating and mounting critical archaeologies. In the remainder of this chapter I deal first with the challenges facing future critical archaeologists and then with several especially promising opportunities for developing new critical archaeologies.

Scholarly Resistance

A segment of the American archaeological community finds critical archaeology, even as it has been practiced in Annapolis, too radical. Here I refer to reactions I have received at professional meetings and in print (Earle and Preucel 1987; Washburn 1987). Leaving aside the name-calling that sometimes characterizes scholarly resistance to critical archaeology, the main criticism is that some of the issues considered by critical archaeologists fall outside the realm of what archaeologists should be thinking about. In other words, critical archaeology is not archaeological enough. Since they assume that archaeology, as science, can be value-free, these critics find fault with the politicizing of archaeology. Generally speaking, critics in this category tend to react strongly, and I expect that few will change their minds. Many critical archaeologists suggest that to hope for a widespread shift in archaeological opinion is beside the point anyway. They argue that a critical approach, like any other, loses its power when it ceases to be radical and outside the mainstream. In any case, the complaint that critical approaches wrongfully politicize archaeology can be answered in two ways: (1) archaeology cannot help but be political, and (2) all that a critical approach does is give the archaeologist a way of monitoring and controlling the political aspect of his or her work rather than leaving it uncontrolled.

Obstacles to Mounting Critical Archaeologies

Not all archaeologists oppose the use of critical theory, and, as already mentioned, Schmidt (1977) and Trigger (1980), among others, have had notable success using ideas similar to those behind Archaeology in Annapolis. For archaeological projects favorably disposed toward a critical perspective, there are both logistical and intellectual obstacles to fully implementing a critical approach.

As I have noted at several points, mounting an effective public interpretive program, one way of creating a critically informed archaeological practice, is costly, and to do so requires a variety of ethnographic and performance skills that archaeologists do not necessarily possess. Deciding to do critical archaeology, with or without an interpretive program, is not like deciding to switch from quarter-inch to half-inch mesh for screening back dirt. When public interpretation is chosen as the most appropriate form of archaeological practice, that is, when interpretation is seen as the most appropriate way of applying archaeological data, it is often necessary to find new sources of funding, locate media consultants, and revise work schedules and the archaeological division of labor—all major adjustments. The necessity of these adjustments is often difficult to comprehend for archaeologists who have not participated directly in a program like Archaeology in Annapolis. It has been our experience that projects that attempt to follow our lead sometimes underestimate the costs involved and cut corners, with generally unsatisfactory results. Other potential forms of archaeological practice, such as direct political action based on archaeologically recovered historical information, are equally difficult for most archaeologists to understand and carry out, as removed as such activities are from the kind of training most archaeologists receive. Despite all this, learning the techniques necessary for planning the applications of archaeology seems to be easier than mastering the intellectual part of such an undertaking.

The intellectual aspect of creating a critical archaeology is particularly challenging for two principal reasons. First, critical archaeologies are intensely local; one size does not fit all. Second, critical archaeology forces those who attempt it to think in ways that are rather different from the patterns of thought that most archaeologists are taught. Given these qualities of critical archaeology, it is not appropriate for a critical interpretation from one context to be "borrowed" and used elsewhere without significant reworking. In most cases, it would not be adequate for a project to depend on critically informed experts to come in and create an interpretation. The techniques for presenting a critical archaeological message can be taught and learned in these ways, but not the message itself. The message needs to be created afresh for each context and created *by* a project internally, rather than *for* a project by consultants from outside. This safeguards localness for the message, but it also ensures that the presentation of the message to the public can be monitored by the authors of the message. This is crucial because critical interpretations are frequently complex, and their effectiveness seems to depend on the continuing attention of their authors. Without this kind of attention, it is easy for an interpretive program to gradually lose its critical edge and slide toward the familiar and the traditional. We have found this to be true both for Archaeology in Annapolis interpretations and for interpretations we have helped other projects create and mount.

To restate, even if its principles were universally accepted, critical archaeology would be unlikely to spread like wildfire across the archaeological landscape. On the technical side, public interpretation costs time and money, and other forms of archaeological practice are equally demanding. On the intellectual side, effective critical archaeologies require sophisticated local knowledge and a strong local commitment to understanding the principles that lie behind critical archaeology. These factors will likely inhibit the spread of critical archaeology, but despite the rigors involved, we will see a slow but steady increase in the application of critical theory to archaeology.

Opportunities for the Next Critical Archaeologies

In previous chapters I have made two assertions that I would now like to bring together: (1) that Annapolis is an almost ideal place to attempt a critical archaeology and (2) that the results of the Annapolis experiment suggest that work on using critical theory in historical archaeology should continue. Certain kinds of contexts and issues are particularly well suited for a critical approach. One of these intellectual environments—but certainly not the only one—is American historical archaeology. Two kinds of factors in particular—logistical and topical—can contribute to the success of critical archaeology in historical archaeology, or any other context.

At least three logistical factors make a situation conducive to a critical approach; it may be helpful to think of these factors as critical masses. These three factors are of approximately equal importance.

One of these factors is a critical mass of research time. A good part of the research necessary for a critical archaeology is ethnographic, ethnohistorical, and historical. That is, a critical archaeology requires research that is not traditionally archaeological. It is possible to perform this kind of research under a broad academic mandate. It is, however, more difficult to do this kind of work under the restrictions imposed by contract archaeology, where a sponsor buys specific archaeological products. This critical mass of research time also refers to the fact that the issues that matter in a community are best learned—perhaps *only* learned—through long-term experience in the community. I am not at all sure that one can enter an unfamiliar community, study it quickly, and produce an appropriate critical archaeology. So, my suggestion here is that the best circumstance for a critical archaeology is a long-term research-oriented project with funding that allows for a relatively unrestricted academic approach. Again, I do not mean to inhibit the development of critical archaeologies in other kinds of situations. If anything, a critical approach is *more* necessary for contract archaeology and government archaeology than for research-oriented archaeology. And, as I have noted at several points, more and more CRM operatives are finding that they have achieved long-term research relationships and experience with particular areas and site types. This kind of familiarity can be used to develop the kinds of local knowledge I presented in chapters 4–7.

A second factor that will contribute to the success of a critical archaeology is a critical mass of historical consciousness. By this I do not mean to suggest that some places have history and other places do not. In fact, I have argued elsewhere (Potter 1984a) that statements like this can be ideological in nature and represent the attempts of certain interests to "corner the market" on a commodity with great value for the tourist trade. When I talk about a critical mass of historical consciousness, I am referring to a tradition of historical discourse, in whatever form it may take in a particular setting. Annapolis was a good place for a critical archaeology because of its long-standing history of thinking of itself as historical; it was relatively easy to sort through the statements Annapolis has made about its past and determine the ways in which the past is used in the present. Any locale will have history and something of a historical consciousness but it is much easier to find out what a critical archaeology must address in a community with a tradition of thinking and talking about the past.

The third important part of the context for a critical archaeology is an audience. A critical archaeology that is done in private and reported only to scholarly colleagues misses the point. Critical archaeology is the creation of an archaeological practice, and an indispensable step in archaeological practice is the application of archaeology to a particular social problem, with the help of a specific audience. This audience can be local residents, tourists, some segment of the reading public, or some portion of a government bureaucracy. All that matters is that archaeological discourse is directed to a segment of the community that needs to hear it and participate in it. The easiest way to guarantee an audience for a critical archaeology is to work someplace where there are lots of people in a mood to take a tour or watch a slide program. However, this should not limit critical archaeology to high-density urban areas. In rural areas, for example, site visits may need to be scheduled rather than casual. Beyond that, there are all kinds of legitimate audiences best reached by media other than archaeological site tours. The issue here is not bringing people on site, but rather determining the appropriate audience for a particular archaeology. In any case, the identification of an audience, and the determination of how to deal with that audience are, for critical archaeologies, not an afterthought but a part of the main thought. The easier it is to identify an appropriate audience in a particular context, the better suited that context is, from a purely technical standpoint, for the creation of a critical archaeology.

Again, I do not mean to set these critical masses up as limiting factors, and I do not want to foreclose the possibility of a critical archaeology anywhere. My point is that in circumstances that do not match these, it will be more difficult to create a critical archaeology but that the task can be made easier by working on the circumstances to find or create these qualities. Where circumstances like these are not the case, a critical archaeology may be more difficult to enact but may be even more necessary, for the very reasons that make it difficult to carry out.

As for the question of what kinds of archaeology or archaeological topics are most suitable for a critical approach, there are three I would like to consider: (1) prehistory, (2) the archaeology of colonialism, and (3) historical archaeology. The idea of a critical prehistory can be viewed in two ways. First, one might deem the task impossible in the same way that Marxist approaches are frequently considered inappropriate for the study of either past or present nonclass societies. However, a number of archaeologists have attempted, with some success, to apply Marxist concepts like ideology and domination to the prehistoric past. But scholarship like that reported in Spriggs (1984), while Marxist, is not necessarily critical, the critical aspect being a consideration of the role played in the present by interpretations of the past. This concept, the appropriation of the past for contemporary purposes, is the key to creating critical prehistories, an undertaking attempted by Handsman (1981a, 1983).

One of the earliest examples of the misuse of data from prehistory was the nineteenth-century idea that the so-called moundbuilders of the Ohio Valley were a superior race wiped out by the ancestors of the American Indians encountered by Europeans at contact (Silverberg 1974: 24). Working in precisely the manner of critical archaeologists, Silverberg (like Trigger 1980: 665) does not just correct errors in scholarship; he also examines the ways in which the myth of the moundbuilders was a tool that whites used to justify the domination of Indians. Other critical prehistories in the United States would carefully examine the contemporary relationships between scholarship on American Indians and the social and political treatment of Indians, on a relatively localized scale. There are certainly topics and contexts that are well suited to the creation of critical prehistories. But the obstacles remain: to do this work requires considerable attention to a wide variety of nonarchaeological data, and this kind of work is at best undervalued and at worst rejected by many prehistorians.

The area in which critical approaches, whether labeled as such or not, have been most productive is the study of colonialism and its aftermaths. Here I include the work of Trigger (1980), D. Miller (1980), and Schmidt (1977, 1983). It may be that domination is easier to identify when it is carried out cross-culturally; Trigger and Schmidt have no difficulty in arguing for a divergence of interests between natives and Europeans. But the ease with which the problems may be identified does not mean that they are particularly easy to solve; critical work in postcolonial settings can mean confronting social issues that have existed unsolved for hundreds of years. A further complication for work such as Schmidt's is the fact that the clash of culture between colonizers and colonized calls into question some basic concepts. For example, before Schmidt can do anything with or about local history in East Africa, he must first combat the Eurocentric bias that often denies oral tradition the status of history. Finally, there is the complex set of issues that flow from Schmidt's being an American working in Africa. Despite, or perhaps because of, these difficulties in working in a postcolonial society, critical work in these settings has been some of the most fruitful to date.

On the face of it, American historical archaeology would seem to be the ideal academic address for critical approaches. It can hardly be argued that Marxist approaches are inappropriate to the historical archaeological record; much of the time span covered by historical archaeology coincides precisely with the period Marx was writing about. But this proximity in time is a disadvantage, as well. Put in a vernacular way, for some people a critical approach to historical archaeology hits too close to home;

Marxist approaches to the recent past often implicate the present, too. Put more broadly, the question is one of how to create a critique of a phenomenon that surrounds us all. Recall Leone's (1986: 432) statement that we have been less than successful at meeting this challenge: "The utter irrelevance of most of historical archaeology today is taken to stand witness to the power of capitalism to disguise its own history."

What Leone is referring to here is the way historical archaeology fails to deal with significant social issues even while it has the best possible archaeological data for doing just that. I would further suggest that within the literature and the discipline, the topics that seem on the surface to be the easiest to tie to significant contemporary social issues are the very topics that have been approached with the most uncritical and thus deadening epistemologies available within historical archaeology. Consider industrial archaeology. This discipline is resolutely object-oriented and almost completely forsakes any kind of social or political analysis, even though it has ideal data to use for the examination of workplace discipline, the standardization and segmentation of labor, alienation, and so on. Somewhat less apolitical but still problematic is another emerging subdiscipline in historical archaeology, namely the archaeology of sites occupied by African-Americans, principally on southern plantations. The archaeology of plantation slavery could be a powerful context in which to examine the roots of contemporary race relations and a wide range of important social issues. But being still in its formative years, it has generally adopted various functionalist approaches that flatten out the inequality on which plantations were based and that ensure that the results of such work have little of real utility to say to most contemporary African-American people (Ferguson 1988; Leone and Potter 1988: 307–9; Potter 1991). Happily, with the increasing visibility of work by archaeologists such as Ferguson (1991, 1992), Orser (1988a, 1988b), and Epperson (1990), this trend is being reversed, perhaps decisively.

In sum, critical approaches are ideally suited to historical archaeology, but at the same time, resistance among historical archaeologists may be even greater than resistance among prehistorians. In general, the best way to assess the value of a critical approach to a project in historical archaeology is to measure the contemporary perceptions of the phenomenon under consideration. Those surrounded by a powerful and long-standing mythology are perfect candidates for a critical approach. The southern plantation, the New England village, the isolated New England hill farm, the California mining town—all of these and many more are historical stereotypes with archaeological remains. One part of a critical archaeology is to test the stereotype with new data, but it is far more important to use the occasion of excavation to examine and discuss with the public the history of the myth, the social currency of the myth (who tells it to whom, and who does not listen), and the social power of the myth. Stories about the past do not survive if they do not have a purpose and are not told if they do not have power. Critical theory is a way of understanding the telling of stories about the past, and to the extent that archaeological results are bound to become a part of those stories, too, it is important for us to understand the process by which our work is made into myth, lest it be used in ways we do not intend.

Concluding the Conclusion

Archaeology in Annapolis demonstrates the promise of critical theory for historical archaeology. As an experiment, the project is neither so unsuccessful that nobody should ever try it again nor so successful that it need never be tried again. The success is that we have found appropriate voices for discussing a more complex and challenging way of thinking about the past than most archaeological interpretations typically use, and also, that members of the public are prepared to consider these ways of thinking. Archaeology does not have to be just neat old stuff from the past that is fun to look at. Until recently, that was the assumption behind a goodly amount of archaeological interpretation. Where Archaeology in Annapolis needs to improve is in refining its message and exploring the limits of the radicalism it can convey in public. Even our most pointed interpretations are passed off by some as insufficiently radical. As for continuing this experiment or conducting very different critical archaeologies, the possibilities are open. There are some constraints; archaeological practice in whatever form it takes requires a variety of serious commitments of time, energy, and intellectual freedom from sponsors, participants, and audiences. However, with the appropriate institutional backup—academic, public, or private—a number of contexts currently under archaeological investigation would serve very well as settings in which to attempt critical archaeologies. When further experiments in critical archaeology are undertaken, the results may be an archaeology that is no longer appropriate for coffee tables and cocktail parties, but it will be an archaeology relevant to contemporary American life, much of which does not belong on a coffee table.

Postscript

On September 27, 1991, I delivered a revised (and nearly final) manuscript of this book to the editorial offices of the Smithsonian Institution Press. Later on that day, two things happened that are worth reporting here, even at the risk of trampling on the rabble-rousing statement about coffee-table books that brings down the curtain on chapter 12.

The two things that happened were a party and a newspaper, both of which I encountered in Annapolis. I was in Annapolis at the invitation of Historic Annapolis, which had decided to update and reuse a citywide archaeology tour I wrote back in 1986. I was invited to Annapolis to give the first of a series of public lectures intended to promote the revival of the archaeology tour, which was offered to the public as Historic Annapolis's annual Historic Hike.

Two days after my lecture, Historic Annapolis threw a garden party fund-raiser at the Paca House. The party featured a silent auction of various arts, crafts, and other local products. One of the items, for which I was the successful bidder, was an editorial cartoon (figure 13.1) by Eric Smith, editorial cartoonist for the *Capital*, both in 1991 and when I was living in Annapolis. In the cartoon, sober conservative Annapolis stares wide-eyed in dismay at the "typical" tourist family. The normalcy of Mr. Annapolis as contrasted with the dementia of Mr. Father Tourist, Mrs. Bee-Hive, and their nose-picking son leaves little doubt as to where Eric Smith thinks his readers have located the moral high ground in the delicate relationship

between residents and visitors. Who could possibly question the need to keep a tight reign on creatures like Eric Smith's tourist family?

Somewhat less colorful but no less important is the editorial that ran in the *Capital* on the same day I bought my Eric Smith cartoon. The editorial was written in the midst of Historic Annapolis's search for a new president. Under the headline "Historic Annapolis Needs Direction from Annapolitans," the editorial says, "Annapolis is a special place to many people. But it is only home to those who live here." After disclosing that only two of the sixteen members of the Historic Annapolis board of directors live in the city, the editorial asks, "Why should a bunch of outsiders decide which buildings in Annapolis are worth renovating?" While the editorial stops short of demanding that the next president of Historic Annapolis be a resident of the city, it strongly suggests that the board should include more locals than it does.

My "discovery" of these two new pieces of data—and I am certain that more frequent visits to Annapolis would have turned up many more—demonstrates that while many things have changed since I left Annapolis in 1987, some things have remained the same. More important, I am more confident than ever that the issues I first began to identify in 1982, transience and visitation in Annapolis, are both significant and unresolved. A program of archaeological interpretation may or may not be an effective vehicle for addressing this set of issues, and Archaeology in Public has by no means solved them. Even so, if the purpose of history and archaeology in Annapolis is to explore and discuss the roots of issues that matter to Annapolitans today, then there are few topics more important than the city's relationships with outsiders.

I have not written this book in an attempt to finish what our interpretive program only started; it will take more than what I have done here to make Eric Smith's cartoon go out of date. The best I can hope for is that this book may serve as a small spark, a tiny catalyst for improving the clarity and the productivity of the local discourse on transience, visitation, and local identity. The real work is to be done in Annapolis, not by me. But if this book helps move the discussion ahead just a bit, I will consider it a success.

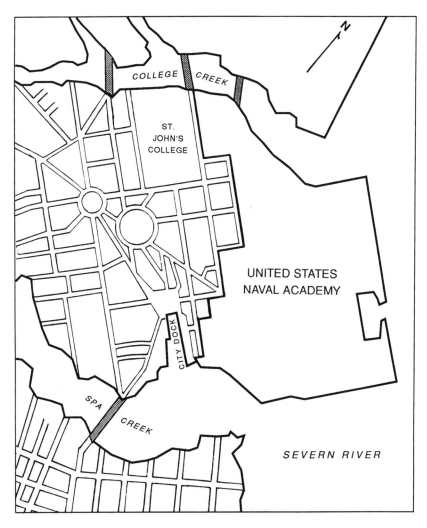

Contemporary Map of Annapolis

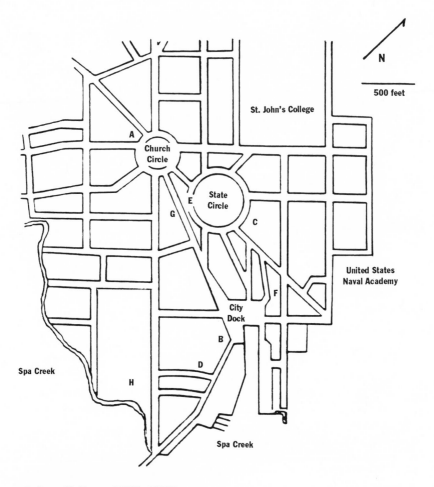

A. Reynolds Tavern (1982, 1983)
B. Victualling Warehouse (1982, 1983, 1984)
C. Calvert House (1984)
D. Newman Street (1984)
E. State House Inn (1985)
F. Shiplap House (1985)
G. Main Street (1986)
H. Carroll House (1987)

Archaeology in Public Sites, 1982-1987

References

Alderson, William T., and Shirley Payne Low
    1976 *Interpretation of Historic Sites*. Nashville, Tenn.: American
        Association for State and Local History.
Alexander, Edward P.
    1979 *Museums in Motion: An Introduction to the History and Functions of*
        Museums. Nashville, Tenn.: American Association for State and Local
        History.
Anderson, Elizabeth B.
    1984 *Annapolis: A Walk through History*. Centreville, Md.: Tidewater.
Baker, Nancy
    1983 Annapolis, Maryland, 1695-1730. In *Annapolis and Anne Arundel*
        County, Maryland: A Study of Urban Development in a Tobacco
        Economy, 1649–1776, edited by Lorena S. Walsh. N.E.H. Grant RS-
        20199-81-1955. On file at Historic Annapolis, Annapolis, Md.
    1986 Annapolis, Maryland, 1695–1730. *Maryland Historical Magazine*
        81(3): 191–209.
Baldridge, Harry A.
    1928 Washington's Visits to Colonial Annapolis. *Naval Institute*
        Proceedings 54(February):90–128.
Barnett, Steve, and Martin G. Silverman
    1979 *Ideology and Everyday Life*. Ann Arbor: University of Michigan Press.
Becker, Carl
    1935 *Everyman His Own Historian*. Chicago: Quadrangle Books.

Bertalanffy, Ludwig von
    1962 General Systems Theory: A Critical Review. *General Systems* 7:1–20.
Binford, Lewis R.
    1962 Archaeology as Anthropology. *American Antiquity* 28(2):217–26.
    1965 Archaeological Systematics and the Study of Cultural Process.
    American Antiquity 31:203–10.
Binford, Sally R., and Lewis R. Binford (eds.)
    1968 *New Perspectives in Archaeology*. New York: Aldine.
Blakely, Michael L.
    1987 Comment on: Toward a Critical Archaeology. *Current Anthropology*
    28(3):292.
Breslaw, Elaine G.
    1975a The Chronicle as Satire: Dr. Hamilton's "History of the Tuesday
    Club." *Maryland Historical Magazine* 70(2):129–48.
    1975b Wit, Whimsy, and Satire: The Uses of Satire by the Tuesday Club of
    Annapolis. *William and Mary Quarterly* (3d ser.) 32:295–306.
Burdett, Harold N.
    1974 *Yesteryear in Annapolis*. Cambridge, Md.: Tidewater.
Burcaw, G. Ellis
    1983 *Introduction to Museum Work*. 2d ed. Nashville, Tenn.: American
    Association for State and Local History.
Carr, Lois Green
    1983 Methodological Procedures for Inventory Analysis. In *Annapolis and
    Anne Arundel County, Maryland: A Study of Urban Development in a
    Tobacco Economy, 1649–1776*, edited by Lorena S. Walsh. N.E.H.
    Grant RS-20199-81-1955. On file at Historic Annapolis, Annapolis,
    Md.
Caton, John Torry
    1971 Baltimore. In *The Old Line State: A History of Maryland*, edited by
    Morris L. Radoff, pp. 192–207. Annapolis, Md.: Hall of Records
    Commission.
Chock, Phyllis Pease
    1986 The Outsider Wife and the Divided Self: The Genesis of Ethnic
    Identities. In *Discourse and the Social Life of Meaning*, edited by Phyllis
    Pease Chock and June R. Wyman, pp. 185–204. Washington, D.C.:
    Smithsonian Institution Press.
Chudacoff, Howard P.
    1981 *The Evolution of American Urban Society*. Englewood Cliffs, N.J.:
    Prentice-Hall.
Churchill, Winston
    1899 *Richard Carvel of Carvel Hall*. New York: Macmillan.
Claassen, Cheryl P.
    1976 Cultural Formation Processes of the Archaeological Record in the

Aleutian Islands. Paper presented at the New England–New York Graduate Student Conference, Storrs, Conn.

Clark, Grahame
1957 *Archaeology and Society*. Cambridge, Mass.: Harvard University Press.

Clark, Lynn
1986 More to Mibs than Meets the Eye. Research paper on file at Historic Annapolis, Annapolis, Md.

Clarke, David L.
1968 *Analytical Archaeology*. London: Methuen.

Clewlow, C. William, Partick S. Hallihan, and Richard D. Ambro
1971 A Crisis in Archaeology. *American Antiquity* 36(4):472–73.

Coles, John
1973 *Archaeology by Experiment*. New York: Scribners.

Colwell, Wayne
1972 Windows on the Past. *Museum News* 50(10):36–38.

Cook, Ebenezer
1708 *The Sot-Weed Factor, or a Voyage to Maryland, a Satire in Burlesque Verse*. London: B. Bragg.

Crosby, Constance A.
1982 Excavations at the Victualling Warehouse Site, AN 14, 1982: Preliminary Report. Manuscript on file at Historic Annapolis, Annapolis, Md.

DeBoer, Warren R.
1982 Archaeology as a Myth-Making and Myth-Serving Profession. In *Directions in Archaeology: A Question of Goals*. Proceedings of the Fourteenth Annual CHACMOOL Conference, edited by P. D. Francis and E. C. Poplin, pp. 363–67. Calgary, Alta.: University of Calgary Archaeological Association.

Deetz, James F.
1971 The Changing Historic House Museum: Can It Live? *Historic Preservation* 23(1):50–54.
1977 *In Small Things Forgotten*. Garden City, N.Y.: Doubleday Anchor Press.
1983 Scientific Humanism and Humanistic Science: A Plea for Paradigmatic Pluralism in Historical Archaeology. *Geoscience and Man* 23(April 29):27–34.
1988 Material Culture and Worldview in Colonial Anglo-America. In *The Recovery of Meaning: Historical Archaeology in the Eastern United States*, edited by Mark P. Leone and Parker B. Potter, Jr., pp. 219–33. Washington, D.C.: Smithsonian Institution Press.

Dixon, Keith A.
1977 Applications of Archaeological Resources: Broadening the Basis of Significance. In *Conservation Archaeology: A Guide for Cultural*

Resource Management Studies, edited by Michael B. Schiffer and George J. Gummerman, pp. 277–90. New York: Academic Press.

Doherty, Kathleen D., and Deborah J. Knox
1986 Buttons in Annapolis: Accessories to the Georgian Order. Term paper, Department of Anthropology, University of Maryland. On file at Historic Annapolis, Annapolis, Md.

Dugan, Mary C.
1902 *Outline History of Annapolis and the Naval Academy*. Baltimore, Md.: B. G. Eichelberger.

Dunnell, R. C.
1971 Sabloff and Smith's "The Importance of Both Analytic and Taxonomic Classification in the Type-Variety System" (*American Antiquity* 34:278–86). *American Antiquity* 36(1):115–18.

Durrans, Brian
1987 Comment on: Toward a Critical Archaeology. *Current Anthropology* 28(3):293–94.

Duval, Ruby
1926 *Guide to Historic Annapolis and the USNA*. Baltimore, Md.: Norman Remington.

Eareckson, Jean Lee
1980 The Six Lords Baltimore and Their Governors. In *Fact Sheets for Interpreters for the Preservation and Restoration of Annapolis*. Annapolis, Md.: Historic Annapolis.

Earle, Timothy K., and Robert W. Preucel
1987 Processual Archaeology and the Radical Critique. *Current Anthropology* 28(4):501–38.

Eddis, William
1969 *Letters from America*. Edited by Aubrey C. Land. Cambridge, Mass.: Harvard University Press.

Emery, Charles E.
1948 *Photogenic Annapolis*. Baltimore, Md.: The Camera.

Epperson, Terrence W.
1990 Race and the Disciplines of the Plantation. *Historical Archaeology* 24(4):29–36.

Ferguson, Leland G.
1988 Review of *The Archaeology of Slavery and Plantation Life*. *American Antiquity* 53(1):195–96.
1991 Struggling with Pots in Colonial South Carolina. In *The Archaeology of Inequality*, edited by Randall H. McGuire and Robert Paynter, pp. 28–39. Oxford: Blackwell.
1992 *Uncommon Ground: Archaeology and Early African America, 1650–1800*. Washington, D.C.: Smithsonian Institution Press.

Flannary, Kent V.
1968 Archaeological Systems Theory and Early Mesoamerica. In

Anthropological Archaeology in the Americas, edited by Betty Meggers, pp. 67–87. Washington D.C.: Anthropological Society of Washington.
1982 The Golden Marshalltown: A Parable for the Archaeology of the 1980s. *American Anthropologist* 84(2):265–78.

Flinders-Petrie, W. M.
1904 *Methods and Aims in Archaeology*. New York: Macmillan.

Fontana, Bernard L.
1973 The Cultural Dimension of Pottery: Ceramics as Social Documents. In *Ceramics in America*, edited by Ian Quimby. Charlottesville: University Press of Virginia.

Ford, James A.
1961 *Menard Site: The Quapaw Village of Osotouy on the Arkansas River*. Anthropological Papers 48(2). New York: American Museum of Natural History.

Fortenbaugh, Robert
1973 *The Nine Capitals of the United States*. York, Pa.: Maple Press.

Fritz, John M., and Fred Plog
1970 The Nature of Archaeological Explanation. *American Antiquity* 35:405–12.

Gardner, William A., and Joan A. Walker
1990 *A Small History of the Forgotten and Never Known*. DelDOT Archaeology Series, No. 84. Wilmington: Delaware Department of Transportation.

Gebhardt, Eike
1982 Introduction to "A Critique of Methodology." In *The Essential Frankfurt School Reader*, edited by Andrew Arato and Eike Gebhardt, pp. 371–406. New York: Continuum.

Geertz, Clifford
1988 Being There, Writing Here. *Harpers* 296(1654):32–38.

Gerlach, L. R.
1975 Making the Past Come Alive. *History News* 30(6):222–23, 225.

Gero, Joan, David Lacy, and Michael Blakey (eds.)
1983 *The Socio-Politics of Archaeology*. Research Report 23, Department of Anthropology, University of Massachusetts at Amherst.

Geuss, Raymond
1981 *The Idea of a Critical Theory*. Cambridge: Cambridge University Press.

Gould, Richard A.
1984 *Toward an Ethnoarchaeology of Modern America*. Research Papers in Anthropology, No. 4, Department of Anthropology, Brown University, Providence, R.I.

Gould, Richard A. and Michael B. Schiffer (eds.)
1981 *Modern Material Culture: The Archaeology of Us*. New York: Academic Press.

Glassie, Henry
    1975 *Folk Housing of Middle Virginia*. Knoxville: University of Tennessee
        Press.
Grady, Mark A.
    1977 Significance Evaluation and the Orme Reservoir Project. In
        *Conservation Archaeology: A Guide for Cultural Resource Management
        Studies*, edited by Michael B. Schiffer and George G. Gummerman, pp.
        259–67. New York: Academic Press.
Handsman, Russell G.
    1980 The Domains of Kinship and Settlement in Historic Goshen: Signs of a
        Past Cultural Order. *Artifacts* 9(1):4–7.
    1981a Processual Theory and Archaeological Patterns: The Search for
        "Structure" in Historic and Prehistoric Archaeology. Paper presented in
        the symposium "New Directions in Archaeology," Middle Atlantic
        Archaeology Conference, Ocean City, Md.
    1981b Early Capitalism and the Center Village of Canaan, Connecticut: A
        Study of Transformations and Separations. *Artifacts* 9(3):1–21.
    1982 The Hot and Cold of Goshen's History. *Artifacts* 10(3):11–20.
    1983 Towards Archaeological Histories of Robbins Swamp. *Artifacts*
        11(3):1–20.
    1987 Comments on "Annapolis, Maryland, and Georgian Order: The
        Archaeology of Colonial Worldview," a symposium at the annual meet-
        ing of the Society for Historical Archaeology, Savannah, Ga.
Handsman, Russell G., and Mark P. Leone
    1990 Living History and Critical Archaeology and the Reconstruction of the
        Past. In *Critical Traditions in Contemporary Archaeology*, edited by
        Valerie Pinsky and Alison Wylie, pp. 117–35. Cambridge: Cambridge
        University Press.
Hanley, Thomas O'Brien
    1982 *Charles Carroll of Carrollton: The Making of a Revolutionary
        Gentleman*. Chicago: Loyola University Press.
    1983 *Revolutionary Statesman: Charles Carroll and the War*. Chicago:
        Loyola University Press.
Harris, Marvin
    1968 *The Rise of Anthropological Theory*. New York: Thomas Y. Crowell.
    1979 *Cultural Materialism: The Struggle for a Science of Culture*. New
        York: Random House.
Heath, Dwight B.
    1973 Economic Aspects of Commercial Archaeology in Costa Rica.
        American Antiquity 38(3):259–65.
Held, David
    1980 *Introduction to Critical Theory: Horkheimer to Habermas*. Berkeley:
        University of California Press.

Hill, James N., and R. K. Evans
1972 A Model for Classification and Typology. In *Models in Archaeology*, edited by David L. Clarke. London: Methuen.

Historic Annapolis, Inc.
1963 *Three Historic Blocks*. Annapolis, Md.: Historic Annapolis, Inc.

Hodder, Ian
1982 Theoretical Archaeology: A Reactionary View. In *Symbolic and Structural Archaeology*, edited by Ian Hodder. Cambridge: Cambridge University Press.
1986 *Reading the Past*. Cambridge: Cambridge University Press.

House, John H., and Michael B. Schiffer
1975 Significance of the Archaeological Resources of the Cache River Basin. In *The Cache River Archaeological Project: An Experiment in Contract Archaeology*. Research Series, No. 8, assembled by Michael B. Schiffer and John H. House, pp. 163–86. Fayetteville: Arkansas Archaeological Survey.

Ingersoll, Daniel, John E. Yellen, and William Macdonald (eds.)
1977 *Experimental Archaeology*. New York: Columbia University Press.

Ives, Sallie Middleton
1977 *A Symbolic Interaction Approach to the Place Meanings in a Historic District: A Case Study of Annapolis, Maryland*. Ph.D. diss., Department of Geography, University of Illinois. Ann Arbor: University Microfilms.
1979 The Formation of a Black Community in Annapolis, 1870–1885. In *Geographical Perspectives on Maryland's Past*. Occasional Papers in Geography, No. 4, edited by Robert D. Mitchell and Edward K. Muller, pp. 129–49. College Park: Department of Geography, University of Maryland.

Jay, Martin
1984 *Marxism and Totality: The Adventures of a Concept from Lukacs to Habermas*. Berkeley: University of California Press.

Kaplin, A.
1964 *The Conduct of Inquiry: Methodology for Behavioral Science*. San Francisco, Calif.: Chandler.

Kelso, William M.
1984 *Kingsmill Plantation 1619–1800: Archaeology of Country Life in Colonial Virginia*. New York: Academic Press.

Kelly, J. H.
1963 Some Thoughts on Amateur Archaeology. *American Antiquity* 28:54–60.

King, Thomas K., Patricia Parker Hickman, and Gary Berg
1977 *Anthropology in Historic Preservation: Caring for Culture's Clutter*. New York: Academic Press.

Klein, Terry C., and Amy Friedlander

1983 *Archaeological Investigations at the Wilmington Boulevard, New Castle County, Delaware*. Wilmington: Delaware Department of Transportation.

Kohl, P. L.
1981 Materialist Approaches in Prehistory. *Annual Review of Anthropology* 10:89–118.

Kubler, George
1962 *The Shape of Time: Remarks on the History of Things*. New Haven, Conn.: Yale University Press.

Land, Aubrey C.
1955 *The Dulanys of Maryland*. Baltimore, Md.: Maryland Historical Society.

Leone, Mark P.
1972 (ed.) *Contemporary Archaeology: A Guide to Theory and Contributions*. Carbondale: Southern Illinois University Press.
1980 The Presence of the Past in St. Mary's City, Maryland. Paper presented at the annual meeting of the American Anthropological Association, Washington, D.C.
1981a Archaeology's Relationship to the Present and the Past. In *Modern Material Culture: The Archaeology of Us*, edited by Richard A. Gould and Michael B. Schiffer, pp. 5–13. New York: Academic Press.
1981b The Relationship between Artifacts and the Public in Outdoor History Museums. *Annals of the New York Academy of Sciences* 376:301–14.
1983a Method as Message: Interpreting the Past with the Public. *Museum News* 62(1):35–41.
1983b Some Factors Establishing the Meaning of Objects in Context. Paper presented at "The Place of Museums in Anthropological Material Culture Studies," at the Heard Museum, Phoenix, Ariz. Ms. in the possession of the author.
1984a The Georgian Order in Annapolis. Paper presented at the annual meeting of the Eastern States Archaeological Federation, Annapolis, Md.
1984b Interpreting Ideology in Historical Archaeology: Using the Rules of Perspective in the William Paca Garden, Annapolis, Maryland. In *Ideology, Power, and Prehistory*, edited by Daniel Miller and Christopher Tilley, pp. 25–35. Cambridge: Cambridge Univeristy Press.
1984c Material Culture of the Georgian World. Paper presented at "The Colonial Experience: The Eighteenth-Century Chesapeake," Baltimore, Md.
1986 Symbolic, Structural, and Critical Archaeology. In *American Archaeology Past and Future: A Celebration of the Society for American Archaeology, 1935–1985*, edited by David J. Meltzer, Don D. Fowler, and Jeremy A. Sabloff, pp. 415–38. Washington. D.C.: Smithsonian Institution Press.

1988 The Georgian Order as the Order of Merchant Capitalism in Annapolis, Maryland. In *The Recovery of Meaning: Historical Archaeology in the Eastern United States*, edited by Mark P. Leone and Parker B. Potter, Jr., pp. 235–61. Washington. D.C.: Smithsonian Institution Press.

n.d. Doubt, Self-Deception, and Psychoanalysis. Unpublished ms. in the possession of the author.

Leone, Mark P., Barbara J. Little, Mark S. Warner, Parker B. Potter, Jr., Paul A. Shackel, George C. Logan, Paul R. Mullins, and Julie A. Ernstein

n.d. The Constituencies for an Archaeology of African Americans in Annapolis, Maryland. In *Studies in African-American Archaeology*, edited by Theresa A. Singleton. Charlottesville: University Press of Virginia.

Leone, Mark P. and Parker B. Potter, Jr.

1984 *Archaeological Annapolis: A Guide to Seeing and Understanding Three Centuries of Change.* Annapolis: Historic Annapolis, Inc.

1988 Issues in Historical Archaeology. In *The Recovery of Meaning: Historical Archaeology in the Eastern United States*, edited by Mark P. Leone and Parker B. Potter, Jr., pp. 1–22. Washington, D. C.: Smithsonian Institution Press.

Leone, Mark P., Parker B. Potter, Jr. and Paul A. Shackel

1987 Toward a Critical Archaeology. *Current Anthropology* 28(3):283–302.

Leone, Mark P., and Paul A. Shackel

1987 Forks, Clocks, and Power. In *Mirror and Metaphor: Material and Social Constructions of Reality*, edited by Daniel Ingersoll, Jr. and Gordon Bronitsky, pp. 45–61. Latham, Md.: University Press of America.

1990 The Georgian Order in Annapolis, Maryland. In *New Perspectives in Maryland Historical Archaeology*, edited by Richard J. Dent and Barbara J. Little. *Maryland Archaeologist* 26:69–84.

Lipe, William D.

1977 A Conservation Model for American Archaeology. In *Conservation Archaeology: A Guide for Cultural Resource Management Studies*, edited by Michael B. Schiffer and George J. Gummerman, pp. 19–42. New York: Academic Press.

Little, Barbara J.

1987 *Ideology and Media: Historical Archaeology of Printing in 18th-Century Annapolis, Maryland.* Ph.D. diss., Department of Anthropology, State University of New York at Buffalo. Ann Arbor: University Microfilms.

1988 Craft and Culture Change in the 18th-Century Chesapeake. In *The Recovery of Meaning: Historical Archaeology in the Eastern United States*, edited by Mark P. Leone and Parker B. Potter, Jr., pp. 263–92. Washington, D.C.: Smithsonian Institution Press.

Little, Barbara J., and Paul A. Shackel
  1989 Scales of Historical Anthropology: An Archaeology of Colonial Anglo-America. *Antiquity* 63(240):495–509.
Lowenthal, David
  1985 *The Past is a Foreign Country*. Cambridge: Cambridge University Press.
Lukacs, George
  1968 *History and Class Consciousness*. Cambridge, Mass.: MIT Press.
MacCannell, Dean
  1976 *The Tourist: A New Theory of the Leisure Class*. New York: Schocken Books.
McGimsey, Charles R., III
  1972 *Public Archaeology*. New York: Academic Press.
McGuire, Randall H.
  1988 The Dead Need Not Speak: Ideology and the Cemetery. In *The Recovery of Meaning: Historical Archaeology in the Eastern United States*, edited by Mark P. Leone and Parker B. Potter, Jr., pp. 435–80. Washington, D.C.: Smithsonian Institution Press.
McKeldin, Theodore R.
  1957 *Washington Bowed*. Baltimore: Maryland Historical Society.
McKendrick, Neil
  1982 Josiah Wedgwood and the Commercialization of the Potteries. In *The Birth of a Consumer Society*, edited by Neil McKendrick, John Brewer, and J. H. Plumb, pp. 100–145. Bloomington: Indiana University Press.
Martin, Paul S.
  1954 Comments. *American Anthropologist* 56:70–72.
  1971 The Revolution in Archaeology. *American Antiquity* 36: 1–8.
Martin, Paul S., and Fred Plog
  1973 *The Archaeology of Arizona*. New York: Natural History Press.
Martin, Paul S., George L. Quimby, and Donald Collier
  1947 *Indians Before Columbus*. Chicago: University of Chicago Press.
Meltzer, David J.
  1979 Paradigms and the Nature of Change in American Archaeology. *American Antiquity* 44:644–57.
Middleton, Arthur Pierce
  1986 Taverns in Eighteenth-Century Annapolis. *Catalogue of the 16th Annual Hunt Valley Antiques Show*, pp. 10–13. Annapolis, Md.
Miller, Daniel
  1980 Archaeology and Development. *Current Anthropology* 21(6):709–15.
Miller, George L.
  1980 Classification and Economic Scaling of 19th-Century Ceramics. *Historical Archaeology* 14:1-41.
  1984 George M. Coates, Pottery Merchant of Philadelphia, 1817–1831. *Winterthur Portfolio* 19(1):31–50.

1991 A Revised Set of CC Index Values for Classification and Economic Scaling of English Ceramics from 1787 to 1880. *Historical Archaeology* 25(1):1–25.

Miller, Henry M.
1988 Baroque Cities in the Wilderness: Archaeology and Urban Development in the Colonial Chesapeake. *Historical Archaeology* 22(2):57–73.

Mitchell, Mary
1969 *Annapolis Visit.* Barre, Mass.: Barre.

Morse, Dan F.
1973 Natives and Anthropologists in Arkansas. In *Anthropology beyond the University*, edited by Alden Redfield. *Proceedings of Southern Anthropological Association* 7:26–39.
1975 Paleo-Indians in the Land of Opportunity: Preliminary Report on the Excavations at the Sloan Site (3GE94). In *The Cache River Archaeological Project: An Experiment in Contract Archaeology.* Research Series, No. 8, assembled by Michael B. Schiffer and John H. House. Fayetteville: Arkansas Archaeological Survey.

Munley, Mary Ellen
1987 Intentions and Accomplishments: Principles of Museum Evaluation Research. In *Past Meets Present: Essays about Historic Interpretation and Public Audiences*, edited by Jo Blatti, pp. 116–30. Washington, D.C.: Smithsonian Institution Press.

Nash, Gary
1986 *The Urban Crucible.* Abr. ed. Cambridge, Mass.: Harvard University Press.

Noel-Hume, Ivor
1973 Creamware to Pearlware: A Williamsburg Perspective. In *Ceramics in America*, edited by Ian Quimby, pp. 217–54. Charlottesville: University Press of Virginia.

Norris, Walter B.
1925 *Annapolis: Its Colonial and Naval Story.* New York: Thomas Y. Crowell.

Oldmixon, John
1708 *The British Empire in America.* London.

Orser, Charles E., Jr.
1987 Plantation Status and Consumer Choice: A Materialist Framework for Historical Archaeology. In *Consumer Choice in Historical Archaeology*, edited by Suzanne Spencer-Wood, pp. 121–37. New York: Plenum Press.
1988a The Archaeological Analysis of Plantation Society: Replacing Status and Caste with Economics and Power. *American Antiquity* 54(4):735–51.
1988b Toward a Theory of Power for Historical Archaeology: Plantations and Space. In *The Recovery of Meaning: Historical Archaeology in the*

Eastern United States, edited by Mark P. Leone and Parker B. Potter, Jr., pp. 313–43. Washington, D.C.: Smithsonian Institution Press.

1989 On Plantations and Patterns. *Historical Archaeology* 23(2):28–40.

Otto, John Solomon

1975 *Status Difference and the Archaeological Record: A Comparison of Planter, Overseer, and Slave Sites from Cannon's Point Plantation (1794–1861), St. Simon's Island, Georgia.* Ph.D. diss., Department of Anthropology, University of Florida. Ann Arbor: University Microfilms.

1984 *Cannon's Point Plantation 1794–1860: Living Conditions and Status Patterns in the Old South.* New York: Academic Press.

Papenfuse, Edward C.

1973 *Mercantile Opportunity and Urban Development in a Planting Society: A Case Study of Annapolis, Maryland, 1763–1805.* Ph.D. diss., Department of History, Johns Hopkins University, Baltimore, Md.

1975 *In Pursuit of Profit: The Annapolis Merchants in the Era of the American Revolution, 1763-1805.* Baltimore, Md.: Johns Hopkins University Press.

Patterson, Thomas C.

1986 The Last Sixty Years: Toward a Social History of Americanist Archaeology in the United States. *American Anthropologist* 88(1):7–26.

Paynter, Robert

1987 Comment on: Toward a Critical Archaeology. *Current Anthropology* 28(3):296–97.

1988 Steps to an Archaeology of Capitalism: Material Change and Class Analysis. In *The Recovery of Meaning: Historical Archaeology in the Eastern United States*, edited by Mark P. Leone and Parker B. Potter, Jr., pp. 407–33, Washington, D.C.: Smithsonian Institution Press.

Pinsky, Valerie and Alison Wylie (eds.)

1989 *Critical Traditions in Contemporary Archaeology: Essays in the History and Philosophy of Archaeology.* Cambridge: Cambridge University Press.

Potter, Parker B., Jr.

1982 The Translation of Archaeological Evidence into Economic Understandings: A Study of Context, Naming, and Nineteenth Century Ceramics in Rockbridge County, Virginia. Unpublished M.A. paper, Department of Anthropology, Brown University.

1984 From Annapolis to Rockbridge: Approaches to Presenting Archaeology to the Public in the Uplands of Virginia. In *Uplands Archaeology in the East: Symposium 2.* Cultural Resources Report, No. 5, edited by Michael B. Barber, pp. 273–83. Atlanta: U.S. Forest Service, Southern Region.

1989 *Archaeology in Public in Annapolis: An Experiment in the Application of Critical Theory to Historical Archaeology.* Ph.D. diss., Department of Anthropology, Brown University. Ann Arbor: University Microfilms.

1991 What Is the Use of Plantation Archaeology? *Historical Archaeology* 23(3):94–107.

Potter, Parker B., Jr., and Mark P. Leone

1986 Liberation Not Replication: "Archaeology in Annapolis" Analyzed. *Journal of the Washington Academy of Sciences* 76(2):97–105.

1987 Archaeology in Public in Annapolis: Four Seasons, Six Sites, Seven Tours and 32,000 Visitors. *American Archaeology* 6(1):51–61.

1992 Establishing the Roots of Historical Consciousness in Modern Annapolis, Maryland. In *Museums and Communities: Debating Public Culture,* edited by Ivan Karp, Christine Mullen Kreamer, and Steven D. Lavine, pp. 476–505. Washington, D.C.: Smithsonian Institution Press.

Price, Barbara J.

1982 Cultural Materialism: A Theoretical Review. *American Antiquity* 47(4):709–41.

Price, J. E., C. R. Price, and S. Harris

1976 *An Assessment of the Cultural Resources of the Fourche Creek Watershed.* Columbia: Archaeological Research Facility, University of Missouri.

Radoff, Morris L.

1971 (ed.) *The Old Line State: A History of Maryland.* Annapolis, Md.: Hall of Records Commission.

1972 *The State House at Annapolis.* Annapolis, Md.: Hall of Records Commission.

Ramirez, Constance Werner

1975 *Urban History for Preservation Planning: The Annapolis Experience.* Ph.D. diss., Department of Urban and Regional Planning, Cornell University. Ann Arbor: University Microfilms.

Randall, John Wirt

1905 *Farmers National Bank of Annapolis: Some Incidents of Its Early History.* Annapolis: Farmers National Bank.

1911 Historic Annapolis. Lecture delivered July 28, 1911, in Baltimore, Md. On file, Maryland State Library.

Rathje, William L.

1974 The Garbage Project: A New Way of Looking at Problems of Archaeology. *Archaeology* 27:236–41.

1978 Archaeological Ethnography: Because Sometimes It Is Better to Give than to Receive. In *Experiments in Ethnoarchaeology,* edited by Richard A. Gould, pp. 49–76. Albuquerque: University of New Mexico Press.

1991 Once and Future Landfills. *National Geographic* 179:116–34.

Rathje, William L., and Michael McCarthy

1977 Regularity and Variability in Contemporary Garbage. In *Research Strategies in Historical Archaeology*, edited by Stanley South, pp. 261–86. New York: Academic Press.

Rathje, William L., W. W. Hughes, D. C. Wilson, M. K. Tani, G. H. Archer, R. G. Hunt, and T. W. Jones
  1992 The Archaeology of Contemporary Landfills. *American Antiquity* 57(3): 437–47.

Reid, J. Jefferson, Michael B. Schiffer, and William L. Rathje
  1975 Behavioral Archaeology: Four Strategies. *American Anthropologist* 77:864–69.

Renfrew, Colin
  1983 Divided We Stand: Aspects of Archaeology and Information. *American Antiquity* 48(1):3–16.

Reps, John
  1965 *The Making of Urban America*. Princeton, N.J.: Princeton University Press.
  1972 *Tidewater Towns: City Planning in Colonial Virginia and Maryland*. Williamsburg, Va.: Colonial Williamsburg Foundation.

Ridgely, David
  1841 *Annals of Annapolis*. Baltimore, Md.: Cushing & Brother.

Riley, Elihu
  1887 *"The Ancient City": A History of Annapolis in Maryland, 1649–1887*. Annapolis, Md.: Record Printing Office. Reprinted in 1976 by the Anne Arundel-Annapolis Bicentennial Committee.
  1897 *Souvenir Volume of the State Conference of Maryland Firemen*. Annapolis, Md.
  1901 *Annapolis, "Ye Ancient Capital of Maryland" 1649–1901*. Annapolis, Md.: Annapolis Publishing.
  1906 *Pictorial Annapolis, Anne Arundel, and the Naval Academy*. Baltimore, Md.: King Brothers.

Robinson, Paul A., Marc A. Kelly, and Patricia E. Rubertone
  1985 Preliminary Bio-Cultural Interpretations from a Seventeenth-Century Narragansett Indian Cemetery in Rhode Island. In *Cultures in Conflict: The European Impact on Native Cultural Institutions, A.D. 1000–1800*, edited by William Fitzhugh, pp. 107–30. Washington, D.C.: Smithsonian Institution Press.

Russo, Jean
  1983 Economy of Anne Arundel County. In *Annapolis and Anne Arundel County, Maryland: A Study of Urban Development in a Tobacco Economy, 1649–1776*, edited by Lorena S. Walsh. N.E.H. Grant RS-20199-81-1955. On file at Historic Annapolis, Annapolis, Md.

Sahlins, Marshall
  1976 *Culture and Practical Reason*. Chicago: University of Chicago Press.

Schaun, George, and Virginia Schaun
  1955 *Compass Pointers and other Streets of Annapolis.* Privately
      published, on file at the West Street Branch, Anne Arundel County
      Library.
Schiffer, Michael B.
  1976 *Behavioral Archaeology.* New York: Academic Press.
  1977 Toward a Unified Science of the Cultural Past. In *Research Strategies
      in Historical Archaeology*, edited by Stanley South, pp. 13–50. New
      York: Academic Press.
  1983 Toward the Identification of Formation Processes. *American Antiquity*
      48(4):675–706.
  1988 The Structure of Archaeological Theory. *American Antiquity*
      53(3):461–86.
Schiffer, Michael B., and George J. Gummerman
  1977 *Conservation Archaeology: A Guide for Cultural Resource
      Management Studies.* New York: Academic Press.
Schiffer, Michael B., and John H. House
  1975 Indirect Impacts of the Channelization Project on the Archaeological
      Resources. In *The Cache River Archaeological Project: An Experiment in
      Contract Archaeology.* Research Series, No. 8, assembled by Michael B.
      Schiffer and John H. House, pp. 277-82. Fayetteville: Arkansas
      Archaeological Survey.
  1977 Assessing Impacts: Examples from the Cache Project. In *Conservation
      Archaeology: A Guide for Cultural Resource Management Studies*,
      edited by Michael B. Schiffer and John H. House, pp. 309–20. New
      York: Academic Press.
Schmidt, Peter R.
  1977 *Historical Archaeology: A Structural Approach to an African Culture.*
      Westport, Conn.: Greenwood Press.
  1981 *The Origins of Iron Smelting in Africa: A Complex Technology in
      Tanzania.* Research Papers in Anthropology, No. 1, Department of
      Anthropology, Brown University, Providence, R.I.
  1983 An Alternative to a Strictly Materialist Perspective: A Review of
      Historical Archaeology, Ethnoarchaeology, and Symbolic Approaches in
      African Archaeology. *American Antiquity* 48(1):62–78.
Schuyler, Robert
  1970 Historic and Historic Sites Archaeology as Anthropology: Basic
      Definitions and Relationships. *Historical Archaeology* 4:83–89.
Shackel, Paul A.
  1986 The Creation of Individuality and Segmentation in Anglo-America.
      Paper presented at the annual meeting of the Northeastern
      Anthropological Association, Buffalo, N.Y.
  1987 *A Historical Archaeology of Personal Discipline.* Ph.D. diss.,

Department of Anthropology, State University of New York at Buffalo. Ann Arbor: University Microfilms.

1993 *Personal Discipline and Material Culture: An Archaeology of Annapolis, Maryland, 1695–1870.* Knoxville, University of Tennessee Press.

Shanks, Michael, and Christopher Tilley

1987 *Re-Constructing Archaeology.* Cambridge: Cambridge University Press.

Sidford, Holly

1974 Stepping into History. *Museum News* 53(3):28–34.

Silverberg, Robert

1974 *The Mound Builders.* New York: Ballantine.

Singleton, Theresa A.

1988 An Archaeological Framework for Slavery and Emancipation. In *The Recovery of Meaning: Historical Archaeology in the Eastern United States*, edited by Mark P. Leone and Parker B. Potter, Jr., pp. 345–70. Washington, D.C.: Smithsonian Institution Press.

Smith, Barbara Clark

1985 *After the Revolution: The Smithsonian History of Everyday Life in the Eighteenth Century.* New York: Pantheon.

Smith, J. Winfree

1983 *A Search for the Liberal College: The Beginning of the St. John's Program.* Annapolis, Md.: St. John's College Press.

South, Stanley

1977 *Method and Theory in Historical Archaeology.* New York: Academic Press.

1988 Santa Elena: Threshold of Conquest. In *The Recovery of Meaning: Historical Archaeology in the Eastern United States*, edited by Mark P. Leone and Parker B. Potter, Jr., pp. 27–71. Washington, D.C.: Smithsonian Institution Press.

Spencer-Wood, Suzanne

1987 *Consumer Choice in Historical Archaeology.* New York: Plenum Press.

Spriggs, Matthew (ed.)

1984 *Marxist Perspectives in Archaeology.* Cambridge: Cambridge University Press.

Stevens, William Oliver

1906 *An Annapolis Alphabet: Pictures and Limericks.* Baltimore, Md.: The Lord Baltimore Press.

1907 *Another Annapolis Alphabet: Pictures and Limericks.* Baltimore, Md.: The Lord Baltimore Press.

1936 *Nantucket: The Far Away Island.* New York: Dodd, Mead & Company.

1937 *Annapolis: Anne Arundel's Town.* New York: Dodd, Mead & Company.

1938 *Old Williamsburg and Her Neighbors.* New York: Dodd, Mead & Company.

1939 *Discovering Long Island.* New York: Dodd, Mead & Company.

Stevens, William Oliver, and Carroll S. Alden

1910 *A Guide to Annapolis and the Naval Academy.* Baltimore, Md.: The Lord Baltimore Press.

Stieff, Frederick

1935 *Baltimore Annapolis Sketchbook.* Baltimore, Md.: H. G. Roebuck and Son.

Stiverson, Gregory A., and Phoebe R. Jacobsen

1976 *William Paca: A Biography.* Baltimore: Maryland Historical Society.

Symonds, Mary Hart

1977 Creation of a Historic District in Annapolis. *Antiques in Annapolis (The Magazine Antiques* January 1977) pp. 146–47.

Taylor, Owen

1872 *History of Annapolis.* Baltimore, Md.: Turnbull.

Taliaferro, Kim

1971 *Colonial Annapolis, 1694–1972.* Annapolis, Md.: Robert Barton & Associates.

Thruston, Mynna

1916 *A Day in Beautiful and Historic Annapolis.* Published by the author. In the library of Historic Annapolis, Annapolis, Md.

Tilghman, Oswald

1925 (1914) *Annapolis: History of ye Ancient City and its Public Buildings.* Annapolis, Md.: Published by order of the Governor.

Tilghman, Tench Francis

1984 *The Early History of St. John's College in Annapolis.* Annapolis, Md.: St. John's College Press.

Tilley, Christopher

1984 Ideology and the Legitimation of Power in the Middle Neolithic of Southern Sweden. In *Ideology, Power, and Prehistory*, edited by Daniel Miller and Christopher Tilley, pp. 111–46. Cambridge: Cambridge University Press.

Trigger, Bruce

1980 Archaeology and the Image of the American Indian. *American Antiquity* 45(4):662–76.

1986 Prehistoric Archaeology and American Society. In *American Archaeology Past and Future: A Celebration of the Society for American Archaeology, 1935–1985*, edited by David J. Meltzer, Don D. Fowler, and Jeremy A. Sabloff, pp. 187–216. Washington, D.C.: Smithsonian Institution Press.

Tubby, Raymond E.

1986 Georgian Order as Reflected in the Tableware of 18th-Century

Annapolis. Paper presented at the annual meeting of the Northeastern Anthropological Association, Buffalo, New York.

Virta, Matthew, and Jennifer Stabler
1986 Marbles in Annapolis, Maryland. Term paper, Department of Anthropology, University of Maryland. On file at Historic Annapolis, Annapolis, Md.

Walsh, Lorena
1983a Annapolis as a Center of Production. In *Annapolis and Anne Arundel County, Maryland: A Study of Urban Development in a Tobacco Economy, 1649–1776*, edited by Lorena S. Walsh. N.E.H. Grant RS-20199-81-1955. On file at Historic Annapolis, Annapolis, Md.
1983b Anne Arundel County Population. In *Annapolis and Anne Arundel County, Maryland: A Study of Urban Development in a Tobacco Economy, 1649–1776*, edited by Lorena S. Walsh. N.E.H. Grant RS-20199-81-1955. On file at Historic Annapolis, Annapolis, Md.

Wallace, Michael
1986 Reflections on the History of Historic Preservation. In *Presenting the Past: Essays on History and the Public,* edited by Susan Porter Benson, Stephen Brier, and Roy Rosensweig, pp. 165–99. Philadelphia, Pa.: Temple University Press.

Ward, Kathryn Painter
1975 The First Professional Theater in Maryland in Its Colonial Setting. *Maryland Historical Magazine* 70(1):29–46.

Warren, Mame, and Marion E. Warren
1981 *Everybody Works but John Paul Jones: A Portrait of the U.S. Naval Academy, 1845–1915.* Annapolis, Md.: Naval Institute Press.

Warren, Marion E., and Mame Warren
1981 *The Train's Done Been and Gone: An Annapolis Portrait, 1859–1910.* Annapolis, Md.: M. E. Warren. Original edition published by David R. Godine in 1976.

Washburn, Wilcomb
1987 A Critical View of Critical Archaeology. *Current Anthropology* 28(4):544–45.

Watson, Patty Jo, Steven A. LeBlanc, and Charles L. Redman
1971 *Explanation in Archaeology: An Explicitly Scientific Approach.* New York: Columbia University Press.

Watson, Richard
1991 What the New Archaeology Has Accomplished. *Current Anthropology* 32(3):275–91.

Wertenbaker, Thomas J.
1942 *The Golden Age of Colonial Culture.* New York: New York University Press.

White, Clarence M., and Evangeline White
1957 *The Years Between*. New York: Exposition Press.
Whitehill, Walter Muir
1968 *Boston: A Topographic History*. Cambridge, Mass.: Belknap Press.
Wildesen, Leslie
1982 A Study of Impacts on Archaeological Sites. In *Advances in Archaeological Method and Theory*, edited by Michael B. Schiffer, pp. 51–96. New York: Academic Press.
Winter, Joseph C.
1980 Indian Heritage Preservation and Archaeologists. *American Antiquity* 45(1):121–31.
Wright, St. Clair
1977a Annapolis: A Brief Historical Summary. In *Antiques in Annapolis* (*The Magazine Antiques* January 1977) p. 146.
1977b Historic Preservation in Annapolis. In *Antiques in Annapolis.* (*The Magazine Antiques* January 1977) pp. 152–57.
Wylie, Alison
1985 Putting Shakertown Back Together: Critical Theory in Archaeology. *Journal of Anthropological Archaeology* 4:133–47.
Zannieri, Paula
1980 Dancing Pilgrims: The Dynamics of Museum Interpretation. Unpublished M.A. paper, Department of Anthropology, Brown University.

Index